China's Thought Management

China's Thought Management argues that by re-emphasizing and moderniz-ing propaganda and thought work since 1989, the CCP has managed to overcome a succession of local and national level crises – the Tiananmen Square protests of 1989, the impact of the collapse of socialism in the Eastern Bloc, SARS, ethnic clashes in Tibet and Xinjiang, to name but a few – emerging re-strengthened and as dominant in Chinese society as ever. The contributors to this book address such crucial issues as the new emphasis on economic propaganda, the continued importance of the PLA propaganda system in China's overall propaganda work and political stability, how the CCP uses "Confu-talk" in its foreign and domestic propaganda, and new approaches to mass persuasion such as "campaigns of mass distraction." Each chapter is a case study of the multiple ways in which the CCP has modified and adjusted its propaganda to reflect China's changed economic and political environment.

Challenging readers to reconceptualize mainstream understandings of the CCP's hold on power and the means the CCP government adopts to maintain its authority to rule, this book will be invaluable reading for anyone interested in the Chinese media and Chinese politics.

Anne-Marie Brady is Associate Professor in the School of Social and Political Sciences at the University of Canterbury, New Zealand.

Routledge studies on China in transition

Series editor: David S. G. Goodman

China's Thought Management

Edited by
Anne-Marie Brady

Routledge
Taylor & Francis Group

LONDON AND NEW YORK

First published 2012 by Routledge
2 Park Square, Milton Park, Abingdon, Oxon OX14 4RN

Simultaneously published in the USA and Canada
by Routledge
711 Third Avenue, New York, NY 10017

Routledge is an imprint of the Taylor & Francis Group, an informa business

First issued in paperback 2014

British Library Cataloguing in Publication Data
A catalogue record for this book is available from the British Library

Library of Congress Cataloging in Publication Data
China's thought management / edited by Anne-Marie Brady.
p. cm. -- (Routledge studies on China in transition ; 40)
Includes bibliographical references and index.
1. Propaganda, Chinese. 2. Propaganda, International. 3. Public relations and politics--China. 4. Social control--China. 5. China--Politics and government--2002- I. Brady, Anne-Marie.
JQ1512.Z13P8526 2011
303.3'750951--dc22
2011011719

ISBN: 978-0-415-61673-7 (hbk)
ISBN: 978-1-138-01700-9 (pbk)
ISBN: 978-0-203-80345-5 (ebk)

Typeset in Times New Roman
by Taylor & Francis Books

Contents

PART II
New methods of control

Figures

Contributors

Anne-Marie Brady is a specialist on Chinese domestic and foreign politics at the School of Social and Political Sciences, University of Canterbury, New Zealand. She is the author of *Marketing Dictatorship: Propaganda and Thought Work in Contemporary China*, (Rowman and Littlefield, 2008); *Making the Foreign Serve China: Managing Foreigners in the People's Republic* (Rowman and Littlefield, 2003); and *Friend of China – the Myth of Rewi Alley* (RoutledgeCurzon, 2002).

He Yong is an Assistant Professor at Communication University of China, in Beijing. From 2008 to 2009 he was a post-doctoral fellow on the Royal Society of New Zealand Marsden Fund project "Propaganda and Thought Work in Contemporary China" in the School of Political Science and Communication, University of Canterbury.

Elaine Jeffreys is an Australian Research Council Future Fellow at the China Research Centre, Faculty of Arts and Social Sciences, University of Technology Sydney. She is co-editor with Louise Edwards of *Celebrity in China* (2010 Hong Kong University Press); editor of *China's Governmentalities: Governing Change, Changing Government* (2011 [2009] Routledge) and *Sex and Sexuality in China* (2009 [2006] Routledge); and author of *China, Sex and Prostitution* (2004 Routledge).

Ji Fengyuan is a Senior Lecturer in the School of Languages and Cultures at the University of Canterbury, Christchurch, New Zealand. She is the author of *Linguistic Engineering: Language and Politics in Mao's China* (University of Hawai'i Press, 2004).

Valérie Niquet is Head of the Asia Department at the Foundation for Strategic Research. She is the author of numerous studies, books and articles dedicated to the evolution of regional balances and to strategic issues in Asia since the end of the Cold War, to the defence policies of the great regional powers, and to the issue of proliferation.

James To is a Lecturer in the International Pacific College, Palmerston North, New Zealand. He completed his doctorate at the School of Social and Political Sciences at the University of Canterbury, New Zealand in 2010. His thesis examined the evolving relationship between Overseas Chinese, China, and Taiwan.

Nicolai Volland is currently a Visiting Fellow at the National University of Singapore. He is the author of the forthcoming book *The Tongue and the Throat: The Origins of Media Control in Modern China*.

Wang Juntao had a career as a political activist and editor in the 1980s until his arrest in 1989 as one of the so-called "black hands" of the student protest movement. He was exiled to the USA and graduated with a Ph.D. in comparative politics from Columbia University in 2006. From 2006 to 2007 he was a post-doctoral fellow on the Royal Society of New Zealand Marsden Fund project "Propaganda and Thought Work in Contemporary China" in the School of Social and Political Sciences, University of Canterbury.

Introduction

Market-friendly, scientific, high tech, and politics-lite: China's new approach to propaganda

Anne-Marie Brady

Propaganda has negative connotations in English, and increasingly, in Chinese. When most of us think of propaganda and China we think of scenes from the Mao years with tens of thousands of young rebels waving Little Red Books in Tiananmen Square and adulating Mao Zedong. In the 1980s China's senior leaders were divided on the issue of whether or not propaganda had a role in China's modernizing economy and polity. That debate was brought to an effective end after the June 4, 1989 crackdown on the pro-democracy movement. The post-June 4 leadership set the bottom line that has been followed up to the present day: that the Party would focus its energy (and base its legitimacy) on both economic growth *and* a renewed emphasis on propaganda.

In the last ten years changes in China's mass communications, media, and cultural economy have become hot topics in Western academic circles and attracted considerable media interest. A common assumption has been that to a greater or lesser extent market reforms and new technology will undermine Party controls. Such assumptions are based on dated preconceptions about the nature of freedom and democracy in our own societies as well as pre-conceptions about the nature of Party–State–Market–Consumer relations in China today. In recent years China has deliberately borrowed from Western methods of mass persuasion and models for funding a cultural economy, at the same time as updating its traditional methods of control and content. China's modern-day propaganda is now market-friendly, scientific, high tech, and politics-lite.

One of the signs of the impact of the new methodologies has been the adoption of new terms to describe propaganda work. By the early 1990s, as China's propaganda specialists noted the negative connotations the word for propaganda had acquired, the terms "publicity" and "information" were increasingly used in Chinese as well as English to describe propaganda activities. In 1998, the Central Propaganda Department officially changed its English language title to the Central Publicity Department (though the Chinese name was not changed). Following the same trend, CCP oral propaganda teams now favor the term "political communication" to describe their activities in promoting the Party line at public forums. Courses on political communication at university level are expanding rapidly.

Many other relevant social science methodologies have been introduced into China's modernized propaganda system in recent years. Some authors have even proposed combining modern management theories with Marxism to improve China's "thought management" (*sixiang guanli*). The title of this edited book is taken from such research, to indicate the seismic shifts which have occurred in the CCP's approach to propaganda and thought work. "Thought management" means

> activities to control, guide, adjust, or develop the social or ideological relationships which influence the shaping (change or development) of people's thinking; to make their thinking conform with the dominant ideology; thereby standardizing people's behaviour; in order to put in place a set of objectives.[1]

"Thought management" epitomizes the CCP government's recent trend of combining traditional methods of persuasion with new methodology more suitable to China's modernized economy and more open society.

The transformation of the CCP's propaganda activities has kept pace with changes in the Chinese economy and certain elements of the political system. China has embraced many new practices and systems from the outside world, especially Western democratic countries, while retaining many key features and practices from the past. China is under increasing pressure to democratize and indeed personal – though not political freedoms – have increased dramatically in recent years; hence introducing the methods of social and political control utilized by modern democratic societies has proven to be a most effective means of maintaining one-party rule. China today, as a direct result of these reforms in propaganda work, has a stable polity and a strong government with a high level of popular support both among the domestic population, and – as James To demonstrates in this volume – internationally among the Overseas Chinese.

The CCP party–state has successfully survived the crisis of 1989; the impact of the collapse of socialism in the Eastern Bloc and the Soviet Union; the painful transition from a state-dominated to a privatized, market economy; the continued opening up of the economy and society to outside influences; the impact of new information communication technology; and various local and national level crises, such as ongoing peasant and worker unrest, the 2002–3 SARS outbreak, ethnic clashes in Tibet in 2008 and in Xinjiang in 2009, the current global economic crisis, and the 2008 poisoned milk powder scandal. The collapse thesis which has dominated Western analysis of China's future since 1989 is clearly erroneous and based on outdated theories.

The essays in this volume discuss the role that propaganda and thought work have had in enabling the CCP to manage major social change and the various crises; emerging re-strengthened and as dominant in Chinese society as ever. *China's Thought Management* examines: (1) the new themes of China's modernized propaganda and thought work; (2) the new methodology being implemented in various fields; and (3) the impact on certain key areas of society of these changed strategies. The CCP has always divided propaganda into two categories: internal and external; as well as four types: political, economic, cultural, and social propaganda. All of these categories and types are discussed in this volume. In order to explore the complexity and differing perspectives on the significance of the issue, *China's Thought Management* incorporates a range of representative views. The contributors, all specialists on Chinese politics, address such crucial issues as the new emphasis on economic propaganda, the continued importance of the PLA propaganda system in China's overall propaganda work and political stability, how the CCP uses "Confu-talk" in its foreign and domestic propaganda, and new approaches to mass persuasion such as "campaigns of mass distraction." Each chapter is a case study of the multiple ways in which the CCP has modified and adjusted its propaganda activities to reflect China's changed economic and political environment. *China's Thought Management* challenges readers to reconceptualize mainstream understandings of the CCP's hold on power and the means the CCP government adopts to maintain its authority to rule.

China's Thought Management builds on discussions explored in my earlier sole-authored monograph *Marketing Dictatorship: Propaganda and Thought Work in Contemporary China* (Rowman and Littlefield, 2008). That book was essentially a survey of the whole Chinese propaganda system, focusing on the period from 1989 to 2007, but also discussing what went before. This new, multi-authored text examines in much more detail key case studies of how and why China's propaganda and thought work has been changed and updated in recent years. Both books form part of a larger project, "Propaganda and Thought Work in Contemporary China," of which I was principal investigator, funded by the Royal Society of New Zealand's Marsden Fund from 2005 to 2009. The two post-docs on that project, Wang Juntao and He Yong, are both contributors to this volume. The three associate investigators on the project, professors Wang Handong and Shan Bo of Wuhan University and Guo Zhenzhi of Qinghua University, have been mentors and early readers of some of the research in this book, as they were on the previous book project.

Part I of *China's Thought Management* focuses on some of the new themes in China's modern propaganda activities. In the first chapter in this section I outline a prominent example of just how much CCP persuasion has changed in recent years: how the Beijing Olympics was both a major sporting event and an opportunity for the CCP to reshape the domestic and foreign public's attitudes to the China. From 2006 to 2008 Chinese society was inundated with Beijing Olympics propaganda. The Beijing Olympics was also the predominant theme of the Chinese government's international publicity in this period. Beijing's Olympic preparations were never only about putting up new sports stadiums; hosting the Olympics was used as an opportunity for a major propaganda effort, what I have called a "campaign of mass distraction." Such campaigns have become a feature of contemporary persuasion; more recent examples are the lead up to and hosting of the Shanghai Expo in 2010 and the 2010 Asian Games in Guangdong. The ultimate goal of propaganda and thought work is manufacturing consent for the continued political status quo. Consent can be active, as shown in societies where citizens choose their governments by election. However in China, passive consent is more appropriate. The Party needs the masses to be as disengaged from politics as possible, and to be optimistic and positive to maintain business confidence and trust in the political status quo. Under these circumstances the role of the Central Propaganda Department has shifted from its Mao era and 1980s role of being the engine house for the political transformation of China, to overseeing the political mummification of the nation.

In Chapter 2 I have teamed up with mass communication specialist and former CCTV editor and journalist, He Yong, to discuss how economic propaganda has come to be one of the leading themes in both China's domestic and foreign propaganda. To many contemporary observers China appears to be a contradiction in terms: a market economy under one-party, communist rule. In this essay we argue that what might appear to be a contradiction is actually regarded as both a strongpoint and a necessity by China's rulers, and indeed, most Chinese people today. The relative success of China's post-1978 economic policies in raising standards of living for many and creating hope of a better future for others has meant that the economy now has a key role in maintaining the CCP's political legitimacy.

In Chapter 3 I explore how, and why, the CCP has introduced selected concepts from Confucianism and "Chinese tradition" into contemporary propaganda and thought work. In Marxist terms, ideology is determined by a society's material conditions. From 1978, and even more so from 1992, China has followed a decidedly different pattern of development from that of the Mao era, and the Chinese Communist Party's (CCP) ideology has progressively evolved to reflect this change. A notable theme in the ongoing evolution of the CCP's contemporary ideology has been the growing influence of Confucian concepts and terminology. Historically, Party ideologues denounced Confucianism and traditional Chinese culture as "feudal" and sought to erase their influence on Chinese society. The chapter explores the role Confucianism and other Chinese philosophies are now playing in the CCP's contemporary propaganda and thought work, and how the new emphasis relates to the revival of popular interest in Chinese traditional philosophy and culture.

Following on from and expanding on the themes in the previous chapter, in Chapter 4 French political scientist Valérie Niquet analyses why, in recent years, the CCP government has introduced traditional Chinese concepts such as "harmony" into the Chinese foreign affairs system and China's foreign propaganda. Niquet coins a new term "Confu-talk" to describe this phenomena. Niquet argues that Beijing's current stress on "harmony" is presented as an antidote to prevailing "China threat" theories which assume that the rise of China will be a threat to the existing global order. A further aspect to this antidote is the Chinese government's embrace of the notion of "soft power." As part of this, since 2004, China has opened hundreds of "Confucius Institutes" worldwide. These are language and culture centers based in foreign universities; which, as Niquet shows, are closely linked to the CCP propaganda system. According to Niquet, the Confucius Institutes and the "harmony" discourse have emerged as a pragmatic and contemporary response to pressures coming both from inside and outside Chinese society. They form part of a new repertoire of survival tools for the CCP in a rapidly changing world.

In Chapter 5, sociolinguist and propaganda specialist Ji Fengyuan discusses how the CCP uses what she calls "linguistic engineering" to build political support and ideological consensus. According to Ji, linguistic engineering is the attempt to affect people's attitudes and beliefs by manipulating the language that they hear, speak, read and write. Linguistic engineering takes a "pluralistic" form in democratic societies; it took a totalitarian form in Mao Zedong's China; and it takes yet a different form in China today. Ji analyses the 2005–6 "Maintain Progressiveness" campaign as an example of how the CCP continues to utilize linguistic engineering in modern day China. Ji's work demonstrates how party political thought work now mainly focuses on Party members and less so on the masses as it did in the Mao years. Meanwhile, as demonstrated in the first four chapters of this book, the masses are now guided by broader, less political themes aimed at building social cohesion, such as the stress on "Chineseness" and "Chinese tradition" and emphasis on consumerism.

Part II of the book looks at new or revised methods of social and political control in China and the role propaganda plays in this. In a further demonstration of how things have changed in the CCP's management of the public sphere, yet somehow remained the same, Chapter 6 discusses the political implications of the marketization of the Chinese media since the 1990s. Nicolai Volland examines developments such as the commercialization and conglomeration of Chinese newspapers, TV stations, film studios, publishing houses, theater companies, art troupes, museums and other cultural organizations, what has come to be known as "Reforms of the Cultural Structure." These changes have fundamentally transformed the Chinese cultural sphere – part of the traditional sphere of influence of the CCP Propaganda Department. The goal of these reforms has been to turn around notoriously unproductive and overstaffed work units, and make them into revenue providers for the local bureaucracies in charge of them. In addition the reforms are part of a strategy to reassert the Party's control over a sector that has, since the mid-1980s, seen broad inroads from private service providers. Volland is cautious in evaluating the effectiveness of the reforms in managing the challenges of China's shift to a more pluralistic marketplace of ideas. New attacks on Party controls constantly appear on the horizon; and the Party's best strategy in dealing with these, one that they have followed since the economic reform period began, is to constantly adapt its policies.

Apart from Party members, one of the other key groups in Chinese society to continue to receive heavy doses of CCP political education is the PLA.[2] The People's Liberation Army is still officially an arm of the Chinese Communist Party. Despite increasing modernization and professionalization in the last twenty years, unlike militaries in most modern industrialized societies, it cannot be said to be under civilian control.[3] In Chapter 7 veteran political activist Wang Juntao and I trace the evolution of propaganda work in the Chinese military from its earliest days to the present. We review the current propaganda agenda and its role in military activities, analyzing the PLA propaganda system's organizational structure and operations, as well as the impact of PLA military propaganda on China's civil sector. The ability of the CCP to maintain control of the PLA in a time of political upheaval is a topic that has interested many observers of Chinese politics in recent years. In 2011 when democratic movements raged throughout the Middle East, it once more became a topic of debate in the media.[4] We argue that, despite increased professionalism within the PLA and the complexities of modern Chinese society, the CCP still has a firm grasp over the Chinese military, and political thought work is the key mechanism for it to do so. Moreover, we assert that the PLA's newly upgraded propaganda and political thought work does not conflict with its military modernization; in fact it co-exists with the rise in professionalism.

Chapter 8, by political scientist Elaine Jeffreys, focuses on a form of social propaganda in contemporary China: contemporary campaigns targeted at prostitutes and their clients. Historically the CCP was strongly opposed to prostitution. The official closing down of the sex industry in the CCP's early years in power was an important symbolic act, drawing a line between New China and the feudal, decadent, past. However, prostitution never actually completely disappeared from China in the Mao years, it simply went underground.[5] The major economic reforms from 1978 on, coupled with widespread unemployment, led to prostitution becoming more open and prevalent. In her essay Elaine Jeffreys utilizes a number of high profile incidents to illustrate the complexity of political and social attitudes towards prostitution in China today and the role government propaganda is playing in helping to shape them. Propaganda campaigns relating to prostitution fall within the responsibility of the Ministry of Health or at other times Public Security, acting in concert with the central and local level propaganda bureaux. The Central Propaganda Department has a leadership role over propaganda matters within the health sector and a guiding role in public security campaigns. CCP social propaganda has always taken a different tack from political, economic, and cultural forms of propaganda; which tend to be more didactic. As Jeffreys notes, when it comes to campaigns relating to prostitution and sexual health "public education" is the goal, not indoctrination. The CCP government's contemporary attitude towards prostitution is neither based on a unitary ideological position nor reflective of a policy-based divorce between rhetoric and reality, and prostitution-related propaganda reflects that.

In Chapter 9, James To reveals how the CCP has modernized its policies and methodology for dealing with Overseas Chinese (OC) communities in the years since the turning point of 1989. Many OC were involved in supporting the pro-democracy movement in China in 1989. The crisis led CCP OC specialists to rethink strategies for influencing and managing the Chinese diaspora. These include new efforts to connect with OC through the promotion of the CCP's version of Chineseness, incorporating idealistic elements of history and civilization, tradition, culture and common biological traits that link ethnicity with nationalism. CCP OC networks promote China's market economy and how the OC can contribute and benefit from it. The CCP has made strenuous efforts to challenge and exterminate any alternative influences coming from the OC community such as Falungong, Taiwan, and pro-democracy groups. James To argues that despite counter-efforts from rival political factions and the OC's gradual assimilation into local societies, CCP thought work has been largely successful in unifying a heterogeneous population of OC in support of a broad range of Party interests.

The final chapter in the volume, Chapter 10, ends the discussion of the place of propaganda and thought work in the CCP's restrengthened hold on power with a survey of the adjusted approaches to social and political control in contemporary China. The essay focuses in particular on the localizing of Party power from the workplace to the residential area; the implications of the reform of the content of mass persuasion messages to the Chinese public; and reform in the means of control/management of the public sphere. In the essay I conclude that China's new order is less violent; hence following Foucault's "physics of power," it engenders less resistance overall. Chinese society is more fragmented than in the past, but the new methods of social and political control draw closely on methods utilized in other modern industrialized societies that are similarly fragmented and individualistic and yet politically stable.

As the chapters in this volume all illustrate, the CCP continues to put a high priority on propaganda as a tool and a task of government. It is a direct result of the Party's renewed emphasis on propaganda as a tool of government in combination with year-on-year double-digit economic growth that, since the events of 1989, CCP legitimacy to rule has stabilized. As the lack of response to calls for a "Jasmine Revolution" in China in 2011 have aptly showed,[6] it is clear that rather than a democratic transition being imminent, the mainstream view among the Chinese populace is that the current political system, despite its many flaws, is still the best one for the country.

Propaganda has an important role in establishing and maintaining the right to govern in all societies. Regardless of whether a government comes to power through force or consent, every regime must garner popular support to continue its rule and that popular support can be built or destroyed through mass persuasion or "propaganda." Governments traditionally maintain power by means of either promulgating ideology or by means of performance-based legitimacy. Most governments utilize a combination of these two approaches to maintain political stability,[7] and contemporary China is no different.

One of the core understandings of the Western Enlightenment project of modernity is that democracy is the ultimate system for a modern developed society. Yet the CCP government now employs much of the same methodology used by modern democratic governments to maintain its legitimacy to rule, meanwhile maintaining its privileged leadership position over Chinese society as ordained by the Chinese Constitution. The Chinese government's cynical and self-serving use of such models should give pause to many critics from Western nations who like to point the finger in judgment at Chinese politics today.

In internal CCP documents, propaganda is described as the "life blood" of the Party–state. It is considered to be one of the key means for guaranteeing the CCP's ongoing purchase on power. The CCP government has found a replacement for revolution as the source for its authority to govern, and it is a source common to democratic societies: popular support. As in democratic societies, in China this support is mediated and molded through many means, not only (but now also including) elections. The CCP has been assisted in its bid to retain its hold on power by careful study of the methodology modern industrial societies utilize to mold public opinion into accepting systemic inequalities within a fixed political system. The CCP may well be able to avoid altogether the need to introduce a genuine multi-party election-based democratic system in China by studying some of the least democratic practices of other modern developed societies.

Notes

1   Zhang Shiwen, Yu Yangtao, and Wang Xinshan, eds., *Xin shiqi sixiang zhengzhi gongzuo yanjiu lunwen ji* (Collected Articles on Political Thought Work Research of the New Era) (Wuhan, Wuhan Daxue Chubanshe, 2001), p. 449.
2   Chinese youth are the other major social group to be the focus of political education in contemporary China.
3   Samuel Huntington's *The Soldier and the State: The Theory and Politics of Civil-Military Relations* (Cambridge MA: Belknap Press, 1957), is the starting point for most discussions on this theme.
4   See for example, Banyan, "The Wind that Will not Subside: Hearing Egyptian Echoes, China's Autocrats Cling to the Hope that They Are Different," *Economist*, February 17, 2011, www.economist.com/node/18178177?story_id=18178177&fsrc=rss
5   See Frank Dikötter, *Mao's Great Famine* (London: Bloomsbury, 2010), pp. 234, 260–61.
6   See Tania Branigan, "The Jasmine Revolution that Never Was," *Guardian Weekly*, March 4, 2011, p. 6.
7   J. H. Schaar, *Legitimacy in the Modern States* (New Brunswick NJ: Transaction Books, 1989), pp. 20–21.

Part I
New themes

1 The Beijing Olympics as a campaign of mass distraction

Anne-Marie Brady

> getting propaganda on the Olympics right will be good for China's international and domestic environment, if Olympics propaganda has a clear direction then China's overall national strength will continually increase and the masses will give us wide support.
>
> (Meeting on Olympics propaganda, 2007[1])

From 2006 to 2008 Chinese society was inundated with Beijing Olympics propaganda. The Beijing Olympics was also the predominant theme of the Chinese government's international publicity in this period. Propaganda and thought work (*xuanchuan yu sixiang gongzuo*) has long been an integral activity in the Chinese Communist Party's (CCP) rule. After undergoing a decline in importance in the 1980s, in the current period it is once again prioritized, albeit updated to reflect changes in Chinese society. For this reason, Beijing's Olympic preparations were never only about putting up new sports stadiums; hosting the Olympics was used as an opportunity for a major propaganda effort, what I call a campaign of mass distraction.

CCP propaganda and thought work has undergone a transformation in recent years, as has the Chinese economy and certain elements of the political system. China has embraced many new practices and systems from the outside world, especially Western democratic countries, while retaining many traditional features and practices from the past. Examining Beijing Olympics propaganda activities is a useful means to reveal the many ways in which China has adapted its political and economic system while maintaining the core political status quo: one-party rule.

Changes in the methodology and goals of the CCP propaganda system (*xuanjiao xitong*) reflect substantial changes in China's system of political control and an adjustment in the nature of the Party's authority to rule. The propaganda system is the most extensive and, arguably, the most important of all the CCP-controlled bureaucratic systems (*xitong*)[2] in China. Hence this chapter analyzes the propaganda activities surrounding the Beijing Olympics as a key to interpreting recent changes in the underpinnings of legitimacy and indeed the whole process of legitimation in contemporary China. It is based on field work trips to China in 1998, 1999, 2000, 2001, 2002–3, 2004, 2005–6,

2007, and 2010, where I conducted formal and informal interviews with propaganda officials, theorists, policy-makers and bureaucrats, academics, journalists and dissidents, as well as ordinary Chinese citizens, while scouring propaganda policy documents, secondary sources in Chinese and English, and relevant information from the Chinese and foreign news media.[3]

The CCP, legitimacy, and the propaganda system

Superficially the two year-long period of "welcome the Beijing Olympics activities" (*ying Aoyun xuanchuan huodong*) looked rather like a Mao-era style mass campaign (*qunzhong yundong*): it involved the whole of Chinese society, received saturation coverage in all sectors of the Chinese propaganda system, it centered on a handful of simple, easily understandable slogans, utilized all tools of mass communication including oral communications, and incorporated both the commercial and non-commercial sectors. However, the Beijing Olympics "mass activities" had some unique features which made them strikingly different from the mass campaigns of the past. Analyzing just what those differences were provides a window on to the new underpinnings of the CCP's right to rule.

One significant difference was avoidance of the term "campaign" (*yundong*) to describe the movement's mass, scripted, series of events. The word *yundong* (when prefixed with either "politics," "mass" or "propaganda") has become a negative term in Chinese official discourse.[4] From the late 1920s and up to the late 1970s, the CCP engaged in a series of mass campaigns, which though aimed at transforming China, often served as the fig leaf for power struggles and purges. The political thought reform of the masses was an essential government task in these years, frequently to the detriment of economic growth. From 1978 to 1989 CCP rule faced a legitimacy crisis;[5] and many critics both within and without China argued that the source of this crisis was the Mao era's (1949–76) excessive emphasis on political thought work and mass campaigns. In response to these pressures, in the 1980s the Chinese government downplayed ideological goals (mass persuasion-based legitimacy) and instead focused its efforts on economic development (performance-based legitimacy). The CCP senior leadership was divided on the issue of whether or not political thought work and propaganda should still have a role in China's modernizing economy and polity.

These debates were brought to a dramatic close with the political crisis of April–June 1989. The post-1989 leadership established the new formula that has been followed up to the present day: that the Party would base its legitimacy on both economic growth *and* a renewed emphasis on propaganda and political thought work.[6] However the debates of the 1980s meant that Party propaganda and thought work in the post-1989 years would be very different from what went before. Since the early 1990s and continuing up to the present day, CCP propaganda and thought work has undergone a dramatic modernization, discarding outdated terminology such as *yundong* and in foreign language publications even avoiding the term "propaganda," meanwhile incorporating the latest technological and methodological innovations.[7]

In terms of propaganda and thought work, the years from 1989 to 1992 were a period of consolidation and reflection on the lessons of the past. However, not long after the Fourteenth Party Congress in 1992, CCP general secretary Jiang Zemin stated that propaganda should be an "extremely important department" with increased powers.[8] The Fourteenth Party Congress is also notable as the moment when China formally designated itself as a market economy. For propaganda officials, the challenge was to create propaganda and thought work suitable for both the market economy and for China's unique political system. For enterprises within the propaganda system, such as sports, media, cultural, and educational organizations, the challenge would be to find new sources of income as state subsidies were progressively withdrawn from this date on.

The period from 1992 to the 2002 Sixteenth Party Congress was a period of substantial reforms in Party propaganda work, reflecting radical, sub-terranean, shifts which were contemporaneously going on in the political sphere. One early shift in thinking occurred in September 1991, when an article in an internal publication argued that instead of calling itself a "revo-lutionary party" and trying to revolutionize Chinese society, the CCP should re-brand itself as a "party in power" with the aim of maintaining this status and the political system it led. The article's suggestions became mainstream opinion by the mid-1990s, and were formally adopted as Party policy during the 2002 Sixteenth Party Congress. This means that propaganda now has an even more crucial role in Chinese politics, as the masses must be persuaded to believe that the party in power and the political system it represents are legitimate and should be sustained.

In the post-1989 years the Central Propaganda Department has overseen the introduction to China of modern methods and tools of mass persuasion more in keeping with the CCP government's re-forged social contract. China's propaganda and thought work now incorporates the methodology of political public relations, advertising, mass communications, social psychology, and other modern forms of mass persuasion utilized in Western democratic societies, but adapted to Chinese conditions and needs.

Modern democratic states commonly use mass persuasion techniques to garner popular support and maintain political legitimacy.[9] According to political scientist Seymour Martin Lipset, "Legitimacy involves the capacity of a political system to engender and maintain the belief that existing political institutions are the most appropriate or proper ones for the society."[10] The governing elite in any given society utilizes mass persuasion techniques – propaganda to its detractors – in order to "manufacture consent" for its continuing rule.[11] Contemporary CCP-sponsored forums promote Lipset's minimalist definition of legitimacy; meanwhile the (conflicting) theories of Max Weber and Jürgen Habermas are downplayed[12] or critiqued as irrelevant for China.[13]

As part of the revival of the importance of propaganda and thought work in China, the CCP has reworked many old traditions as well as introducing new approaches. An example of this is the CCP's revival of the practice of launching periodic mass campaigns in order to guide the public mind. However, since the term *yundong* is no longer used, the ambiguous *huodong* (which can be translated as "activities" as well as "campaign") is now preferred. The Chinese term for PR campaign is "gong guan *huodong*" and the new-style mass campaigns do have much in common with PR efforts. The campaign to welcome the Beijing Olympics was particularly reminiscent of a PR promotion for a new product. This campaign was formally launched in February 2006 and ended in the last seconds before the opening ceremony.[14] It was the final stage of a long-term effort to link China's successful Olympics bid to ongoing efforts to maintain the political credibility of the CCP government.

Following the pattern of the Mao era, some contemporary propaganda campaigns are targeted at party members while others are aimed at the Chinese population as a whole. Since 1994, every two years or so, Party members and senior non-Party state officials have had to down tools to engage in concentrated political study, sometimes for periods as long as eighteen months. In 1994 Party members were instructed to "Study Deng Xiaoping Theory," in 1998 they studied Jiang Zemin's "Three Stresses," in 2000 and again in 2003 they crammed Jiang's theories on "The Three Represents," from 2005 to 2006 they took part in the record-breaking eighteen-month-long "Maintaining the Progressiveness of Party Members Education," and from 2007 to 2008 they studied the theory of "Scientific Development." Instead of political study, the masses are now targeted with soft propaganda messages aimed at garnering social and political stability such as the two-year long "Welcome the Beijing Olympics Campaign."

Beijing Olympic propaganda activities reflect the changed circumstances in the justifications for maintaining the political status quo in China. Rather than being a campaign of political indoctrination, Beijing Olympics propaganda was a campaign of mass distraction, designed to distract the population from more troubling issues such as political representation, inflation, unemployment, corruption, and environmental degradation. It is a form of what Freudenberg and Allario call "diversionary framing," whereby public opinion is shaped, in part, by distraction.[15] In China today the ultimate goal of propaganda and thought work is manufacturing consent for the continued political status quo. Consent can be active, as shown in societies where citizens choose their governments by election. However, in China passive consent is more appropriate. The Party needs the masses to be as disengaged from politics as possible, and to be optimistic and positive to maintain business confidence and trust in the political status quo. Under these circumstances the role of the Central Propaganda Department has shifted from being the engine house for the political transformation of China, to overseeing the political mummification of the nation.

"Mass distraction" is a common political tactic which was known as far back as the Romans when the poet Juvenal spoke scathingly of the authorities using "bread and circuses" to distract the masses from political concerns. Many commentators have referred to the Bush administration's 2003 invasion of Iraq as a "weapon of mass distraction" with the real goal being to secure Iraq's oil reserves.[16] North Korea's mass games are another example of mass distraction and diversionary framing.

Recent research into how performance magic works can give some insight into why "mass distraction" can be so effective at diverting attention from other issues.[17] Magicians engage audiences with smoke, mirrors, and other sensory distractions while sleights of hand are performed. Audiences focus on the display while being robbed of their senses. Just like magicians who distract audiences and steal their wallets, politicians and their spin doctors create spectacular events or seek out scandalous information on opponents while simultaneously working on other goals. For those who follow Lipset in believing that a government is legitimate if its people believe it to be so, then studies of "magic" help to explain why people within a given political system might ignore obvious inequities in their society which are glaring to outside observers. Freudenberg and Allario state that mass distraction can help to make the whole issue of legitimation disappear from sight altogether. This makes it an extremely useful tool for governments in countries like China and North Korea, which are under pressure to democratize, or like the US, when it engages in an activity illegal under international law.

China and the Olympics

The People's Republic of China (PRC)'s Olympic participation and performance was long ago politicized due to the PRC being excluded from the international system for much of the Cold War and even before that, China's reputation as the "sick man of Asia" in the late imperial and republican period.[18] It is significant that Mao Zedong's first published paper was on the part sports education plays in building national strength.[19] In China, propaganda officials value sport as an "important means of engaging in mass political thought work, particularly towards youth."[20] Since the crisis of 1989, the CCP has singled out Chinese youth as one of the main target groups for political thought work.[21] Sport is an important means to build patriotism, which since 1989 has been one of the main themes of CCP propaganda.

PRC athletes first participated in an Olympic Games in Helsinki in 1952, though Beijing resigned from the International Olympic Committee (IOC) in 1958, due to the "two China's issue." This early experience has cast a political shadow over China's Olympic involvement, which remains to this day. It rejoined in 1979. In 1993 Beijing's application to host the 2000 Olympics was turned down, in part because of international criticism of the Chinese government's actions to crush the pro-democracy movement in 1989. China's 1993 Olympics bid was headed by Chen Xitong, widely reviled for his role in the crackdown on the 1989 student protest movement. For this, and other reasons the bid was a public relations disaster, vividly demonstrating the extent of China's post-1989 international image problem. Yet in China the popular reaction to the failed bid added fuel to government efforts to unify the country through promoting nationalism. For the CCP government, and indeed for many Chinese citizens, hosting the Olympics was always more about international and domestic image and prestige than it was about sport. Success in Olympic sport is, however, commonly regarded as a mark of a nation's power and China's Olympic sporting achievements have always been used to build nationalism. In 2001, Project 119 was launched by the State General Administration of Sport, which identified 119 gold medals (later expanded to 122) which China focused its energies on winning in 2008.[22] In the end China obtained the highest number of gold medals of any other country at the Beijing Olympics, outranking its nearest competitor the USA by 51 to 36, and gathering a total of 100 medals overall. China's Beijing Olympic medal tally was a source of great national pride.

In marked contrast to 1993, and demonstrating just how much CCP propaganda methodology had changed in the intervening years, Beijing's 2008 bid was advised by two leading international PR firms, Weber Shandwick Worldwide of the United States, and Britain's Bell Pottinger. The two firms even lobbied the International Olympic Committee on Beijing's behalf. In the lead-up to the bid for the 2008 games, China's well-prepared spin doctors made a point of stating that granting Beijing the Games in 2008 would help to improve China's human rights situation.[23] This argument was not, however, widely promoted within China; indeed when I once mentioned it to a class of Chinese undergraduates they laughed in disbelief.

Re-branding China

It is no accident that the person chosen to head the Beijing Organizing Committee of the Olympic Games (BOCOG) from 2005, Liu Peng, was from 1997 to 2002 a deputy-director in the Central Propaganda Department.[24] Liu was also concurrently head of the State General Administration of Sports, which in terms of its place in the Party-state system, is under the guidance (*zhidao*)[25] of the Central Propaganda Department and is part of the Chinese propaganda system. China had lost the last Olympic bid because of perceived image problems, so this time round, Chinese (and Western) spin doctors worked hard to manage the bid process all the way through. Hosting the Olympics offered a golden opportunity to reshape China's national image. BOCOG has its own propaganda bureau, led by officials who concurrently head the propaganda sections of the Beijing Party Committee and the State General Administration of Sports. In 2005 another layer of bureaucracy was added to Olympics propaganda in the form of the "Beijing Olympics News Propaganda Work Coordinating Group" (*Beijing xinwen xuanchuan gongzuo xietiao xiaozu*, official English title Beijing Olympic News and Communications Coordination Group).[26] The group was headed by Li Dongsheng, who is currently a deputy-director in the Central Propaganda Department in charge of the news media. Equivalent committees were set up at the provincial and local level all over China, to coordinate all aspects of Olympic propaganda. In a 2007 meeting on Olympic propaganda jointly hosted by the Central Propaganda Department, the Central Office for Spiritual Civilization, and BOCOG, it was emphasized that, "getting propaganda on the Olympics right will be good for China's international and domestic environment, if Olympics propaganda has a clear direction then China's overall national strength will continually increase and the masses will give us wide support."[27]

The CCP divides propaganda and thought work into two categories: internal (*duinei*), targeted at Chinese people; and external (*duiwai*), targeted at foreigners in China, Overseas Chinese, and the outside world in general; as well as four types: political, economic, cultural, and social. China's internal and external propaganda activities are frequently different, directed at different audiences and different goals. Reflecting the goals of China's foreign propaganda activities, Beijing Olympics propaganda targeted at the outside world focused on cultural and economic themes. In recent years China has been placing increasing emphasis on the role of culture to promote its national image.[28] Promoting a new national image (*guojia xingxiang*) internationally was one of the key strategic goals of China hosting the Olympics.[29] In 2006 the Central Propaganda Department sub-organization the National Planning Office of Philosophy and Social Science (the main body for social science research funding in China) commissioned a major two-year scholarly research project (2006–8) on how the Olympics might help to improve China's national image.[30] The new image aimed to allay international fears about China's increasing political, economic and military power, at the same time as projecting awareness of China's renewed strength and prosperity. In 2003 Party theorists put forward a theory which matches the new national image: the concept of China's "peaceful rise."[31] This concept and the debate on the need to improve China's national image have been widely embraced by China's intellectual class, as it closely reflects their own heartfelt anxieties. This collaboration between Party-state interests and elite concerns is an example of the CCP's success in recent years in regaining the support of many of those, who only a few years before, were its harshest critics.[32]

China's new national image has political as well as economic implications and the government's efforts have been closely co-ordinated with Chinese and foreign firms who hoped to use the Olympics to increase international awareness and acceptance of their products. During the lead up to August 2008, Chinese Olympic sponsors such as Lenovo put together ad campaigns which were almost indistinguishable from government political advertising on the Olympics theme. This reflects the close relationship between advertising and propaganda in China. International PR companies such as Hill and Knowlton, Ogilvie and Maher, and Saatchi and Saatchi were also eager to help China re-launch what they call "the China brand."[33] The State Council Information Office (in charge of China's foreign propaganda activities) supports the notion of "re-branding China." However, officials from its sister organization, the Central Propaganda Department, have expressed objections to this terminology being associated with changing China's national image, as "China is not a brand."[34]

An important aspect of promoting the so-called "China brand" was to shift international perceptions of China from dated stereotypes such as pictures of "Tank Man,"[35] the individual who stood down a tank in Beijing in 1989; scenes of the demonstrators on Tiananmen Square in 1989; and ubiquitous images of Mao Zedong. The image of "Tank Man" has been shown repeatedly in the Western media and is constantly referred to in Western-led debate on China as both a symbol of modern China and of the battle of the individual against authoritarianism. Yet in China "Tank Man" is virtually unknown. The image was only briefly played on Chinese television in June 1989, and it was shown as an example of the "tolerance" of the Chinese authorities towards the protesters.[36] Few in China today, whether dissidents or not, would agree that "Tank Man" or the protests of 1989 are appropriate symbols for China's contemporary international profile. Similarly, China has now spent more years under the policies of "reform and opening up" (1978–present) than it did under Mao (1949–76). It is no accident that in 2008 the PRC Ministry of Culture refused to cooperate with the New York Asia Society's exhibition "Art and China's Revolution," which included numerous images of Mao[37] or that Olympic commemorative 10 yuan bank notes (which normally display Mao's image) featured a picture of the Bird's Nest Olympic Stadium.[38] Despite Western fascination with the Great Helmsman and his impact on Chinese culture and society, Mao Zedong long ago disappeared from China's foreign propaganda efforts, and these days is only selectively used in its domestic propaganda.

Olympics propaganda aimed at Chinese audiences was designed to garner popular consent for the continuance of CCP rule and build national pride.[39] Like foreigners, the Chinese people were also being persuaded to "buy in" to the "China brand," but for different reasons. Domestic Olympic propaganda activities focused on economic, cultural and social themes. Hosting the Olympics was an opportunity to step-up the ongoing efforts to educate the Chinese public to embrace the new "brand values" appropriate for this new, New China, such as innovation, industry, civil obedience, and national unity. It also served as an opportunity for the Chinese authorities to showcase the achievements of the government in recent years, while editing out the problems of past and present. Although the Olympics feature elite sports, a strong theme of China's domestic Olympics propaganda was inclusiveness and participation. This is in keeping with current government thinking on the need to build a (managed) civil society in China.[40]

Reflecting the complexity and reach of the CCP propaganda system Beijing Olympics propaganda activities began long before any sports stadiums were built and incorporated a lot more than media content. This is because the CCP-led propaganda system includes not only the media, but also advertising and all forms of publications, the education, cultural, science, sport, health, and technology sectors; as well as the network of propaganda cadres installed in Party committees and branches at all levels of organizations in both the state bureaucracy, non-state enterprises with CCP cells, the political department system of the People's Liberation Army, and all mass organizations. Beijing Olympics propaganda activities were a massive, long-term effort, with many strands. I do not have space to discuss them all, but in the following sections, I will analyze a few key threads of this "campaign of mass distraction" as examples of China's changed social pact.

Beijing Olympic slogans

Every successful propaganda or PR campaign must have simple, easily understandable catchwords which sum up the underlying message. In the past the CCP galvanized Chinese people with phrases such as "Smash the Four Olds!" or "Surpass Britain in Fifteen Years!" and targeted certain groups for demonizing. In the current era, CCP propaganda slogans are deliberately inclusive of everyone in Chinese society and avoid offending foreign sensibilities. Rather than revolution and radical social transformation, the goal of China's propaganda work is now social unity and cohesion – what the Hu administration calls "harmony" (*hexie*) and "harmonious society" (*hexie shehui*). The slogans of Beijing Olympics domestic propaganda: "Welcome the Olympics, Be Civilized, and Follow the New Trend" (*ying aoyun, jiang wenming, shu xinfeng*) and "I Participate, I Contribute and I am Happy" (*wocanyu, wo fengxian, wo kuaile*) are hard to oppose. The first slogan refers to efforts to prepare the Chinese people to be good hosts during the Olympics, while the second relates to the government's efforts to guide, and encourage, the development of civil society in China.

The Beijing Olympics foreign propaganda slogan "One World, One Dream" (*tong yige shijie, tong yige mengxiang*) and "New Beijing, New Olympics" (*xin Beijing, xin Aoyun*) is also hard to disagree with. The images associated with the first slogan reveal what the ideals of the "same dream" are: world peace and social harmony. In the last few years the theory of "harmonious society" has also been introduced into China's foreign policy as building a "harmonious world."[41] The second slogan reflects China's increasing desire to promote its own views and values internationally. This is a defensive strategy on China's part. In the post-Cold War era, China has felt increasingly challenged by successive US administrations' international promotion of "democracy"; through force if necessary. The 1999 conflict in Kosovo – when the US used the "right to protect" as a justification for intervening in ethnic conflict in Serbia – brought about a major shift in Chinese foreign policy. After 1989 China adopted a "lie low" strategy to deal with Western criticism, but from 1999 the new foreign policy line was to "use two hands to combat two hands."[42] This meant that China would be proactive in both political and economic activities in order to combat what were perceived as strong attacks from the West on both political and economic fronts.

It is noticeable that neither China's domestic nor its foreign-targeted Olympic propaganda featured political messages. Non-political propaganda and thought work have always been an important theme in the Chinese propaganda system. An example of this from the Mao years are the numerous "hygiene campaigns" (*weisheng yundong*) aimed at educating the Chinese population about various healthcare messages. However the fact that politics were downplayed at the Beijing Olympics is in and of itself political. Many voices inside and outside China sought to use the Beijing Olympics as a vehicle for political reform, encouraged by China's Olympic bid promises. However, the Chinese authorities were extremely strict on anyone, Chinese or non-Chinese, who linked dissent on any theme – including the demolition of housing to make way for Olympic buildings – to the Beijing Olympics. There was surprisingly strong public support in China for this stance, as shown by the public response to protests along the international Olympic torch relay and subsequent events. The CCP government explicitly linked support for the Olympics to patriotism, so to oppose or in any way criticize the Olympics was to be unpatriotic or for foreigners, anti-China.

Olympics media strategy

In the crucial two-year lead up to the Olympics, propaganda officials devised a complex media strategy aimed at both building positive international and national public opinion, as well as deflecting any "anti-China" attacks (the code word for negative reports on China and its government). In August 2006 the News Department of the Central Propaganda Department issued instructions to the Chinese media that for the next two years they should focus their energies on promoting the Beijing Olympics.[43] The Chinese media were instructed to report on how the Olympics were improving China's international image, improving relations between the peoples of the world and the Chinese people, and helping to push forward China's economic transformation. All Chinese Olympic reporters had to attend classes on "Olympic News Propaganda." The classes provided background on the Olympics as well as the dos and don'ts of Olympic reporting. Only politically reliable Chinese journalists were permitted to report on Olympic topics. Chinese media organisations were forbidden to employ journalists to work on Olympic-related stories who did not have journalist registration.[44]

The Chinese media were given strict instructions on what they should and should not cover during the two-year lead up to the Olympics. They were told they should not publish negative stories on problems with food and medicine safety, city construction, environmental protection, labor matters and major disasters, other than to use the official reports of the relevant departments, and that at all times they should follow the "news management bottom line" (*xinwen guanli dixian*) which means: censorship, check the origins of articles, and the accuracy of stories.[45] Propaganda officials urged Chinese journalists to focus on positive news when reporting the Olympics.[46] This is another way of saying that they should only promote news stories on how well China's Olympics preparations were going and ignore any negative stories about hosting the Olympics. This instruction was faithfully obeyed by the Chinese media. "Focus on positive propaganda" has been a phrase repeated like a mantra by successive leaders in propaganda work since 1989. Positive propaganda is regarded as an essential tool for maintaining Chinese citizens' confidence in their political and economic system. Negative news is only allowed to be reported very selectively, as it risks undermining public faith in the system. Journalists were urged to create emotionally moving stories about Olympic preparations in order to "draw in, touch, and move people."[47]

Olympic restrictions meant that through much of 2008 the Chinese media were banned from reporting on a simmering scandal about adulterated infant formula produced by one of China's major milk companies, San Lu, which is 43 percent owned by the New Zealand company Fonterra.[48] The scandal was only allowed to be publicized when the New Zealand government put pressure on Beijing to publicly withdraw the product and allow the media to discuss what had happened.[49] Three hundred thousand infants suffered kidney damage from the formula and at least six have died. It appears that in this case, commercial as well as political interests profited from the propaganda ban on bad news during the Olympics.

Any sensitive topics directly related to the Olympics needed the approval of BOCOG's Propaganda Department before being published. Stories relating to foreign tourists at the Olympics were particularly delicate. Chinese journalists were told that if there were any incidents involving foreign tourists they could only report the official line, and if there was no official line, they were not to report anything.[50] On August 10, 2008, a US tourist in Beijing, the father-in-law of one of the US Olympics coaches, was stabbed to death by a Chinese attacker. BOCOG officials confiscated the notebooks and tapes of Chinese reporters who covered a press conference where the US team talked about the killing. However, online reports were allowed greater freedom to cover such sensitive stories than the print media.[51] This is due to the different audiences in the print and online media, and the porous nature of the Internet, which meant that foreign reports on the same story were available to Chinese netizens.

While Olympic propaganda officials had the means to control the Chinese media, it was much harder to influence what the foreign media was saying about China during the lead up to the Olympics. As the opening ceremony drew closer, international and domestic pressure increased on Beijing to live up to its earlier promises linking hosting the Olympics and improving human rights in China. At a 2007 meeting to discuss Olympics propaganda, officials complained that "anti-China forces" (foreigners) were using the Olympics to attack China's "national image," as were Tibetan, Xinjiang and Taiwan independence groups, Falungong and democracy activists.[52] As an antidote to this the Chinese media were instructed to contradict foreign negative reports on China's human rights situation and religious policies by promoting "the achievements of the construction of a harmonious society."[53] They were told they should write about the important role of the Olympics in China's economic reforms and how the whole nation was preparing for the Olympics. They should also continually note the superiority of the socialist system in organizing important events. This theme was heard repeatedly as the Games drew near, and gained international attention when Zhang Yimou, artistic director of the opening and closing ceremonies, mentioned it as an explanation for the success of the opening ceremony.[54] Such rhetoric is a literal example of what I have called elsewhere "marketing dictatorship"[55] in China, the ongoing efforts to persuade the Chinese population to accept the current political system.

Ironically, the barrage of negative foreign reporting on China's hosting of the Olympics – which like the government's own campaign intensified as the countdown to the opening ceremony progressed – ultimately turned out to be in Beijing's favor. Western reporting on politically timed protests in Tibetan areas in March 2008 and on the protests that dogged the international route of the Olympic torch relay from March to May 2008, were perceived by many Chinese, in China and abroad, to be prejudiced and hostile. Their response was an outpouring of nationalistic support for both China and the Beijing Olympics using online forums, public rallies outside China, and even a few within China.[56] It was a resounding confirmation that the CCP's post-1989 strategy of indoctrinating Chinese youth with pro-PRC nationalism had worked and that hosting the Olympics could help to unite the Chinese people around their government.[57]

In principle, Beijing Olympics organizers tried to adopt a positive attitude towards the massive influx of foreign journalists who came to report on China and the Olympics. In the crucial period of August 2008 there were more than 20,000 foreign journalists registered to report in China – usually there are only 600–700 foreign journalists based in the country. The strategy advocated for managing the large numbers of foreign media coming to China to report the Olympics reflected traditional CCP political hospitality techniques directed at foreigners.[58] Beijing Olympics media managers were instructed to

> be good at looking after the media, be good at using the media. Utilise all-encompassing and detailed hospitality work on the media as a means to get the media to represent our views, "borrow a boat to go out on the seas," and report objectively on China and the Olympics. Pay special attention to cultural matters, small details, and courtesy; be warm and people-focused.[59]

However, in practice, during the Olympics many foreign journalists reported feeling suffocated by the excessive hospitality from volunteers who even followed them into toilets, and they were frustrated by continual stonewalling from Beijing Olympics press officials when raising any "political" questions.[60] In 2007 BOCOG announced that foreign journalists would be able to report unrestricted in China during the year leading up to the Olympics. Many foreign journalists found that this policy was interpreted very differently on the ground. When it came to politically sensitive topics, foreign journalists were just as constrained as usual. A further concession on a matter of interest to the foreign media contingent was the announcement that during the Olympic period restrictions would be lifted on many English-language websites which are normally blocked in China, such as the website of Amnesty International.[61] However, censorship of sensitive Chinese language websites continued unabated.[62]

Olympic volunteers

In the Mao years activism and volunteering formed an essential role in the construction of New China, helping to both build new social values and new infrastructure in a relatively short space of time. In the 1950s and 1960s thousands of Chinese volunteers worked on projects such as the Miyun Reservoir or joined in bringing in autumn harvests. Participation in such activities reflected Mao's ideas on education; that people could, and should, learn through labor. The backlash against the extremes of the Mao years meant that these practices fell out of favor in Chinese society in the 1980s and 1990s, though they continued on a much smaller scale. However since 2005, the CCP is again advocating and overseeing large-scale volunteering projects. This is in response to the ever-increasing rise in the numbers of non-governmental organizations in China and the government's awareness that such groups could become agents for political change, as they have been in other authoritarian societies.

There were 1.47 million volunteers (*zhiyuanzhe*) involved in the Beijing Olympics, 400, 000 in Beijing alone. Volunteers did everything from performing at the Olympic opening and closing ceremonies, doing translation work, acting as "go-fors" during Olympic events, and even providing security in the case of People's Armed Police (*wujing*) students who were selected to accompany the worldwide Olympic torch relay.

Volunteering is an important part of the Olympic tradition. In the 2000 Sydney Olympics, as in previous Games, volunteers came from a wide range of ages and social groups. However, at the Beijing Olympics volunteers were primarily selected from university students, mostly those based in Beijing.[63] This reflected the post-1989 emphasis on the political education of youth, particularly educated youth. Despite the restricted pool of applicants, more than 2 million people applied to be Beijing Olympics volunteers. They had to undergo a rigorous series of theoretical and physical examinations before being chosen.[64] All Olympics volunteers had to undergo extensive training in Olympic etiquette and protocol. The courses emphasized patriotism and provided participants with model answers on issues such as the status of Taiwan.[65]

Volunteering is under the "guidance" of the Central Propaganda Department and the network of controls and checks within the propaganda system.

Volunteer groups (non-governmental and government-directed) are considered to be mass organisations (*qunzhong tuanti*). The recent emphasis on volunteering is a response to the lessons learned from the series of "color revolutions" in a number of former communist states in the early 2000s. The color revolutions deeply worried the CCP leadership and have been studied as an anti-model for what China should avoid if it wants to maintain political stability.[66] Since 2005 the Party-state has been working on building up civil society in China, albeit one which is managed by the Party rather than one which will undermine it.[67] This is why Beijing Olympic propaganda emphasizes "participation" and state-managed volunteerism has expanded at the same time as controls have been increased on genuine non-governmental organizations.

Civilizing Beijing

Although they couldn't all be Olympics volunteers, from February 2006 ordinary Chinese people were still drawn into preparations for the Olympics through a massive public etiquette movement, aimed at "civilizing" Beijing.[68] This campaign formed part of the "welcoming the Beijing Olympics activities." It was also part of a larger and even more ambitious effort, the "Construction of Spiritual Civilization" (*jingshen wenming jianshe*) in China.[69] The Jiang administration launched the Construction of Spiritual Civilization (*jingshen wenming jianshe*) in 1996. It added a new layer of bureaucracy to the existing system of social and political control.[70] The Spiritual Civilization project aims to build a new, modern set of values for Chinese society to match China's modern "material civilization" – economic development and infrastructure.[71] Spiritual civilization is a form of mass education which replaces the political indoctrination of the Mao era with social education. Spiritual civilization activities are administered by the Office of Spiritual Civilization (*Jingshen wenming bangongshi*), a sub-agency of the Central Propaganda Department. Discussion on the need for "spiritual civilization work" (a code word for the CCP continuing to engage in ideological education and persuasion) began in the early 1980s as China began to embark on its new economic path and rejected the political excesses of the Mao years.

The Civilize Beijing campaign targeted indiscretions such as spitting in public, queue-jumping, and littering, it also promoted public-spirited values such as helping others in difficulty. It wasn't only directed at Beijing residents, though hosting the Beijing Olympics was the focus. The movement was given saturation coverage in a series of public advertisements on CCTV and local stations. The ads educated Chinese people on topics such as how to be a "good sport" by cheering for other's teams, how to clap, appropriate chants at Olympic sporting events, what to do with their rubbish in public places, and how to look after lost foreigners.

Another aspect of the campaign utilized Olympic English classes to promote the desired values of the movement. Taxi drivers, police, Olympic volunteers, and other relevant groups had to enroll in Olympic English, which combined practical vocabulary for managing everyday interactions with foreign tourists with set phrases on what to say if an Olympic visitor asked them a tricky political question. According to one Beijing taxi driver, if this happened, his brief was to stick to "the five goods": "the Olympics are good, the Communist Party is good, the government is good, and the taxi company is good."[72] Such attention to detail reflected the CCP's long tradition of carefully managing the foreign presence in China and maintaining a certain distance between foreigners and Chinese. Local residents' associations (*juweihui*), the lowest rung of the Chinese Party-state, also ran Olympic English classes for locals in the lead up to the Games. The classes weren't just confined to the able-bodied who might possibly be out on the streets and encounter a foreigner during the Olympics – special sessions were also held for the blind, physically disabled, and mentally handicapped.[73] The classes were a means to further engage in spiritual civilization education and involve as a great a number of Chinese people as possible in the Olympics.

As a result of these strenuous efforts to "civilize Beijing," during the mid-two weeks of August 2008, Beijing and other Olympic venues were effectively turned into massive Potemkin Villages. The popular response to the tightened official controls was generally resigned and good-humored.[74] The authorities had long ago signaled that any protests relating to the Olympics would be quickly quashed. During the Olympics, protesters who persisted in raising the issue of inadequate compensation for housing demolished as part of the Olympic preparations were sentenced to a year's re-education through labor.[75] Jokes circulated through mass text messaging and popular blogs told of Beijing residents taking a special drug so they could go to sleep and wake up when the Olympics were over and of other ways in which they tried to *bi yun*. This was a pun on two words with the same sound in Chinese but different meanings: the first meaning to "to use contraception" and the other to "avoid the Olympics."[76]

During the two-year countdown to the Olympics local Spiritual Civilization Offices organized and/or supervised a multitude of local level Olympics-related events, and Olympic-themed propaganda was the main theme of local public bulletin boards and other local propaganda formats.[77] One of the most visible ways in which the Olympics was promoted at the grassroots level was through countdown clocks, which recorded the number of days, minutes, and seconds till the opening of the Games. The first Olympic countdown clock – which was donated by watchmakers Omega – was installed in Tiananmen Square on September 22, 2004. Like so many aspects of the Olympics, the clock intertwined both political and commercial interests. From 2004 to 2008 Olympic countdown clocks were ubiquitous throughout China, but especially in Beijing. Counting down to the Olympic opening ceremony became an officially encouraged national pastime, and served as a useful diversion from other less positive social and economic issues.

The opening and closing ceremonies of the Beijing Olympics

The August 8 opening ceremony was the climax of years of building excitement. The two-hour ceremony surpassed all expectations, combining stupendous special effects with 14,000 performers. Many commentators had predicted that the opening ceremony would be Beijing's "coming out party," the one event which signaled China's re-launched national image. But the word "party" has connotations of spontaneity and fun, the very opposite of Beijing's awe-inspiring, highly scripted ceremony. In fact the 2008 Beijing Olympics opening ceremony was very like a product launch, on a scale that no company could ever hope to replicate. New, New China emerged to an international television audience estimated to have been the largest of all time. Approximately 2 billion viewers worldwide watched the August 8 ceremony.[78]

In a 1998 speech in Beijing at the China International Brand Strategy Conference, Kevin Roberts, CEO of Saatchi and Saatchi, suggested that the brand values of "new" China should be "eternity, wisdom, mystery, harmony, invention, energy, high intelligence, high craft, industriousness, pragmatism." He went on to say,

> As a consumer I have high expectations of this brand. I can't get these values from the West, especially as they are backed by 6,000 years of culture. This is the society that centuries ago invented paper and the printing press, gunpowder, the mechanical clock, acupuncture, the magnetic compass and so on. But the brand also offers the promise of the New China, the excitement of a country re-inventing itself, and the allure of a country which is returning to its central place in the world.[79]

Read ten years later, Roberts' advice reads like a detailed description of the program for Beijing's 8 p.m., August 8, 2008, Olympics opening ceremony. Even the timing for this ceremony was chosen to reflect traditional Chinese ideas on numerology, concepts which, only a few years before, were denounced as feudal and superstitious.[80]

The opening ceremony closely reflected recent readjustments in China's national narrative.[81] The central themes were the richness and the mystique of China's historical culture, and the strength of its current economic development. The first part of the ceremony was a stylized chronology of Chinese history. In this narrative the Mao era was virtually elided, with only a few oblique references, such as the faux Mao suits worn by one set of performers, and a blank (electronic) scroll which was unfurled and gradually filled in throughout the performance. This referenced a famous Mao quote that the Chinese people were like a blank sheet of paper. According to Mao: "On a blank sheet of paper free from any mark, the freshest and most beautiful characters can be written, the freshest and most beautiful pictures can be painted."[82] Throughout the opening ceremony the "blank screen" of China was painted into a landscape picture by the steps of dancers, then colored in by the tracking of Olympic athletes across the LCD screen. The ceremony also appeared to hint at another famous dictum, Deng Xiaoping's advice to Chinese people on how to deal with the pain of earlier eras: "Put the past behind you and look to the future."[83]

The ceremony highlighted the power of the masses, which reflects yet another Mao adage: "The people have strength."[84] Individuals only featured in the ceremony when they were supported by the masses. This was particularly emphasized when a single female dancer in Tang Dynasty costume was borne aloft around the stadium on a platform lifted by thousands of male supporters. In a tragic twist, only days before the opening ceremony the original dancer who was to perform this piece fell in rehearsals and became a paraplegic. The Chinese media were initially forbidden from reporting on this story, along with other Olympics-related controversies such as having another key performer mime her performance because it was believed that the singer with the better voice was less photogenic.[85]

In accordance with Olympic tradition, the second half of the ceremony consisted of the athletes from the various countries filing in to the stadium. This part of the ceremony was enlivened by the dancing and smiling of hundreds of identically dressed and styled young Chinese women, who lined the route as the athletes walked in, then formed a guard of honor enclosing them into an area at the center of the stadium. The young women's presence (and their discreet security role) made the ceremony seem even more like a product launch than a sporting event. Chinese companies frequently utilize bevies of identically clad beauties as a decorative feature in PR functions. The young women danced and smiled for hours. Like all Olympic performers they would have had to rehearse for up to a year to perform their role in the opening ceremony, they received no pay, and had only an Olympic certificate to thank them for their effort.[86] The event's artistic director, Zhang Yimou, praised all the opening ceremony performers and what they had achieved, saying that "uniformity brings beauty" and to follow orders "is the Chinese spirit" which he said, "many foreigners can not achieve."[87] Nine thousand of the 14,000 performers were soldiers in the People's Liberation Army.[88] PLA General Political Department Propaganda Department deputy head Zhang Jigang was the executive director of the Olympics opening ceremony.[89]

The program for the opening ceremony was so sensitive that it had to be vetted and approved by the most senior leaders of the CCP, the Standing Committee of the Politburo. According to Zhang Yimou, "No other artistic activity has had this many layers, and such a high level review."[90] During the closing ceremony the former general secretary of the CCP, Jiang Zemin, appeared second after the current general secretary Hu Jintao, an indication of Jiang's continued prominence in the senior leadership. The closing ceremony also featured Jiang's favourite singer Song Zuying in a duet with Placido Domingo. Both these moves were an attempt to appease the Shanghai clique within the senior leadership. I was able to watch the US broadcast of the opening ceremony and the New Zealand broadcast of the closing ceremony as well as the CCTV broadcast of both. Non-Chinese broadcast coverage focused on the performers and the sports people; however, the CCTV coverage frequently flashed back from scenes of the performers to show the Chinese leadership impassively viewing the spectacle from their red and gold throne-like seats. It was a subliminal reminder to the Chinese people of the continued importance of the role of the CCP in overseeing this new, New China, a China which promises prosperity and opportunities for all who work hard in the Chinese equivalent of the American dream.

The Olympics closing ceremony had considerably less hoopla than the opening ceremony. The propaganda messages were more muted this time round and entertainment appeared to be the main goal. Following the trend set by the opening ceremony, the closing ceremony fused the traditional with visions of the future. The highlight of the show was a "memory tower," a futuristic pagoda reminiscent of the Integral in Zamyatin's dystopian novel *We*,[91] which seethed with men in silver suits. It was an echo of another stereotypical image from the Mao era which has now been summarily renounced:[92] that of the Chinese people as hundreds of thousands of "little blue ants."[93] The men in silver suits climbing and performing gravity-defying acrobatics over the tower referred to China's aspirations to send an astronaut to the moon by 2020. Towards the end of the closing ceremony the same band of female *erhu* players who had featured in China's 2008 Olympics promo at the 2004 Athens Olympics closing ceremony reappeared. After the Athens performance Zhang Yimou was pilloried for approving the musicians' skimpy outfits and risqué dancing.[94] This time the women were discretely clothed in sports outfits and gently swayed rather than doing the "can can" they performed previously. Beijing's Olympic ceremonies were noticeable for their lack of sex and humor.

Many Chinese families got together to have dinner and watch the opening ceremony similar to the way in recent years they have celebrated Chinese New Year by watching the CCTV New Year extravaganza. "Live sites" for showing the opening ceremony on big screens were also set up around Beijing at various locations. Twenty-one thousand gathered to view the opening ceremony at the Temple of Heaven site.[95] The Olympic opening ceremony had record TV audiences in China, quite possibly the largest audience ever.[96] All Olympic broadcasts had extremely tight security nationwide.[97] The fear was that some dissident group might attempt to take over the broadcasts, as the outlawed spiritual group Falungong had done on several occasions in recent years.

Exactly how many people in China were watching the Olympics coverage was a political matter, as well as being commercially sensitive. Chinese journalists were instructed to use CCTV's figures only. The higher the ratings, the more CCTV can charge for their advertising in future. The CCTV figures on the audience for the opening ceremony were considerably higher than those estimated by foreign firms. Figures for viewer turnout ranged from 39.5 percent from AGB Nielsen Media Research to 68.8 percent from CSM Media

Research – a partnership between London-based TNS Group and CCTV-affiliated CTR Market Research.[98] According to AGB Nielsen, Chinese viewing levels during the actual sporting events were high; they were up 45 percent on usual television viewing on day three of the Olympics alone.[99]

Conclusion

In a mid-2008 propaganda cadres meeting, Li Dongsheng, chair of the Beijing Olympics News Propaganda Work Coordinating Group, commented that the CCP had faced its greatest risk of "peaceful evolution" when the "third" or "fourth generation" of children born after 1949, came of age. That danger passed in the 1980s and 1990s, and the CCP-led political system has survived. Now the fifth and sixth generations, born in the 1980s and 1990s, are coming of age, but Li asserted that there is "basically not a chance [of peaceful evolution]."[100] "Peaceful evolution" is a code word for the Party's fear that a mass-led democratic transition will occur in China and that they will lose power. The phrase originates from a series of speeches made by former US secretary of state John Foster Dulles in the 1950s that communist governments will be gradually be undermined by their population's exposure to Western culture, leading to a "peaceful evolution" rather than a violent revolution. The popular response to the perceived Western media bias during the Olympic torch relay shows that Li's confidence in Chinese youth is not misplaced.[101]

In July 2008 a Pew survey announced that 86 percent of Chinese people were satisfied with their country's development, while in 2004 only 42 percent of Chinese people had agreed with this sentiment.[102] Despite facing multiple troubles China's "party-in-power," the CCP, has regained public support for its continued rule. According to the Pew survey, China now ranks number one in the world in terms of public support for a government. As a result of assiduous attention to the techniques of mass persuasion, since the events of 1989, CCP legitimacy to rule has stabilized – though the foundations of that legitimacy have changed. Rather than a mass-led democratic transition being imminent, the Chinese equivalent of Walter Lippmann's "group mind"[103] has now crystallized around the view that the current political system, despite its flaws, is the best one for the country.

Hosting the Olympics was supposed to improve China's international profile as well as domestic support for the government. The two weeks of the August 2008 Olympics were indeed a sporting and PR triumph for Beijing. Despite the controversies surrounding hosting the Olympics in Beijing – human rights, the environment, food safety and other issues – the Chinese government actually managed to increase its public approval in China and has succeeded in reshaping its image on the international scene.

The successful hosting of the Beijing Olympics and the two-year campaign that preceded it mark a new watershed in China's propaganda work. It is the culmination of years of work in multiple aspects such as the refinement of media management techniques, the "re-branding" of China, the Party's efforts to forge a relationship between commercial and political interests, the renewed role of the PLA in propaganda work, and the CCP's achievements in regaining the support of leading intellectuals and artists such as director Zhang Yimou.

In the two-year build up to the events of 2008, China's saturation-style Olympics domestic propaganda dominated the Chinese public sphere, deliberately drowning out other issues and voices and denying them the opportunity to promote an alternative political agenda to the Chinese public. We should be prepared for more such campaigns. The countdown to the Shanghai 2010 World Expo and the hoopla during the year of the Expo achieved similar goals. China's ongoing space efforts are also being highly publicized domestically and internationally for similar reasons. Such campaigns help to redirect attention from other more troubling topics and build confidence and pride in the existing system.

Out of the Beijing Olympics, with many plumes of smoke and multiple flashes of fireworks, China re-launched itself as a determined, united, powerful, wealthy, culturally rich nation (apparently) singing harmoniously as one. As the audience's senses were distracted by the spectacle of China's rebirth they may have neglected to ponder the human, cultural, economic and political cost which lay beneath this drama. What we now know about the actions taken behind the scene to prepare for the Beijing Olympics takes some of the shine off that triumph.

Notes

1 *Neibu tongxin* (hereafter *NBTX*), 2007/15, p. 1. This publication is a bi-monthly classified bulletin issued by the News Department of the Central Propaganda Department which instructs the Chinese media on the current propaganda line.

2 On the role of the *xitong* in the Chinese bureaucratic system, see Kenneth Lieberthal, *Governing China: From Revolution through Reform* (New York: W. W. Norton, 1995), pp. 192–208.

3 The project "Propaganda and Thought Work in Contemporary China," funded by the Royal Society of New Zealand Marsden Fund.

4 See "Zhonggong bu qi bu gao zhengzhi yundong kao zhidu fan fubai de xinlu" (The CCP won't launch or engage in political movements and is following the new path of relying on the system to deal with corruption), *Liaowang*, July 9, 2008, http://cpc.people.com.cn/GB/64093/64099/7490432.html. See also Michael Schoenhals, "Political Movements, Change and Stability: The Communist Party in Power, 1949–1999," *China Quarterly*, no. 159 (September 1999), pp. 595–605.

5 Ding Xueliang, *The Decline of Communism in China: Legitimacy Crisis, 1977–1989* (Cambridge: Cambridge University Press, 1994).

6 Deng Xiaoping, "Address to Officers at the Rank of General and Above in Command of the Troops Enforcing Martial Law in Beijing," *Deng Xiaoping wenxuan* (Deng Xiaoping: Selected Works), vol. 3, accessible at http://english.peopledaily.com.cn/dengxp/

7 For more on this topic see, Anne-Marie Brady, *Marketing Dictatorship: Propaganda and Thought Work in Contemporary China* (Lanham MD: Rowman and Littlefield, 2008).

8   Zhonggong zhongyang xuanchuanbu zhengce fagui yanjiushi, *Shisi Da yilai xuanchuan sixiang gongzuo de lilun yu shixian* (Theory and Practice in Propaganda and Thought Work since the 14th Party Congress) (Beijing: Xuexi Chubanshe, 1997), p. 367.

9   Harold D. Lasswell, "The Theory of Political Propaganda," *American Political Science Review*, 21 (1927), pp. 627–631.

10 Seymour Martin Lipset, "Some Social Requisites of Democracy: Economic Development and Political Legitimacy," *American Political Science Review*, 53, 1 (1959), p. 86.

11 Edward Bernays, *Propaganda* (New York, n.p., 1928), and "The Engineering of Consent," *Annals of the American Academy of Political and Social Science*, 1947, 250 (March 1947), pp. 113–120; Noam Chomsky and Edward S. Herman, *Manufacturing Consent: The Political Economy of the Mass Media* (New York: Pantheon Books, 1988); Jacques Ellul, *Propaganda: The Formation of Men's Attitudes* (New York: Vintage, 1973); Walter Lippmann [1925], "The Phantom Public," in *Propaganda*, edited by Robert Jackall (New York: New York University Press, 1995), pp. 47–53; Edward Sapir, *Culture, Language and Personality* (Berkeley: University of California Press, 1961); Benjamin Lee Whorf, "The Relation of Habitual Thought and Behavior to Language," in *Language, Thought, and Reality*, edited by J. B. Caroll (Cambridge MA: Technology Press of Massachusetts Institute of Technology, 1956), pp. 134–159.

12 Jiang Jingyi, "Zhengzhi hefaxing: Gongchandang zhizheng jianshe de zhongyao keti" (Political Legitimacy: An Important Issue for the Establishment of the CCP as a Party in Power), *Makesizhuyi yanjiu wang* (Marxist Research Online), January 12, 2006, http://myy.cass.cn/file/206011221059.html; Wu Kefeng, "Zheng ji kunju: gainian, yuanyin, ji qi pojie" (Political Achievement and Political Difficulties: Perspectives, Causes and Solutions), *Makesizhuyi yu xianshi* (Marxism and Reality) no. 6 (2006); Xie Fangyi, "Zhengzhi zhuanxing zhong zhengzhi hefaxing wenti tanxi" (English title: On Political Legitimacy in the Transformation of the Party), *Zhonggong Zhejiang shenwei dangxiao xuebao* (Journal of the CCP Zhejiang Party School) no. 5 (2004).

13 Yang Guangbin, "Hefaxing zhebi shenme?" (What's Behind "Legitimacy"?), *Xuexi shibao* (Study Times), October 23, 2007.

14 "Zhongyang wenmingwei Beijing Aozuwei fachu tongzhi guangfan kaizhan 'ying Aoyun, jiang wenming, shu xinfeng' huodong"(Central Spiritual Civilization Office, BOCOG, issue a notice to launch a broad movement to "Welcome the Olympics, be civilized, and follow the new trend") February 13, 2006, www.qlwmw.com/show.asp?id=2424

15 William R. Freudenberg and Maria Allario, "Weapons of Mass Distraction: Magicianship, Misdirection, and the Dark Side of Legitimation," *Sociological Forum*, 22, 2 (2007), pp. 146–173.

16 See Connie Rice's top ten list of "weapons of mass distraction" at www.npr.org/templates/story/story.php?storyId=3384070

17 Stephen L. Macknik, Mac King, James Randi, Apollo Robbins, Teller, John Thompson, and Susana Martinez-Conde, "Attention and Awareness in Stage Magic: Turning Tricks into Research," *Nature*, July 30, 2008, www.nature.com/nrn/journal/vaop/ncurrent/full/nrn2473.html

18 On the politics of China and the Olympics see Susan Brownell, *Beijing Games; What the Olympics mean for China* (Lanham MD: Rowman and Littlefield, 2008); Sun Wanning, "Semiotic Over-determination or 'Indoctritainment': Television, Citizenship, and the Olympic Games," in *Media in China: Consumption, Content and Crisis*, edited by Stephanie Hemelryk Donald, Michael Keane and Yin Hong (London: RoutledgeCurzon, 2002); Xu Guoqi, *Olympic Dreams: China and Sports, 1895–2008* (Cambridge MA: Harvard University Press, 2008).

19   Mao Zedong, "A Study of Physical Education," *Xin qingnian* (New Youth) 1917, www.marxists.org/reference/archive/mao/selected-works/volume-6/mswv6_01. htm#s2
20   Chen Junhong, ed., *Jiaqiang he gaijin sixiang zhengzhi gongzuo xuexi duben* (A reader on Strengthening and Reforming Political Thought Work) (Beijing: Zhonggong Zhongyang Dangxiao Chubanshe, 1999), p. 169.
21   Deng Xiaoping, "We Are Confident That We Can Handle China's Affairs Well," http://english.peopledaily.com.cn/dengxp/vol3/text/d1040.html See also Xuanchuan Wenhua Zhengce Fagui Bianweihui, ed., *Xuanchuan wenhua zhengce fagui* (Policies and Regulations on Propaganda and Culture) (Kunming: Yunnan Renmin Chubanshe, 1999), p. 10.
22   Lindsey Hilsum, "The Patriot Games," *New Statesman*, July 31, 2008. On the medal tally see http://results.beijing2008.cn/WRM/ENG/INF/GL/95A/GL0000000. shtml
23   Jeremy Page, "Olympics – Beijing's PR Team Pats Itself on the Back," *Reuters Financial Report*, July 14, 2001, www.prfirms.org/resources/news/olympics071401.asp.
24   See www.Chinavitae.com/biography/Liu_Peng
25   The Central Propaganda Department (CPD) has a leadership (*lingdao*) relationship with some sectors of the propaganda system such as the media, and "guidance" relations with other sectors such as sport or health. "Guidance" means just that, the General Administration of Sport is not under orders from the CPD. The CPD is not concerned with sporting issues *per se*, but in a more abstract sense where they touch on ideological concerns or are connected to propaganda.
26   The following is a report from the meeting of a local level Beijing Olympic News Co-ordinating Group, accessed via a cache site. http://209.85.141.104/search? q=cache:DrQA_aZUl9sJ:www.chuzhou.gov.cn/art
27   *NBTX*, 2007/15, p. 1.
28   An example of this is the establishment of China's Confucius Institutes, which were first set up in 2004. The Institutes promote Chinese language and culture. As of 2011, there are 322 Confucius Institutes worldwide.
29   "Beijing Aozuwei guwen: Aoyunhui shi tuichu guojia xingxiang zhanlue qiji" (BOCOG Adviser: The Olympics Is a Turning Point for the Strategy of Promoting the National Image), *Zhongguo jingji jikan*, August 4, 2008, http://news.xinhuanet. com/politics/2008-08/04/content_8934954.htm. See also Wang Hongying, "National Image-building and Chinese Foreign Policy," *China: An International Journal*, 1, 1 (2003), pp. 46–72.
30   www.npopss-cn.gov.cn/zhongdaxiangmu/20071213bjayxxgj.htm
31   The phrase "peaceful rise" (*heping jueqi*) was first used in the speech of Zheng Bijian, at the Bo'ao Forum on November 23, 2003.
32   On the improvement in relations between the CCP and the Chinese intelligentsia from the mid-1990s, see Joseph Fewsmith, *China since Tiananmen: The Politics of Transition* (Cambridge: Cambridge University Press, 2001).
33   See Joshua Cooper Ramo, "Brand China," a report sponsored by Hill and Knowlton, February 2007, http://joshuaramo.com/_files/pdf/Brand-China.pdf; "Saatchi Eyes Branding China Inc.," *China Daily*, October 22, 2004, www.chinadaily. com.cn/english/doc/2004-10/22/content_384654.htm
34   Interview with SCIO adviser, September 2007.
35   In 2006 PBS produced a documentary on how "Tank Man" had helped shape Western perceptions of contemporary China, see www.pbs.org/wgbh/pages/frontline/ tankman/view/
36   Scenes from the CCTV reporting on "Tank Man" appear in the documentary *Gate of Heavenly Peace* (1996).
37   Robin Pogrebin, "China Won't Lend Art Works to Asia Society Exhibition," August 20, 2008, www.nytimes.com/2008/08/20/arts/design/20soci.html

38   "China Debuts New 10 Yuan Note," Associated Press, July 7, 2008, www.msnbc. msn.com/id/25571090/

39   *NBTX*, 2007/15, p. 1.

40   See Gao Yanqing, "Gongmin shehui yu sixiang zhengzhi gongzuo fazhan de xin qushi" (New Developments in Civil Society and Political Thought Work), *Dang zheng ganbu luntan* (Political Cadre Forum) (September 2007), pp. 28–30. Interview with thought work policy adviser, December 2007.

41   Zheng Yongnian and Sow Keat Tok, "Harmonious Society and Harmonious World: China's Policy Discourse Under Hu Jintao," October 2007, Briefing Series 26, China Policy Institute, Nottingham University.

42   Chen Junhong, ed., *Jiaqiang he gaijin sixiang zhengzhi gongzuo xuexi duben* (A Reader on Strengthening and Reforming Political Thought Work) (Beijing: Zhonggong Zhongyang Dangxiao Chubanshe, 1999), p. 30.

43   *NBTX*, 2006/15, p. 9 and 2007/15, p. 1.

44   *NBTX*, 2006/15, p. 9.

45   *NBTX*, 2007/15, p.1. See also "Censors Make News in PR battle," *South China Morning Post*, August 14, 2008, which reproduced a copy of instructions from the CPD with a detailed list of propaganda dos and don'ts in the period leading up to and during the Olympics.

46   *NBTX*, 2005/2, p. 9.

47   *NBTX*, 2007/15, p. 1.

48   Documents relevant to this scandal are available here: www.chinasmack.com/ stories/kidney-stone-gate-fake-baby-milk-powder-sanlu-baidu/

49   "Fonterra: We Acted Responsibly on Killer Milk," *New Zealand Herald*, September 16, 2008. www.nzherald.co.nz/nz/news/article.cfm?c_id=1& objectid = 10532373

50   Jacquelin Magnay, "Censors Make News in Public Relations Battle," *South China Morning Post*, August 14, 2008.

51   Rebecca Mackinnon, "The Chinese Censorship Foreigners Don't See," *Wall St Journal Asia*, August 14, 2008.

52   *NBTX*, 2007/15, p. 1.

53   *NBTX*, 2007/15, p. 1.

54   "Only China Can Produce This: An Interview with Zhang Yimou," *Southern Weekend*, August 18, 2008, translated by China Digital Times.

55   Anne-Marie Brady, *Marketing Dictatorship: Propaganda and Thought Work in Contemporary China* (Lanham MD: Rowman and Littlefield, 2008).

56   There are many examples of this sentiment online; the following video clip, made by a UK-based Chinese student is representative. See Jordan Chen, "Unfair Media London," www.youtube.com/watch?v=fNgT5HdCqg4

57   See for example "Red Heart China Appears in Netizens MSN Signatures," *Xinhua*, April 18, 2008.

58   See Anne-Marie Brady, *Making the Foreign Serve China: Managing Foreigners in the People's Republic* (Lanham MD: Rowman and Littlefield, 2003).

59   *NBTX*, 2007/15, p. 1.

60   Email communications with journalists from AFP, *The Australian*, *Sydney Morning Herald*, and the *Jutland Post* based in Beijing during the Olympics, August 2008. See also http://blogs.afp.com/?post/2008/08/16/Beware-threat-of-exploding-Olympic-muffins

61   "Hu Says China Stands by Games Pledges, Web Curbs Lifted," Reuters, August 1, 2008.

62   Rebecca Mackinnon, "The Chinese Censorship Foreigners Don't See," *Wall St Journal Asia*, August 14, 2008.

63   http://en.beijing2008.cn/20/95/article212019520.shtml

64   Carol Huang, "For Beijing's Olympic Volunteers, the Rules are Many," *Christian Science Monitor*, July 21, 2008, www.csmonitor.com/2008/0717/p04s01-woap.html

65   For an example of the training volunteers received, see www.beijing2008.com/04/
      56/article212035604.shtml, accessed February 5, 2007.
66   Liu, Ming, ed., *Jietou zhengzhi yu 'yanse geming'* (Street Politics and the 'Color
      Revolutions') (Beijing: Zhongguo Chuanmei Chubanshe, 2006). Interviews with
      government policy advisers in Beijing, October and December 2007.
67   Gao Yanqing, "Gongmin shehui yu sixiang zhenzhi gongzuo fazhan de xin
      qushi" (New Developments in Civil Society and Political Thought Work), *Dang
      zheng ganbu luntan* (Political Cadre Forum) (September 2007), pp. 28–30.
68   "Beijing tries to 'civilize' residents ahead of Olympics," AFP, February 21, 2006.
69   *NBTX*, 2007/15, p. 6.
70   A number of authors have discussed the emergence of spiritual civilization ideology.
      See Anne Anagnost, "Constructing the Civilized Community," in Theodore Huters,
      R. Bin Wong, and Pauline Yu, eds., *Culture and the State in Chinese History: Con-
      ventions, Accommodations and Critiques* (Stanford CA: Stanford University Press,
      1997); Borge Bakken, *The Exemplary Society: Human Improvement, Social Control,
      and the Dangers of Modernity in China* (Oxford and New York: Oxford University
      Press, 2000); Anne-Marie Brady, *Marketing Dictatorship: Propaganda and Thought
      Work in Contemporary China* (Lanham, MD: Rowman and Littlefield, 2008);
      Nicholas Dynon, "'Four Civilizations' and the Evolution of Post-Mao Chinese
      Socialist Ideology," *China Journal*, no. 60, July 2008, pp. 83–109; Sara Friedman,
      "Embodying Civility: Civilizing Processes and Symbolic Citizenship in Southeastern
      China," *Journal of Asian Studies*, 63, 3 (August 2004), pp. 687–718; Stig Thogersen,
      "Parasites or Civilisers: The Legitimacy of the Chinese Communist Party in Rural
      Areas," *China: An International Journal*, 1, 2 (September 2003), pp. 200–223.
71   Interview with thought work policy adviser, December 2007.
72   Lindsey Hilsum, "The Patriot Games," *New Statesman*, July 31, 2008.
73   See www.beijing2008.cn/63/08/article214020863.shtml accessed September 22,
      2008. Interview, Residents Association Propaganda Section Director, Beijing,
      September 2007.
74   Anita Chang, "Chinese Grumble About the Olympics, but Quietly," Associated
      Press, August 4, 2008. Phone interviews with two Beijing-based former activists,
      April 2008 and August 2008.
75   Nick Venter, "China – Orwell's Dream Come True," *The Dominion Post*, August
      25, 2008.
76   Ben Blanchard, "Two Great Olympic Jokes Circulating in Beijing," Reuters,
      August 1, 2008.
77   Interviews at several residents' associations in Beijing, September 2007.
78   http://blog.nielsen.com/nielsenwire/media_entertainment/beijing-opening-ceremonys-
      global-tv-audience-hit-2-billion/
79   See Kevin Roberts, 1998 speech, www.saatchikevin.com/Brand_China_Beijing/;
      see also Tsinghua-Ogilvie Project for Public Branding, School of Journalism and
      Communication, Tsinghua University. www.tsjc.tsinghua.edu.cn/index.php?
      id=128& styleid = 2
80   Xuanchuan wenhua zhengce fagui bianweihui, ed., *Xuanchuan wenhua zhengce
      fagui* (Policies and Regulations on Propaganda and Culture) (Kunming: Yunnan
      Renmin Chubanshe, 1999), p. 305.
81   On the politics of China's national narrative see Ann Anagnost, *National Past-
      times: Narrative, Representation, and Power in Modern China* (Durham NC and
      London: Duke University Press, 1997).
82   Mao Zedong, "Introducing a Co-operative," April 15, 1958, *Quotations from
      Chairman Mao* (Peking: Foreign Languages Press, 1966), p. 36.
83   Deng Xiaoping, September 5, 1988, http://zhanyi.gov.cn/youth/dxp/c1890.html
84   "Zhongguo renmin you liliang zhishi qinlue zhanzheng," *Renmin Ribao* (People's
      Daily), November 7, 1950.

85   Barbara Demick, "Officials: Dancer Paralyzed, Organisers Take Flak for Belated Reporting," *Chicago Tribune*, August 15, 2008, www.chicagotribune.com/news/nationworld/chi-chinese-danceraug15,0,2964490.story
86   "Olympic Artists Angry," August 14, 2008, www.aftenposten.no/english/sports/article2592984.ece
87   "Only China Can Produce This: An Interview with Zhang Yimou," *Southern Weekend*, August 16, 2008, translated by China Digital Times.
88   "Chinese Whispers," www.stuff.co.nz/4661348a26500.html
89   http://english.chinamil.com.cn/site2/special-reports/2008-08/27/content_1446479.htm; http://gb.cri.cn/17844/2008/09/09/1945s2233537.htm
90   "The Way Art Works: An Interview with Zhang Yimou," *Southern Weekend*, August 16, 2008, translated by China Digital Times.
91   Yevgeny Zamyatin [1924], *We*, Gregory Zilboorg, trans. (New York: Dutton Books, 1959).
92   See Cheng Yunjie, "Memoirs Give Glimpse of China's Farewell to 'Blue-Ants' era," http://news.xinhuanet.com/english/2008-09/11/content_9930398.htm
93   Robert Guillain, *The Blue Ants: 600 Million Chinese under the Red Flag*, translated by Mervyn Savill (London: Secker and Warburg, 1957).
94   www.chinatoday.com.cn/English/e2008/e200803/p52.htm
95   Sixth IOC/BOCOG press conference, August 14, 2008.
96   David Barboza, "The Games Are Golden for a Chinese Network," *International Herald Tribune*, August 21, 2008.
97   "Shi guangdianju zhaokai huiyi quanmian bushu Aoyunhui qijian guangbo dianshi xuanchuan, anquan bochu gongzuo" (City Administration of Radio Film and Television Host a Meeting on Deploying Radio, Film and Television Propaganda and Secure Broadcasting During the Olympics), August 8, 2008, www.chuzhou.gov.cn/art2008/08/08/art_51
98   Jonathan Landreth, "World Audience Huge for Games Opener, China Breaks Record, German Viewership Lacklustre," *The Hollywood Reporter*, August 10, 2008.
99   "Chinese Viewing Levels up 45% During Olympics," August 12, 2008, http://blog.nielsen.com/nielsenwirc/tag/tv-rating/
100 http://blog.newsweek.com/blogs/beijing/archive/2008/08/04/even-state-media-must-break-records.aspx
101 Melinda Liu and Duncan Hewitt, "China's Most Modern Citizens Aren't Drawing It Any Closer to the West," *Newsweek*, August 9, 2008.
102 http://pewglobal.org/reports/display.php?ReportID=261
103 Walter Lippmann [1925], "The Phantom Public," pp. 47–53 in *Propaganda*, edited by Robert Jackall (New York: New York University Press, 1995).

2 Talking up the market

Economic propaganda in contemporary China

Anne-Marie Brady and He Yong

The relative success of China's post-1978 economic policies in raising standards of living for many and creating hope of a better future for others has meant that the economy now has a key role in CCP political legitimacy. Yet the transition from a socialist economy to a capitalist society has come at great cost; many of the economic achievements of the socialist era have been lost as part of this process. In the years from 1949 to 1978 Chinese people were told that markets and capitalism were exploitative and must be abolished in China. Since 1978, and even more so after 1992, Chinese people have been educated to accept the opposite view: that "the socialist market economy" (a euphemism for CCP-controlled capitalism) is a necessary stage for China's (now mythical) socialist future.

Economic matters are now a key focus of both China's domestic and foreign propaganda activities. Economic propaganda is a politically sensitive matter in China. There are obvious long-standing sensitivities around the radical shift in CCP policies which the era of "reform and opening up" represents. But even more sensitive in the current period of global economic crisis is the role of economic propaganda in talking up the market and maintaining market confidence within and without China. Despite the importance of this form of propaganda in China, it is a surprisingly understudied subject, whether in Western or Chinese scholarly sources. This chapter utilizes internal policy papers, interviews with experts, and relevant secondary sources to analyze the role and impact of economic propaganda in China's contemporary "thought management" and how the policies on promoting economic propaganda play out in key papers within the Chinese media, particularly during a period of crisis such as the current global economic crisis and during the San Lu tainted milk powder scandal of 2007–8.

Economic thought reform

The current importance of economic propaganda in China reflects the fact that in the post-Mao era, economic development has become the core political task of the Chinese government.[1] Initially this new direction was highly controversial among Party conservatives. It effectively negated the Mao era's emphasis on the political thought reform of China, meanwhile progressively undermining many of the economic-related achievements of the Mao years including equal opportunity for women in employment and the egalitarian social and education policies that helped to raise the standard of living of millions of Chinese people. Party leaders dealt with these tensions both in the 1980s and the years that followed by avoiding linking the Party's new economic direction with capitalistic phraseology and emphasizing the CCP's guiding role throughout the whole process. For example, at the 13th Party Congress in 1987 General Party Secretary Zhao Ziyang announced a new slogan "One focus, two basic points" (*yi ge zhongxin, liang ge jiben dian*). These were: focus on economic development, stick to the Four Cardinal Principles,[2] and press ahead with reform and opening-up.[3] In real terms this meant that China would maintain its one-party communist government at the same time as engaging in a market economy. This was a totally new form of political economy which necessitated multi-level adjustments in China's system of governance.

One aspect where adjustments were made was in the system of economic propaganda media management. Traditionally, economic propaganda themes had always been guided by the Central Propaganda Department, while the concrete details of new policies were issued by state agencies engaged in economic affairs. However China's development of a more market-oriented economy required a media management system for economic matters which could respond more rapidly to crisis situations. In 1987 the State Administration for Commodity Prices (SACP), a subordinate of the State Council, discovered some Chinese newspapers were disclosing the government's Consumer Price Index (CPI) control targets for the following year, and that some reports had mistakenly replaced the official figure of 6 percent with 60 percent.[4] After this incident the SACP issued guidelines on how the media ought to portray commodity price information in the future. However since SACP had no authority over the media within the propaganda system it was unable to enforce its suggestions. The SACP had to submit its views to both the State Council and the Central Propaganda Department before action was taken. The SACP advice was eventually jointly approved by both the State Council and Central Propaganda Department, which instructed the whole propaganda system to follow these new guidelines.

The clumsiness of this system and its inability to respond in a timely manner to economic crises is why, in February 1989, the Central Committee of the CCP ordered the Research Office of the State Council to supervise economic propaganda instead of the Central Propaganda Department. The document issued by the General Office of the State Council defined the authority of the State Council on economic propaganda as follows:

1 The Research Office of the State Council will host a biweekly press symposium introducing the current economic situation and issuing instructions on how to report current economic policies.

2   All economics-related editorials, important commentaries, and significant reports published in the media will be censored by the Research Office of the State Council.

3   The propaganda work of professional economic publishing outlets such as *Economic Daily* and *Economic Information Daily* will be supervised by the Research Office of the State Council.[5]

The Research Office of the State Council is the primary policy-making organization of the government. It drafts the *Government Work Report* every year for the premier, which is submitted to the National People's Congress. It has eight sub-units to deal with key state issues, including long-term planning, macroeconomic policies, agriculture, and so on. Following the ruling each sub-unit was in charge of drafting news briefings for their relevant area of responsibility and supervising how issues within these areas were reported by the Chinese media.[6]

Yet despite the new ruling, the Central Propaganda Department did not give up its activities of guiding the overall strategy on economic propaganda and its crucial role in delineating the boundaries of what could and could not be said on any topic within the public sphere, and this continued to include economic matters. The Central Propaganda Department has overlapping duties with many state bodies, so the adjustment in roles was nothing new. However the adjustments do reflect internal debates circulating within the CCP at the time about whether, in the light of China's changed economic and political direction, it was still necessary to continue Party propaganda activities and to allow the Central Propaganda Department and its local equivalents to have so much influence over China's public sphere.[7] Zhao and his advisers preferred to downplay propaganda activities and focus on economic development, while Party conservatives argued for the continued importance of propaganda and thought work. However, it should be noted that the new delineation of responsibilities was not altered after Zhao fell from power and it continues to the present day.[8]

In June 1989, within days of the military crackdown on the pro-democracy protest movement, the reformed Party leadership announced a new slogan summing up China's political management: "Seize with two hands, both hands must be strong." This meant that, in a turn-around from the policies of the previous leadership, the government would now emphasize *both* economic development *and* propaganda and thought work.[9] The two are interlinked, so that in a clear about-face from the Mao years, one of the key tasks of Party propaganda activities became promoting economic development, while one of the key tasks of China's economic development became ensuring that the population maintained its faith in the existing political system.[10]

In 1991 yet another notice jointly issued by the State Council and the Central Propaganda Department further clarified their working relationship on economic propaganda matters:

The Premier's Office working meeting has defined that the *Economic Daily* belongs within the State Council system. The Research Office is in charge of the paper's professional guidance, while the General Office takes charge of the paper's management. The paper's overall propaganda work is still supervised by the Central Propaganda Department.[11]

This ruling set the standard for the new order in media management on economic issues: a dual supervision system which provides technical guidance from the relevant state bodies and ideological guidance from the Central Propaganda Department. Yet while the Central Propaganda Department was technically only responsible for offering guidance on economic issues when they touched on ideological concerns, most economic reporting has an element of ideology, so the new system meant that the Central Propaganda Department's role had not declined, rather it had been redefined. This was in line with overall trends in the growth of the powers of the CCP's Central Propaganda Department after 1989. The Central Propaganda Department also continued its role in supervising the economic thought reform of Chinese citizens, educating them to embrace the new economic order and all it entailed.

From the early 1990s the saying "politics tight, economics relaxed" (*zhengzhi jin, jingji song*) became commonly heard among Chinese journalists and editors.[12] Popular perception was that the government would strictly control reporting on political affairs, but on economic matters more leeway would be allowed. However the perceived difference in levels of control between the two was only relative. Essentially journalists were only free to report on economic matters as long as they were focusing on positive reports and took a line which promoted market reforms. Marxist economic analysis was banned[13] and most negative reports were restricted to the system of classified journals only available to top officials (*nei can*). Chinese journalists were given precise instructions on exactly how they should report China's economic development, in much the same way that they were given precise instructions on how to report political affairs. For example in a 1991 article Fan Jingyi – who would soon after be promoted to chief editor of *People's Daily* from 1993 to 1998 – placed maintaining social stability as the core task for China's economic propaganda. He outlined four styles of reporting in order to achieve this. These were: (1) achievement reports; (2) economic circumstances reports; (3) promoting new policies; and (4) critical reports.[14] Fan argued that in order to improve the quality of economic propaganda the Chinese media should: relate the state's economic achievement reports to the ordinary life of the people, put state economic policies into terms understandable to ordinary people, and any critical stories on the economy should carefully consider social stability and must receive government approval before going to press.[15] Despite the passage of years, Fan's guidelines on economic reporting are still the basic desired approach promoted by Party propaganda leaders up to the present day.

In February 1992 Deng Xiaoping came out of retirement to launch further economic reforms. A new term, "the socialist market economy," was created to describe China's new economic model. In September 1992, after a special meeting of the Politburo of the CCP Central Committee to promote the change in terminology it was announced that "propaganda and thought work should place economic development as the core task."[16] At the same time talking up the Chinese economy and encouraging further foreign investment and trade also became the primary task of foreign propaganda work.[17]

In 2006 Zeng Jianhui, a journalist and bureaucrat with a long involvement in China's foreign propaganda activities, published a classified (*neibu*) text on how to improve China's foreign propaganda work. The sensitivity of the topic is indicated by the security classification, which is relatively rare these days for a published book. Zeng issued nine themes that China's foreign economic propaganda should concentrate on including, (1) introducing the Party's targets and policies for economic development; (2) publicizing major state projects; (3) utilizing data from China's agricultural [under] development to fight back against international "China Threat" critics; (4) articles on China's policies to develop hinterland provinces; and (5) publicizing the reform and opening-up policy, state-owned enterprise (SOE) reform, and the rapid changes in ordinary people's lives that have come about as a result of China's economic changes.[18] Zeng instructed the media to coordinate their output with Party policies because, "in foreign propaganda, the basic tone and statement should completely conform to the Central Committee."[19] In an earlier book on similar themes, Zhu Muzhi, former president of the State Council News Office/Office for Foreign Propaganda, summarized the basic two goals of foreign economic propaganda as follows: "first, let everyone know China is secure; and second, that China is profitable."[20] In recent years, with the advent of the Internet and China's increasing globalization and internationalization, the boundaries between domestic and foreign propaganda have been growing less and less obvious. This means that Chinese journalists must be mindful that they now have a foreign audience alongside their domestic audience and that their foreign reports are read by an ever-growing, foreign-language-speaking Chinese audience.

China's modern economic propaganda has both political and economic goals. It must provide "spiritual impetus, intellectual support and positive public opinion on economic development," as well as introducing "successful methods and experiences for accelerating economic development."[21] China's transformed economy required a whole new approach to propaganda and thought work. New methodologies and technologies were progressively introduced, while China's mass communication specialists studied the mass persuasion model of other modern industrialized societies. Copying the approach followed in many Western countries, from 2004 on a legion of government spin doctors were trained to present China's official perspective in times of crisis. Instead of speaking in slogans as in the past, "speaking with truth" (*yong shishi shuo hua*)[22] was advocated as a better means of mass persuasion than indoctrination and didacticism. As part of this new approach the Central Propaganda Department began to tolerate the release of a certain amount of negative news, as well as following the more traditional positive propaganda line that everything is under control. China's modern propaganda specialists argue that releasing information during crisis situations creates popular confidence in the government's ability to manage.[23] The CCP learnt this the hard way after the global pandemic SARS was exacerbated by Party information controls from 2002 to 2003. Economic propaganda, which contains both true information and an ideological slant towards promoting specific economic policies, now plays a crucial role in efforts to maintain political stability.

Economic crisis or political opportunity?

Since the global economic crisis began in July 2007, the CCP government has done relatively well in handling the current economic situation, certainly when compared with other leading economic powers such as the U.S. and Japan. In the following section we will survey three leading newspapers in China during the peak of the global economic crisis, from October 1 to 20, 2008 – a time when global stock markets were crashing and leading banks, insurance, and finance companies were failing – in order to analyze how the Chinese media reports such a serious crisis with national and international implications.

The survey of 20 days of the front pages of *People's Daily* (*Renmin ribao*) in October 2008 illustrates the extent to which economic propaganda has now become the key topic for the Party's leading newspaper (Figure 2.1). In the survey *People's Daily* front page reports were categorized as follows: politics, society, technology, environment, ethnic minority affairs, and sport. In 137 articles on the front page over 20 days, economic reports made up 39.4 percent of the total reports. Political reports, including foreign affairs activities and meetings of leaders, accounted for 39.4 percent. Back in the year 2000, during the same time period, the percentage of economic propaganda on the

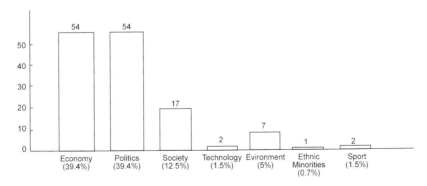

Figure 2.1 Proportional distribution of front page topics in the *People's Daily* in October 2008

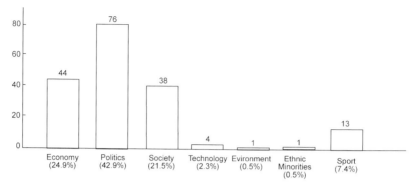

Figure 2.2 Proportional distribution of front page reports in the *People's Daily* in October 2000

front page of *People's Daily* was 24.9 percent, and political propaganda was 42.9 percent of a total of 177 articles (Figure 2.2).

In the 2008 sample, *People's Daily* economic propaganda mainly focused on five themes as shown in Figure 2.3 agriculture (25.9 percent), the current political/economic campaign the "Concept of Scientific Development" (16.7 percent), national development projects (*guojia jichu jianshe*) (16.7 percent), reports on industry (13 percent), and on market conditions (13 percent).

The promotion of agricultural achievements is a traditional theme for *People's Daily*. Large numbers of the rural population have migrated to urban areas to work in the industrial and service sectors. This "floating population" is hard to reach in propaganda terms and it is also a major potential source of political instability. In 14 agricultural articles in *People's Daily*, six focused on grain increases, information about harvesting, and sowing seeds. China's grain production affects social and market stability. Though *People's Daily* is unlikely to be read by many rural residents, the articles published by the paper are a model to other media outlets on the themes they should focus on in their reports and news programs. *People's Daily* is the official mouthpiece of the CCP (*dang bao*); it has a different audience and agenda to other papers

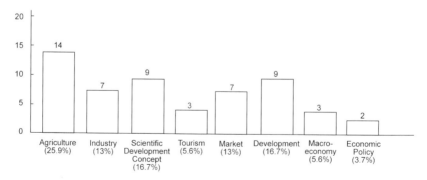

Figure 2.3 Economic propaganda themes

in China. It is less a newspaper than a platform for CCP policy transmission. *People's Daily* articles are also understood as the voice of the CCP government, so are extremely influential internationally. Reflecting its role in promoting China's national image and policies, since the mid-1990s *People's Daily* online has expanded to include versions in English, Russian, Japanese, French, Arabic, and Spanish.

In the same 2008 sample, *People's Daily* featured a significant number of articles on the topic of the "Concept of Scientific Development." The "Concept of Scientific Development" refers to the goal of creating more sustainable methods of economic development in China and the roll-out of social welfare policies to deal with the ever-growing gap between rich and poor which has developed as a result of China's market reforms.[24] *People's Daily* editorials set the line for how the rest of the country debates new theoretical approaches.[25] When a new policy is being promoted, *People's Daily* articles illustrate the policy with practical examples that are a model for other newspapers to follow.

Articles promoting national development projects mainly focus on the successes of China's current economic model. This type of article and other industrial and market reports make up a picture of prosperity and harmony, which underlines the success of the CCP's current policies and direction. There were no negative reports on the front page of *People's Daily* in the time periods we analyzed.

Local level newspapers have a somewhat different focus to national newspapers such as *People's Daily*. Two popular local newspapers were sampled over the same period; one was Beijing's *New Capital News* (*Xinjing Bao*) and the other was Shanghai's *New People's Evening News* (*Xinmin Wanbao*) (Figures 2.4 and 2.5). In these papers social news made up the majority of reports (61 percent and 34.7 percent respectively). Economic reporting was ranked in second place (14.6 percent and 34.7 percent respectively). This difference in the level of coverage of economic news between *People's Daily* and

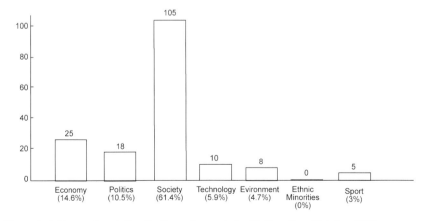

Figure 2.4 Proportional distribution of reports in *Xinjing Bao*, October 2008

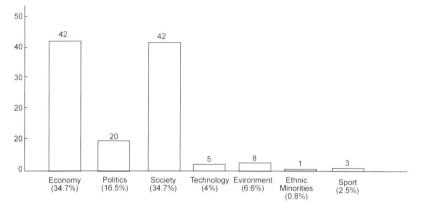

Figure 2.5 Proportional distribution of reports in *Xinmin Wanbao*, October 2008

these two local papers reflects their differing target readership and differing political roles. In contrast to *People's Daily's* Party mouthpiece role, the two local papers are supposed to be the "tongue and throat of the people" (*renmin de houshe/baixing de houshe*). This means that they are targeted at mainstream readers and deal in "soft" propaganda, that is, information which fits in with the Party propaganda guidelines but it is put in a more user-friendly form. These papers also need to focus much more on the "bottom line" than *People's Daily*; which is heavily subsidized both by the Party-state and by the more commercially focused newspapers within its media group.

In the period we surveyed not only did these local papers cover less economic news, there was also a big difference in the type of economic reports featured in the three papers. From October 1 to 20 the two local newspapers focused on the global financial crisis while *People's Daily* continued to talk up China's economic performance. More than 80 percent of the local papers' economic reports were foreign reports, covering bankruptcies in the US and trouble in foreign stock markets. In this respect the papers were in line with the CCP's guidelines on promoting economic propaganda. A standard technique of China's current soft propaganda methodology is to use international stories to mold public opinion on issues related to China.[26] The emphasis on the failure of the Western economic system to prevent the financial tsunami served as a subtle means to emphasize the success of the China model (*Zhongguo moshi*). This has been a strong theme in the Chinese media since the global economic crisis began. From Beijing's point of view, the global economic crisis has in many ways proven to be a political opportunity to celebrate China's chosen economic and political path.

"Go" and "no-go" zones in economic reporting

The main emphasis of China's economic propaganda is positive reporting; so if there is nothing good to be said about a current economic issue in China, the Chinese media must say as little as possible and avoid editorializing. Censorship was a traditional method of control in the Mao years. However, on most matters of strong public interest in the current period, the CCP propaganda strategy is more a matter of information management and damage control than it is about strict censorship.

Different sectors of the propaganda system are now "managed" to different levels. For example: television is much more strictly controlled as it is the main propaganda tool for communicating with the masses; the Internet, which is dominated by China's young, educated, urban youth is carefully guided, but allowed somewhat more freedom of debate; certain newspapers are permitted to be more frank than others; and the scholarly world is allowed even more latitude, as long as it keeps to accepted boundaries such as not questioning the leadership of the CCP over Chinese society.

China's propaganda has three levels of taboo. These are: "forbidden content," "content which should be reported prudently," and "topics which should only be reported by Xinhua."[27] The Chinese media must be "socially responsible" and what propaganda officials call "social efficiency" must take precedent over "economic efficiency" (i.e. audience) when it comes to making decisions about what is and isn't acceptable for publication in the Chinese media.[28] The majority of the Chinese media stick within the designated limits for reporting on economic affairs and follow Party directives. There is a multitude of banned topics in China's economic propaganda. In the following section we will discuss some recent representative "go" and "no-go" zones in China's economic journalism and analyze why they are so sensitive.

The Central Propaganda Department gives strict instructions to editors that they must control or suppress any stories which might cause instability.[29] In late 2007 rising food inflation, especially in pork and cooking oil prices, led to social unrest throughout China. Inflation is a highly sensitive matter and during such crises the media must follow the central authorities' line on this – meaning that they should only use Xinhua reports.[30] There is no charge for relaying Xinhua reports in the Chinese media, just one of many ways in which Party propaganda policies subsidize the commercially focused Chinese media conglomerates. In 2007 the Central Propaganda Department instructed the Chinese media to promote government policies on managing problems in pork production such as offering food subsidies for poor university students, and explain to consumers the changes in the pork market that were causing the price rises.[31]

China's banking sector has been under intense pressure in recent years, as it is lumbered with large numbers of bad loans that were often made for political reasons rather than on market terms. In 2005 the Chinese media were instructed to promote reforms in the banking sector including increased supervision. The China Banking Regulatory Commission (*Zhongguo yinhangye jiandu guanli weiyuanhui*) announced the policy and the Central Propaganda Department informed the media. The Chinese media were instructed to promote stories on banking related crimes that were already resolved. Not for publication was the fact that the Chinese banking system had "suffered a severe test." A Chinese paper that reported on a 300 billion yuan bail-out of Chinese banks was punished for breaching "financial propaganda discipline" and creating a "negative influence" in society.[32] According to propaganda guidelines, runs on banks are not allowed to be reported in the Chinese media.[33]

It is forbidden to report on banking fraud cases under investigation, and even banking cases that have been tried can only be reported with the permission of the bank concerned.[34] The media are instructed that they must "protect local banks' international image. In order to avoid creating an unhelpful impression of the finance industry in the overseas market and damage national interests, don't publish information about problems in the domestic finance industry in dealing with money laundering."[35] Banking sector issues could potentially affect social stability and must be managed carefully; when discussing particular banking corruption cases the media must adopt the correct slogans and follow the guidelines of the propaganda department and banking supervision units.

All reports on the stock market and the *renminbi* exchange rate must be strictly managed.[36] The proposal to expand China's capital markets is a key strategic plan of the Party and state, and the media are instructed to consider promoting this initiative as a "political task."[37] Propaganda guidelines warn that, "One cannot be too careful in reporting financial issues."[38] Moreover, "financial issues impact on everything, financial policy-making is extremely sensitive as it impacts on a wide range of interests and has a major social impact."[39]

On April 2, 2008, the CCTV show *30 Minute Economic Update* (*Jingji ban xiaoshi*), appealed to the government to prop up the market during the stock market crisis. During the program well known economist Wu Xiaoqiu critiqued the government's extraction of high taxes from stock market transactions at the same time as it was claiming that it was trying to encourage stock market development, calling government stock market policies a "big fat lie" (*tian da huang*).[40] The following day the program was closed down with no explanation. Three months later in the same year, a leading economic newspaper, *Financial Times* (*Caijing bao*) was forced to suspend publication for three months. This paper had exposed illegal operations in the China Agricultural Bank. Although it was well known to industry insiders why the newspaper was punished, the General Administration of Press and Publications (GAPP, the state body in charge of managing print publications) gave out a very special reason: that the newspaper had been supervised outside its area of operations, which is not permitted by press regulations. The punishment was issued by the government of the Inner Mongolian Autonomous Region because the newspaper was registered there, though *Financial Times* is published in Beijing. Having the paper registered in Inner Mongolia was meant to be a strategy to avoid stricter censorship guidelines in Beijing, but it had clearly failed. According to GAPP regulations, as a "provincial paper," *Financial Times* must not publish critical reports of events that occur in Beijing.[41]

In mid-2008, leading financial websites on the mainland were given oral instructions by the Central Propaganda Department to avoid publishing negative and sensitive commentaries, reports, or headlines about China's stock markets.[42] In order to avoid a paper trail the Central Propaganda Department and its local equivalents increasingly use oral instructions to convey their "guidance."[43]

Ever since China began its economic reform project, outside observers have continually queried China's statistics.[44] Since the global financial crisis began such voices have become more insistent.[45] China's secrecy regulations explicitly restrict the release of sensitive statistics to do with the national economy and social development.[46] In 2009 some outside observers noted that there appeared to be a mismatch between China's current electrical consumption and figures on industrial output. Throughout early 2009 the Chinese administration constantly reiterated that China's industrial value-added growth (IVA) was growing smoothly, which indicated that China was less influenced by the global economic crisis. However, according to an article of May 2009 in the *Wall Street Journal*, China's IVA statistics were not in line with electricity consumption: electricity use was still seeing negative growth, while the IVA was growing at a positive rate. Eventually China stopped publishing data on electricity consumption.[47] Following this report, Shao Bingwen, the former vice-president of China's Electricity Supervision Committee (*Dianjianhui*), confirmed that some statistics reported by local government were untrue.[48] Soon after, the central government also announced that a new law on the public release of statistical information would be implemented in 2010. However, the new law was focused more on concerns about statistical information being politically correct, than accurate.[49]

Statistics on the level of unemployment in China are an issue affecting social stability. In the past 10 years the restructuring of China's state-owned enterprises has resulted in massive lay-offs. In 1997 and 1998, when the lay-off process first began, journalists were instructed to report on the successful "reform" of the SOEs and the "successful" redeployment of laid-off staff. Reflecting China's precarious economic situation at the time, in 1999 the Central Propaganda Department made a ruling that the media must not openly discuss economic problems, such as the overheating of the economy or unemployment figures.[50] In the News Propaganda Guide for the first quarter of 2006 the news media were instructed to "promote that the Party centre is putting expanding employment opportunities at the centre of socio-economic development."[51] They were also told to promote model stories of laid-off workers who have found work in the new economy and to promote awareness of China's new social welfare policies in urban areas.[52]

The actual unemployment figures in China have been consistently under-reported throughout more than a decade of radical economic restructuring. Since the global economic crisis began, large numbers of China's privately owned small to medium sized factories that were producing goods for the export market have closed down. Many of the workers were from the countryside, so technically officials could argue that such people were not "unemployed" as they could return home to their farming communities if they lose their jobs in the city. The so-called "floating population" and rural residents are excluded from China's unemployment statistics. In November 2008, a current affairs program on Linfeng Television, a broadcaster in Shanxi Province, reported that laid-off workers had demonstrated outside local government offices. The program was closed down and four staff – the anchor, program editor and two reporters – were dismissed.[53] In late 2008 the government announced in the official media that China's unemployment rate was now 4.2 percent. In December 2008 Chinese Academy of Social Sciences researchers claimed that China now had 9.4 percent unemployment.[54] Even this figure was widely regarded by outside observers as an underestimate; some say China's actual unemployment rate could be as high as 27 percent.[55]

Despite the success of China's economic reform policies in raising standards of living in many parts of China, there are still large numbers of people living below the poverty line. However, this too is a taboo topic in the Chinese media. Rather than allow open discussions on the issue of poverty in China, the government tacitly acknowledged the problem at the 16th Party Congress in 2002 by announcing new policies aimed at poverty alleviation and stressed the need to build a prosperous society for all (*xiao kang shehui*). The media were instructed to thoroughly promote these new policies.[56] In 2006 the Chinese media were given detailed instructions on covering issues to do with China's disadvantaged groups:

> don't report on extremely poor areas or groups of people, don't report on the population of poor areas without permission, don't report irresponsible analysis of poverty policies, and any serious matters should be reported to Central departments [to inform them, not for permission to publish about these matters].[57]

Although China's economic growth largely comes from the development of private companies, use of the term "private sector" (*siren jingji*) is discouraged in the Chinese public sphere because it is opposite to the fundamental notions of socialism. The Chinese media are told to instead use the term "non-state sector" (*fei gong you zhi jingji*).[58] The Chinese media are instructed to promote stories on the "non-state sector" in China in order to create a good external environment for business but also to guide private companies to "do business legally, pay their taxes, and be socially responsible."[59] Propaganda about private firms must feature model workers as in the state sector.[60]

Since the mid-2000s the party has accepted the suggestions of a number of "New Left" economists to introduce more social welfare policies into its economic development plan.[61] The current global financial crisis has led to a resurgence of the influence of Chinese critics of market liberalism and the government's tendency in the Jiang years to slavishly follow the Western, especially the U.S., economic model. Such controversy adds to the existing sensitivities around the apparent contradiction of a communist party over-seeing the dismantling of a socialist economy. Reflecting these concerns, on May 14, 2009 a report in *Qiu shi* (*Seeking Truth*), the leading CCP theoretical journal, reiterated that China's economic system would maintain the empha-sis on public ownership as the leading force in the economy, while allowing diverse forms of ownership to develop side by side. The report emphasized that China's "national conditions" (*guoqing*) meant that it could never com-pletely privatize industry.[62] One month later the Central Propaganda Department issued a booklet entitled the "Six Whys: Answers to Six Impor-tant Questions" to further explain why China would not privatize public assets.[63] The global economic crisis is proving to be a boon to proponents of the China model, as well as adding fuel to the arguments of those within the country who argue that China should become more, not less, socialistic.

When political and economic interests collude

A topic of long-standing interest to many Western analysts of Chinese politics is whether or not the CCP's unleashing of the market will threaten its own hold on power. In 2008 a shocking scandal over adulterated milk products illustrated how, when it comes to the Party propaganda system and its current emphasis on economic propaganda, some commercial interests profit from it as much as political interests do. According to official statistics, close to 300,000 infants suffered from kidney damage after consuming tainted San Lu milk powder from 2007 to 2008, while six infants died. The non-official fig-ures are even higher, with many other families coming forward to say that their children had died after drinking San Lu products.

The adulteration of the milk occurred during the lead up to the 2008 Beij-ing Olympics when the Central Propaganda Department had explicitly banned the media from publishing stories on food safety issues.[64] The CCP's strict censorship on politically sensitive economic matters fits in well with the needs of big business to hush up commercially sensitive stories and to be constantly talking up the market. The company involved in the scandal, San Lu, a major Chinese dairy producer based in Shijiazhuang, knew that its milk products were tainted, and which ones, as early as December 2007. Instead of recalling products, it initially paid off consumers who complained to keep them quiet, asked local government to gag the media, and avoided telling its foreign partner what was going on for eight months. After the story got into the news San Lu offered 3 million *renminbi* as a "public relations" payment to a number of Chinese web portals to blackout or otherwise screen negative reports on the company.[65]

The Shijiazhuang government did not inform central health authorities and made only desultory efforts to deal with the gangs, enabling them to continue operations until August 2008.[66] Central health authorities knew of the situation by at least June 2008, after a report from Gansu health officials, but did not release the information to the Chinese media or recall the tainted products.[67]

San Lu milk was adulterated with melamine, a substance used in the production of plastics and fertilizer. San Lu got its milk supplies from scores of local peasants who farm a few cows on their smallholdings. The milk produced from these farmlets was collected by middlemen contractors. Both farmers and the middlemen added melamine and other substances to the milk, in order to conceal that it had been diluted with water. When melamine is added it makes it appear as if the watered down milk has high protein levels, enabling the milk producers to conceal that they were trying to earn more for less milk. As a result of rising inflation in 2007, the Chinese dairy industry had been instructed by the government to keep dairy prices low, at the same time as feed and fuel prices were rising. It had long been rumored that Chinese milk and other food producers added such substances in order to boost profits, but never before on such a scale and with such disastrous results.

The poisoned milk scandal erupted into the media in September 2008. Chinese consumers went into uproar over news that local officials, the central authorities, and San Lu had colluded to suppress information on the scandal. Until the scandal became known, San Lu was the largest producer of infant formula in China, with over 50 years of experience marketing dairy products there. San Lu dairy products were formerly rated very highly in China. They were the official supplier of milk powder to Chinese astronauts.

In February 2008 rumors began to circulate that babies were getting sick from drinking San Lu formula. The Shijiazhuang government forbade its local media from reporting on the story, while the non-Shijiazhuang media were also excluded from covering the story due to the GAPP regulations which forbid the Chinese media from publishing critical stories on areas outside their own region. In July 2008 a *Southern Daily* reporter tried to do a story on the large numbers of babies suffering from kidney damage after drinking San Lu formula but was prohibited by the propaganda ban.[68] In the same month a worker at a San Lu milk collection point in Jiangsu sent a whistleblower report on what was happening to Chinese food safety authorities.[69] Also in July, a Hunan TV news program report on alarmingly high levels of infants suffering from kidney disease showed images of San Lu powder without making any comment. In early August San Lu informed its board of directors that melamine had been found in its milk powder. It was only from this date that a trade recall (meaning San Lu contacted suppliers asking them to return products but did not inform the media or the public who were still consuming the milk powder) was ordered of the affected products. San Lu's 43 percent foreign stakeholder Fonterra objected to San Lu's approach to handling the situation, but did not go public with what it knew.

The story was forced out into the open on September 11, 2008 after blogs in China named San Lu infant formula as the product which was damaging the health of large numbers of Chinese infants. In order to avoid a public relations disaster which would affect its own reputation, Fonterra asked the New Zealand government to contact the Chinese central authorities and urge them to take proper measures to deal with the crisis, including ordering a public recall of the milk products.[70] On the same day that news of the scandal became public the Central Propaganda Department issued instructions that the Chinese media were only allowed to use Xinhua News Service stories – the Party line – on the story.[71]

After the story became public San Lu's foreign investor, Fonterra, went into damage control mode. In media interviews Fonterra CEO Andrew Ferrier used the word "sabotage"[72] to describe what had happened and portrayed Fonterra and San Lu as victims.[73] But sabotage has connotations of malicious damage by a competitor and that is not what had happened in this case. And the true victims were 300,000 or more Chinese infants and their families. Even the Chinese official line was that the melamine was deliberately put into milk powder by San Lu producers in order to increase the protein content of milk that had been diluted with water. This was done to make greater profit, not to "sabotage" San Lu or Fonterra.

The Chinese population responded with outrage and anguish to the news that infant formula had been contaminated with melamine. Thousands of angry consumers queued outside San Lu headquarters demanding redress. All over China scores of anxious parents took their children to hospitals to check if they had been harmed by consuming milk products. In the days after the scandal became known, online discussion in China harshly criticized the government's handling of the crisis.

Ms Tian Wenhua, chair of the San Lu board, was also the company's general manager and Communist Party secretary. As a senior Party leader she would have received classified Communist Party publications informing her of the propaganda edicts banning public discussion of food safety issues during the Olympic period. Party discipline would have kept her from relaying this crucial information to her Fonterra business partners. On September 16, 2008 Ms Tian was fired from all her posts. The following day she was arrested. Nineteen others were arrested in connection with the San Lu scandal.

Ms Tian was singled out as a scapegoat for national policies which were out of her control. The Chinese authorities were concerned about issues of state security and national image in the lead up to the Olympics. Local officials had effectively been told by Beijing that on food safety concerns, "don't tell us, we don't want to know." The suppression of information about the tainted formula was on a national scale; it ranged over several provinces and included the central government.

San Lu was not the only company to be affected; after the news went public Chinese food safety authorities inspected the dairy products of all other companies available on the Chinese market. Twenty-two out of 109 were found to be contaminated, though only San Lu products had dangerous levels. The Chinese dairy industry was in a state of disaster and by the end of 2008 consumer confidence in food safety in China was at an all-time low.

Chinese web censors went into overdrive to control the crisis, which deeply challenged public confidence in the government. Web managers were instructed to "guide public opinion" on the San Lu tainted formula scandal. Internet news sites were ordered not to feature the story prominently and told that any reports should emphasize that the government had the situation under control. While comments and reports critical of the government's role were removed, hundreds of thousands of vitriolic postings railing against Tian Wenhua, the CEO of San Lu, were not.

In December 2008 *China Daily* reported that Chinese dairy employees were now taking an oath to adhere to business ethics.[74] This was part of efforts to reassure foreign and domestic consumers that China's food safety was under control. The trial of Ms Tian and three of her fellow directors (notably, the three foreign directors who represented Fonterra on the San Lu board were not charged) was a one-day session which was closed to the victims of the tragedy.[75] Tian and her accomplices weren't on trial for information about the tainted milk suppressed from May to September, rather for selling "fake and shoddy" products.[76] Tian was sentenced to life in prison for her role in the affair.

A finance website, *Wang yi caijing*, reported that Tian Wenhua took "full responsibility" for the tainted milk tragedy and this story was posted on the website of the CCP Office for Foreign Propaganda.[77] However, *First Financial Daily (Diyi caijing ribao)*, a newspaper aimed at Chinese investors and backed by liberal forces within the CCP, reported Tian Wenhua as saying Fonterra should take some of the blame for the tragedy. Ms Tian said that Fonterra participated in the decision to continue selling tainted milk from August 2 to September 12, when the company knew about the levels of contamination but before the information went public. The article was reposted on the *People's Daily* website; an indication that this version of events had some official approval.[78] However, Xinhua News Service reporting gave a much watered down version of Ms Tian's claims, and avoided naming Fonterra at all.[79] For a few weeks non-official websites showed Chinese television reports on the San Lu trials, as well as home-made videos satirizing official handling of the tragedy, but these were soon taken down.[80] The Chinese media did not report on a press conference held on January 2, 2009 by some of the families of the victims of the tragedy, or that some of them were detained for attempting to meet with foreign journalists.[81] In November 2010, Zhao Lianhai, the father of one victim, was sentenced to two and a half years in jail for his attempts to raise awareness about the ongoing problems of the children who had been affected by drinking poisoned milk.[82]

The San Lu tragedy illustrates the risks inherent in the overlapping relationships between Party, state, market, and criminal interests within the Chinese political system. It is a tale of government interference in the market economy for political interests; large scale local and national level corruption of political figures by criminal groups and business interests; and severe weaknesses in the role of the nation's watchdog organizations as a result of political interference. The cost to large numbers of ordinary people, not only those whose babies were affected, but all who could no longer feel safe consuming Chinese milk products, was unacceptably high. If it had occurred in a democratic country, heads would have rolled in all these agencies for covering up what was happening and it may even have led to a change of government. Yet remarkably, despite the phenomenal scale of the tragedy, none of this has occurred. The government's efforts to close down public debate about the issue have been successful and public anger appears to have been appeased by the arrest of Ms Tian and a handful of other scapegoats. The voices of the families of the victims have been suppressed. The San Lu poisoned milk scandal is a stark example of how effective China's propaganda system is at managing public opinion on politically damaging economic news, even in a situation when the system itself was a factor in causing the tragedy. It is also a reminder that commercial, as much as political interests, benefit from the CCP's media management and constant talking-up of the market.

Conclusion

At the National Conference on Propaganda and Thought Work in January 2008, Hu Jintao defined propaganda work as one of two key tasks that the Party requires to maintain its leading position, while the second task is economic development.[83] As China recovers from the global economic crisis and deals with serious incidents such as the poisoned milk powder scandal, economic propaganda plays a crucial role in maintaining political stability. The government uses a range of tools to manage the problems it faces; including both economic handouts (carrot), and force (stick), but one of the most crucial of them all is persuasion. The Chinese people must be made to continue to believe that the current political and economic system is the best one for them and that there is at present, no alternative, whatever hardships the country may suffer. China's trading partners must also be encouraged to maintain their faith in the strength of the Chinese economy and the government's ability to deal with the current problems.

Despite the challenges China faces, as noted, the popular mood is very optimistic about the nation's future. This optimism is certainly encouraged by the ongoing emphasis on positive propaganda, but it is also based on an awareness of how far China has come since the turning points of 1911, 1949, 1978–79, 1989, 1992, and 2008. China's economic propaganda is effective because its underlying premise is basically true; the CCP government has made major progress in improving the economic livelihoods of large numbers of Chinese people and they continue to be the only viable political force able to lead and unite China.

Notes

1   Deng Xiaoping, "Some Points on Economic Work" (*Guanyu jingji gongzuo de jidian yijian*), October 4, 1979. See http://cpc.people.com.cn/GB/69112/69113/69710/4725544.html
2   These are: the principle of upholding the socialist path, the principle of upholding the people's democratic dictatorship, the principle of upholding the leadership

of the Communist Party of China, and the principle of upholding Marxist–Leninist–Mao Zedong Thought.

3   http://news.qq.com/a/20090723/001137.htm

4   Zhongyang xuanchuanbu bangongting, *Dang de xuanchuan gongzuo wenjian xuanbian wenjian pian 1949–1993* (Party Propaganda Work Documents 1949–1993), volume 4 (hereafter *DDXC*) 4 vols., Zhonggong zhongyang dangxiao chubanshe, 1994, p. 1686.

5   Ibid., p. 1848.

6   www.gov.cn/gjjg/2005-12/26/content_137261.htm

7   Interview with Zhu Houze, former head of the Central Propaganda Department, 1985–1987, December 18, 2005.

8   This delineation of responsibilities is still current. See: www.fsou.com.cn/html/text/bmyg/ … /805306425.html (now only available cached).

9   "Quanguo xuanchuan buzhang huiyi" (National Meeting of Propaganda Department Directors), July 1–21, 1989, available at http://bjds.bjdj.gov.cn/ShowArticle.asp?ArticleID=7541

10   Ding Guan'gen, "Guanyu xuanchuan sixiang gongzuo de jiben silu," June 25, 1993, in Zhonggong zhongyang xuanchuanbu zhengce fagui yanjiushi, ed. Shisi Da yilai xuanchuan sixiang gongzuo de lilun yu shixian (Theory and Practice in Propaganda and Thought Work Since the 14th Party Congress) (Beijing: Xuexi chubanshe, 1997), p. 84.

11   *DDXC*, 2037.

12   Interview, propaganda policy analyst, December 2002.

13   In March 1992, Deng Xiaoping stated in an internal document, "the main task is to prevent Leftism from slowing reform," Alison Liu-Jernow, "Don't Force Us to Lie: The Struggle of Chinese Journalists in the Reform Era," New York Committee to Protect Journalists, 1993, p. 79.

14   Fan Jingyi, "Improving Economic Propaganda," *Xinwen zhanxian* (Journalism Battlefront), vol.1, 1991, pp. 22–25.

15   Ibid.

16   *DDXC*, pp. 2104–2105.

17   *DDXC*, pp. 1815–1816; *Shandong sheng duiwai xuanchuan gongzuo huibian ziliao 1992–1998* (Shandong Province Foreign Propaganda Work Reference Materials 1992–1998) (hereafter *SSDWXC*) (Shandong: n.p., 1998), vol. 2, 1676–1677; Wang Zhongshen, *Duiwai xuanchuan chulun* (Introduction to Foreign Propaganda) (hereafter *DWXCCL*) (Fuzhou: Fujian renmin chubanshe, 2000), p. 145, see also Zeng Jianhui, *Rongbing, jiaqiao, tuwei* (Melting the Ice, Building a Bridge and Breaking Through) (Beijing: Wuzhou Communication Press, 2006), p. 33.

18   Zeng Jianhui, *Rongbing, jiaqiao, tuwei*, pp. 33–40.

19   Zeng Jianhui, *Rongbing, jiaqiao, tuwei*, p. 42.

20   Zhu Muzhi, *Lun duiwai xuanchuan* (On Foreign Propaganda) (Beijing: Wuzhou Communication Press, 1995), p. 465.

21   *Neibu tongxin* (hereafter *NBTX*), 2005/4, p. 1.

22   See http://news.xinhuanet.com/newmedia/2004-03/09/content_1354467.htm

23   Dong Guanpeng, ed., *Zhengwu gongkai lilun yu shiwu* (English title, Theory and Practices of Transparent Government) (Beijing: Xinhua chubanshe, 2007), p. 380.

24   *Bulletin of Third Plenary Session of the Sixteenth Central Committee*, www.cnr.cn/home/column/sgdb/xxdt/200310290389.html.

25   Interview with journalist, Beijing, January 2003.

26   Chen Junhong, ed., *Jiaqiang he gaijin sixiang zhengzhi gongzuo xuexi duben* (A Reader on Strengthening and Reforming Political Thought Work) (Beijing: Zhonggong zhongyang dangxiao chubanshe), 1999, p. 117.

27   See www.epochtimes.com/b5/2/6/21/n197672.htm

28   *NBTX* 2006/8, p. 14.

29 *NBTX* 2003/5, p. 13.
30 Interview with journalist, Beijing, January 2003.
31 *NBTX* 2007/15, p. 11.
32 *NBTX* 2005/3, p. 4.
33 *NBTX* 2005/2, p. 10.
34 *NBTX* 2005/16, pp. 2–4.
35 *NBTX* 2006/13, p. 13.
36 *NBTX* 2006/14, p. 5.
37 *NBTX* 2005/10, p. 3.
38 *NBTX* 2005/3, p. 4.
39 Ibid, p. 4.
40 See http://hi.baidu.com/msohu/blog/item/352527978f9b3f6855fb96f7.html
41 See http://blog.sina.com.cn/s/blog_56c0cdfd0100b8my.html
42 Daniel Ren, "Beijing Censors Financial Websites," *South China Morning Post*, September 10, 2008, online.
43 Interviews with Chinese media specialists, January 2006.
44 Carlston A. Holz, "'Fast, Clear and Accurate': How Reliable Are Chinese Output and Economic Growth Statistics?" *The China Quarterly* (2003), p. 173: 122–63; S. Lee Travers, "Bias in Chinese Economic Statistics: The Case of the Typical Example Investigation," *The China Quarterly* (1982), 91, pp. 478–485.
45 Albert Keidel, "The Limits of a Smaller, Poorer China," *Financial Times*, November 13, 2007.
46 "Xinwen chuban baomi guiding," June 13, 1992, in Beijingshi xinwen chubanju, ed., *Xinwen chuban shiyong fagui shouce* (A Practical Handbook of Regulations and Laws for the News Media) (Beijing: Jinghua chubanshe, 1998), p. 5.
47 "Making Sausages, Data in China," *The Wall Street Journal*, May 29, 2009, http://online.wsj.com/article/SB124350326977562001.html
48 http://finance.sina.com.cn/review/20090605/22136312071.shtml In August 2009 the Chinese National Bureau of Statistics announced that electricity use by China's small and medium size enterprises (the companies which have fueled China's export-led growth in the last 15 years) was down 48.9 percent in the first half of the year. www.caijing.com.cn/2009-08-03/110220099.html
49 www.theepochtimes.com/n2/content/view/19289/
50 *NBTX* 1999/4, p. 15.
51 *NBTX* 2006/2, p. 10.
52 Ibid, p. 10.
53 www.rfa.org/cantonese/news/china_media_reporter-01062009112631.html?encoding=simplified
54 See http://zqb.cyol.com/content/2009-01/02/content_2492566.htm
55 www.theepochtimes.com/n2/content/view/11375/
56 *NBTX* 2003/1, pp. 1–9.
57 *NBTX* 2006/13, p. 10.
58 *NBTX* 2005/20, p. 15.
59 Ibid, p. 15.
60 Ibid, p. 15.
61 See Zhao Yuezhi, *Communication in China, Political Economy, Power, and Conflict* (Lanham MD: Rowman and Littlefield, 2008), pp. 293–294.
62 http://cn.chinareviewnews.com/doc/1009/6/8/4/100968455.html?coluid=45& kindid = 0& docid = 100968455& mdate = 0514111930
63 See www.zaobao.com/special/china/cnpol/pages2/cnpol090531.shtml and http://theory.people.com.cn/GB/index.html
64 *NBTX* 2007/14, p. 25.
65 www.chinasmack.com/stories/kidney-stone-gate-sanlu-paid-consumers-to-keep-quiet/

66   Email correspondence with a China-based, Hong Kong journalist, October 2008.
67   http://english.caijing.com.cn/2008-12-31/110044273.html
68   www.rfi.fr/actucn/articles/105/article_9593.asp
69   www.chinasmack.com/stories/kidney-stone-gate-fake-baby-milk-powder-sanlu-baidu/
70   "China: Adulterated Milk: Fonterra," New Zealand Ministry of Foreign Affairs and Trade, September 10, 2008.
71   www.chinafreepress.org/publish/cfpnews/China_Starts_Censoring_Tainted_Milk_Powder_Scandal_Reporting.shtml,   http://chrdnet.org/wp-content/uploads/2009/04/china-human-rights-briefing-september-i-edition.pdf
72   www.nbr.co.nz/article/fonterra-claims-milk-was-sabotaged-another-baby-dies-35243
73   www.efluxmedia.com/news_-New_Zealand_Chinese_Dairy_Company_Is_Victim_of_Criminal_Action_24493.html
74   www.chinadaily.com.cn/china/2008–12/19/content_7323889.htm
75   www.china.org.cn/china/news/2009-01/01/content_17041521.htm
76   www.google.com/hostednews/ap/article/ALeqM5jL7mHkJcSHVOLlejm-s7eQS2xXDiwD95AIF8O0
77   http://cn.china.cn/article/n381277,de7cc1,d1614_4867.html
78   www.chinanews.com.cn/jk/kong/news/2009/01-05/1513741.shtml
79   http://news.xinhuanet.com/english/2008-12/31/content_10584145.htm
80   http://v.ku6.com/show/UJPIafPDVa-4YSxA.html
81   www.google.com/hostednews/afp/article/ALeqM5hO2jlYTFpymNoMqrJlLbAsXvSntA
82   Christopher Bodeen, "China Food Safety Activist Given 2½ year prison sentence for 'inciting social disorder,'" November 10, 2010, Canada Press.
83   http://news.xinhuanet.com/newscenter/2008-01/22/content_7475040.htm

3 State Confucianism, Chineseness, and tradition in CCP propaganda

Anne-Marie Brady

Introduction

In the history of China's politically fraught debate over what constitutes modernity, Confucianism and Chinese tradition have frequently been portrayed as an obstruction to China's path towards becoming a modern nation state. The CCP was long at the forefront of those in China who desired the elimination of such influences from Chinese society. However, the CCP is now in the vanguard of those who promote a revival of Confucian and other traditional values in Chinese society. In his authoritative 2008 survey of the rise of Confucianism in contemporary Chinese academic discourse, John Makeham stated that "there are no policy documents and programs that promote the idea of an officially sanctioned 'Confucianized' national identity in mainland China."[1] Makeham's bold assertion might make readers overlook the fact that since the mid-1980s, the CCP has been directly involved in supporting the return of Confucianism[2] and other aspects of traditional Chinese thought as a mainstream discourse in Chinese society. As I will show in this chapter, a careful reading of pertinent Party policy documents from the 1980s to the present reveals that the current popular Confucian revival began with the imprimatur of Chinese Communist Party (CCP) support, and in recent years it has now been fully incorporated into official discourse. The Party's adoption of these concepts parallels the popular revival of interest within Chinese society towards China's traditional philosophical and cultural norms. The debate over what "modernity" means continues within China, but some are now raising concepts such as "alternative modernity," "socialist modernity" and "multi-modernity." Instead of mimicking the experience and systems of other modern nation states China is now seeking to forge its own distinctive path, one which incorporates Chinese tradition within modernity, rather than rejecting it outright.

In Marxist terms, ideology is determined by a society's material conditions. From 1978, and even more so from 1992, China followed a decidedly different pattern of development from that of the Mao era, and CCP ideology has progressively evolved to reflect this change. Historically, Party ideologues denounced Confucianism and traditional Chinese culture as "feudal" and sought to erase their influence on Chinese society. So how is it that the CCP now embraces certain concepts of Confucianism and Chinese tradition, when in the past it rejected them and sought to reverse their influence in Chinese society? In the following chapter I will explore the role Confucianism and other traditional Chinese philosophies now play in the CCP's contemporary propaganda and thought work, and consider in what way the new emphasis relates to the revival of popular interest in Chinese traditional philosophy and culture. While there has been much discussion of the popular revival of Confucianism, there has been very little analysis so far of the CCP government's point of view on this new social trend. The chapter concludes with an analysis of what this shift in ideological content can tell us about the changing nature of political power in the People's Republic of China today.

A chronology of CCP–Confucian interactions

It is well known that the CCP and Confucianists are old foes. In many ways the two are diametrically opposite philosophies: Marxism opposes "morality" and class hierarchy. Confucianism accepts class inequity, emphasizes moral behavior, and uses the concept of "harmony" to explain social inequity. So it might be considered somewhat unusual to combine the two philosophies into one ideology. However, the ongoing project of Chinese Marxists from Mao Zedong in 1938[3] to Hu Jintao in 2008[4] has been to Sinicize Marxism. For key CCP ideologists such as Mao Zedong, Confucianism was part of the culture and heritage of all Chinese people. Certain aspects of Confucianism have long been utilized as part of CCP thought work. Nonetheless, historically, the relationship between Confucian thought and Chinese Marxism could only be said to be one of relatively subtle influence. But in the last 20 years the CCP has engaged itself in actively promoting the study of Confucianism and recently it has even adapted certain Confucian terminology into its ideology.

The CCP's attitude towards Confucianism has been markedly different in various eras. We can categorize the chronology of CCP–Confucian interactions from the May Fourth era to the present into five different phases: (1) the period of the 1920s and 1940s when the CCP rejected Confucianism as part of the old order it hoped to overthrow; (2) the Mao years when the CCP sought to construct a New China and eradicate influences from the past; (3) the immediate post-Mao years when China faced an identity crisis, rejecting Maoist radicalism but unsure of what its alternative was to be; (4) the crisis of 1989 which forced the CCP leadership to rethink the underpinnings of its authority to rule; and (5) the post-1989 era when the CCP formally began to adopt a new approach to its political rule and adjusted its ideology accordingly.

Phase 1: "Rejecting Confucius"

The CCP arose out of the May Fourth Movement, with its slogan of "Smash Confucianism" (*zalan Kongjia dian*).[5] Yet CCP theorists rejected

Confucianism and many other aspects from China's traditional culture, while at the same time adopting some of their key concepts such as the rectification of names (*zhengming*) and the concept of the Ancestral Land, *zuguo*.[6] In his 1940 essay "On New Democracy" Mao Zedong opposed "the worship of Confucius, the study of the Confucian canon, the old ethical code and the old ideas."[7] Paradoxically, it is well known that Mao's favourite bedside reading was the Confucian governance classic *A Mirror for Governance* (*Zizhi tongqian*) and the *Twenty-Four Dynastic Histories* (*Ershi shi*).[8] A 1964 study of *The Selected Works of Mao Tse-tung* found that 22 percent of the quotes and analogies used in his published works came from Confucian thought.[9]

From the 1920s to the 1940s China was in a state of flux and upheaval. The CCP's perspective on Confucianism was just one of many in Chinese society. Other voices, such as the scholar Liang Shuming, sought to utilize the best of Confucian ideas with the best of Western philosophy to create a New Confucianism more suitable for modern China.[10] These suggestions were part of a possible "third way" in China's modernity, a democratic, multi-party political system which would be both Chinese and modern.

Phase 2: constructing "New China"

These discussions ended in the late 1940s when the CCP won the Chinese Civil War. The CCP came to power with a strong desire to transform China into a socialist society, what they called "New China." Not only the institutions, but also the people, had to be transformed to create New China. As a consequence, from 1949 to 1976 Chinese people underwent nearly 30 years of political thought reform (*sixiang gaizao*), suffered annual mass political campaigns (*zhengzhi yundong*), and compulsory weekly political study (*zhengzhi xuexi*). The outcome of all this incessant political education was not, as CCP leaders such as Mao had once hoped, the creation of Socialist Chinese people. Instead, by the end of the Mao years, the populace had become politically jaded and somewhat cynical of Party propaganda.

Phase 3: "Rejecting Maoism"

In the immediate post-Mao era of the late 1970s and 1980s the CCP cast off the political radicalism of the previous decades, and took an experimental approach to what might replace it as the guiding ideology and indeed the whole issue as to whether a guiding ideology was still a requirement in a modern industrial society such as China. China's foreign propaganda changed radically once the new economic policies were rolled out, dropping references to Marxism–Leninism–Maoism and emphasizing "Chineseness."[11] This soon came to include a selective use of Chinese traditional thought. China's opening up to the outside world after years of self-imposed isolation had a major impact on the CCP's attitude towards Confucianism and other aspects of traditional Chinese culture. I do not have the space to elucidate all the ways that this was so, but below are a few significant examples.

From 1978 China opened up its borders to foreign tourists and foreign investment, which led to ever-increasing numbers of ethnic Chinese traveling to China in search of their roots (*xun gen*). Tourists needed places to visit and they came because they were attracted to Chinese culture and civilization. And so it was that temples and other traditional Chinese buildings which in the Mao years had symbolically been put to practical use as schools or factories, or even destroyed, in the immediate post-Mao era had to be patched together to create tourist attractions for the burgeoning tourist market. In this way, what had only so recently been rejected by CCP ideologues as feudal eventually came to be seen as useful; and when it came to the Overseas Chinese, even strategically important. The Chinese foreign affairs bureaucracy began incorporating phrases from Confucian classics such as "Is it not delightful to have friends coming from afar? (*you peng zi yuanfang lai, bu yi le hu*) from the early 1980s.[12] This was part of efforts to stress "Chineseness" to foreign visitors, in contrast to the Maoism which had been the main theme of Chinese propaganda in the 1960s and early 1970s.[13]

The 1980s was an "age of enlightenment" in China, when all sorts of contending ideas were introduced and debated. Chinese intellectuals were highly critical of what had gone before, yet were divided as to what alternative path should be followed. Some advocated what their critics labeled "complete Westernization" (*quanpan Xihua*), that is the introduction of multi-party democracy and a complete break with the traditions of the past;[14] others wanted less radical change but rejected the ideological controls of the Mao years; while still others emphasized that the CCP must focus on both economic development at the same time as retaining its traditional emphasis on ideology, albeit an updated ideology to match China's changed economic environment. The U.S. scholar Du Weiming was extremely influential in stirring interest in Confucianism in China in the mid-to-late 1980s through his networking, and conference presentations.[15]

In 1984, the Academy of Chinese Culture (*Zhongguo wenhua shuyuan*) was set up in the Chinese Academy of Social Sciences (CASS) to investigate contemporary Confucianism. According to the chain of command in the CCP propaganda system, the CASS is under the "guidance" of the Central Propaganda Department, while provincial academies of social science are under the direct leadership of their local equivalents. The Academy of Chinese Culture was part of a joint project between scholars in Beijing, Qinghua, Renmin, Beijing Normal University and CASS to engage in Chinese cultural research and organize conferences. Over the years the academy published a series of books on Chinese culture by Hong Kong, Taiwan and Overseas Chinese authors. A further important body involved in the discussion of Confucian values in the 1980s was the Chinese Confucius Research Institute (*Zhonghua Kongzi yanjiusuo*) established in 1985.[16] In 1985 the Institute's director Zhang Dainian explicitly linked the ongoing spiritual civilization campaign with the attempt to critically inherit the Chinese cultural legacy.[17] At the Institute's second national conference in 1987 Zhang called for the "revival of cultural syncreticism" (*wenhua zonghe chuanxin*).[18]

In 1986 the Academy of Chinese Culture's research program on contemporary neo-Confucianism was sponsored as a key project in the five-year plan of the National Social Sciences Foundation.[19] In China social science is regarded as "ideological work" which must be guided by CCP propaganda authorities.[20] Chinese social science must follow the same guidelines on what can and can not be researched and published as the Chinese media. The National Social Sciences Foundation is directly under the leadership of the CCP's Central Propaganda Department. Its address gives it away; it is located in the same office as the Central Propaganda Department at 5 Chang'an Boulevarde. This body enables the CCP to generate high-quality policy-relevant social science research. It is significant that the Party-state's investment in publishing on Confucianism was not simultaneous with similar investments in research on Daoism, Buddhism, or even Islam or democracy. Confucianism was given the official imprimatur of support, and while other philosophies were not banned as they had been in the past, they have yet to be given the same level of support or prominence.

Usually outsiders associate the CCP's Central Propaganda Department with conservatism, but in the 1980s the Central Propaganda Department was an engine house for reform, especially under the leadership of Zhu Houze (1985–87). Zhu Houze's guiding principle in this period was "tolerance" (*kuanrong*).[21] Under Zhu's management the Chinese public sphere was permitted to experiment with a wide range of new or rediscovered concepts and methodologies towards the goal of helping to rebuild China after the excesses of the Mao years. However, in China, as in the Soviet Union in the same period, this openness inevitably unleashed a diversity of views that were not all supportive of maintaining the CCP's dominance in the Chinese political system. The outcome was the crisis of 1989.

Phase 4: CCP legitimacy crisis

As discussed in previous chapters, from 1978 to 1989 the CCP government faced an ever-escalating legitimacy crisis; which came to a head in June 1989. The events of 1989 prompted a further questioning in inner-Party circles as to why the Party's hold on political power had become so weak, and what remedies might be implemented to re-strengthen it. In 1990 a classified publication raised the concept of the CCP as the "Party in power"; to signal that the Party was now in the post-revolutionary era and must, like any government, work to maintain the support of the people.[22] From 1989 to 1990 the CCP launched a campaign against "peaceful evolution," the notion that the West was trying to undermine China by exposure to Western ideas and ways of life. This official rejection of the Western model came at the same time as the development of a growing popular interest in traditional Chinese studies (*guo xue*) and the beginnings of what became an outpouring of scholarly and popular books on Confucianism and other aspects of Chinese tradition.

In 1992, the Central Propaganda Department-led funding body, the National Social Sciences Foundation, made a further investment in funding a large-scale Confucian research project, which was important in symbolizing official support in the post-1989 era for the popular and scholarly interest in the topic. The 1986 and 1992 Confucian studies projects involved more than 50 scholars from more than 10 provinces in China. The outcome was the introduction of Confucian thought to the mass market. From 1986 to 1996, 61 books by New Confucians and 54 books on New Confucianism were published by this group.[23]

Phase 5: "Embracing Confucius"

Throughout the 1990s the "Chinese studies fever" (*guoxue re*) grew from strength to strength. Popular demand brought back the teaching of Confucian classics in many Chinese schools;[24] and more and more elaborate celebrations to commemorate the Yellow Emperor (see below) and the birth of Confucius. All of these were permitted, and even subsidized, by the Chinese Party-state. All public events, especially those involving Overseas Chinese and Taiwanese, must have the permission of the local propaganda department.[25] The CCP's support for such activities was not, as some speculated, because it was turning itself into the "Chinese Confucian Party."[26] Instead it was for good practical reasons, such as because they served as an antidote to Western ideas and culture and they were also attractive to crucial interest groups such as the Taiwanese and Overseas Chinese.[27]

In 1996, as part of the Party's renewed "nation-building" project, Jiang Zemin proposed a return to "traditional" socialist and "Chinese" values. Behind the scenes Chinese scholars were commissioned to write internal reports analyzing in what way "traditional values" could be utilized in contemporary thought work.[28] The decision to incorporate these values into domestic propaganda and thought work was proposed by the influential CCP Central Policy Research Office (*ZhonggongZhongyang zhengce yanjiushi*) in the late 1990s.[29]

In 2001 the project for the Construction of Moral Education for Chinese Citizens was announced. This project aimed to further extend the Party's new approach to thought work in China by incorporating a number of key Confucian concepts. This new approach utilized methodology from civics education used in the Western world.[30] The project aspired to promote a system of morals and new model figures to suit the contemporary era. Moral education themes covered matters of interest to ordinary people such as food safety, health matters, education and training, travel services, and environmental matters.[31] The project gave new impetus to the existing trend to incorporate traditional Chinese concepts into contemporary propaganda. Beginning in 2005, 20 September was marked as "National Citizens Morals Propaganda Day (*Gongmin daode xuanchuan ri*). On this day the Chinese media are supposed to promote stories on moral Chinese youth, such as how they are volunteering to go and work in the countryside to help the peasants, as well as stories about China's socialist democratic system of law, and China's People's Assemblies and how they are elected. It is argued that such reports help to "strengthen political awareness and protect stability."[32]

The 2008 Beijing Olympics opening ceremony showcased a plethora of phrases and symbols from Chinese, especially Confucian, tradition. It opened with 2,008 drummers chanting *you peng zi yuanfang lai, bu yi le hu!* ("Is it not delightful to have friends coming from afar?) and featured the term "harmony" (*he*) displayed in 897 giant moveable type blocks.[33] The utilization of Confucian concepts in CCP ideology has become increasingly sophisticated in recent years. For example in March 2009, in a conference supported by the CCP Policy Research Office, experts in various fields explored ways in which Confucian concepts could be utilized to build social compliance.[34] The goal of all these activities is not to replace socialist ideas with Confucianism or any other value system, rather to combine the best of them all.[35] The value systems of Confucianism and other aspects of Chinese tradition have now become so mainstream that in 2007 the CCP Politburo prepared detailed reading materials for mid- and upper level cadres on topics such as why China's "traditional thought" is so important today, and "the value of Confucianism in contemporary China."[36]

The Party's selective use of terminology from Chinese tradition

The Chinese Party-state's selective use of terminology from traditional Chinese thought is most commonly found in China's domestic propaganda (*duinei xuanchuan*), though it first featured in propaganda directed at Overseas Chinese, the Taiwanese, and non-Chinese foreigners from the early 1980s.[37] In the following sections I will discuss some of these terms and how they are utilized in CCP contemporary thought work.

Civilization: wenming

In late Imperial China the notion of civilization (*wenming*) was used to define just who was part of the inner group of the Sinic world order, and who wasn't. However in the current period it doesn't quite have that meaning, though there are overlaps with previous usage. From the late 1970s Party theorists debated the relationship between "material civilization" (economic prosperity) and "spiritual civilization" (superior ideology). Conservatives argued that in the post-Mao era, while the government needed to focus on material civilization, it should not forget the need for spiritual civilization. The mini political campaigns of the 1980s such as the 1983 Campaign Against Spiritual Pollution were all couched in these terms.

In the mid 1990s this terminology was brought to life again under the leadership of Jiang Zemin with his "Spiritual Civilization Construction Project."

Spiritual Civilization Offices at the local level supervise many aspects of Chinese society, in co-ordination with State bodies. These range from social, cultural, and educational activities, to public security, family planning, marriage guidance, and social welfare. Although these activities are not necessarily explicitly political, by excluding unapproved social forces from organizing events or dominating community groups, they prevent other organizations from promoting an alternative political agenda and alternative values to the Chinese public. Approved activities are "*wenming*" (civilized), unapproved activities are "*bu wenming*" (uncivilized).

Nowadays Spiritual Civilization activities are one of the main means to engage in thought work on the masses. The emphasis is on creating a value system which suits China's modern society. The introduction of Confucian and other traditional Chinese concepts into CCP thought work is predominantly, but not exclusively channeled through spiritual civilization activities. Party theorists regard social stability as the key to political stability. Spiritual civilization is a soft form of social control, which is backed up by the law and police system.[38]

Filial piety: xiao

Filial piety is one of the most central aspects of Confucian thought. Filial piety does not just concern an individual's relationship with their parents; it also reflects their attitude towards their immediate superiors and the nation's rulers. Since 1996 the CCP has promoted the notion of filial piety through popular "competitions" to find the "Top Ten Most Virtuous Sons and Daughters" (*shi da xiaozi*). This activity was initially trialed in Hubei, Hebei, and Guangdong provinces.[39] In a 2006 report the Guangdong Propaganda Department noted that this competition-cum-campaign was an effective means to "stir people's emotions." The Guangdong campaign lasted from March to June 2006 and was conducted through TV programs, newspaper articles, and online debates. Guangdong officials praised the promotion of filial piety as an effective means for the Party to get close to the Chinese people and claimed that propaganda about it had achieved good outcomes.[40]

Filial piety education has since become an important theme of youth "thought education."[41] The Top Ten Most Virtuous Sons and Daughters has now become a nationwide program. Every year each province selects prominent individuals to be celebrated as "filial sons and daughters" and they compete with those selected from other provinces to win a national title. Concepts of filial piety are further promoted through an annual television show which selects well known performers and other media stars as filial paragons.[42] CCP propaganda activities frequently feature mainstream media stars, just as PR campaigns do in the Western world. According to the Central Propaganda Department's *Internal Digest* (*Neibu tongxin*), "when media stars participate it extends the influence [of the campaign]."[43]

Filial models have long been a part of traditional Chinese culture. One of the most well known texts of pre-1949 China was the book of moral exemplars *Twenty-Four Virtuous Sons and Daughters*.[44] The CCP has re-introduced such education, updating it to reflect the changes in Chinese society with the goal of resolving some of the acute social problems in Chinese society. Fifty percent of all murders in Anhui Province are committed by criminals from broken homes, while for youth crime the figure is 75 percent. Based on such research, Chinese policy-makers argue that "without civilized families there will be no civilized society." It is believed that family education can develop an individual's moral knowledge, physical health, and aesthetics, as well as attitude towards work and the law."[45]

In 2006 Jinchang City in Gansu Province adopted a new promotion system; all officials who were judged as not showing proper filial piety to their parents or failed to care adequately for their spouses and children were to be denied the chance of promotion. A total of 12 aspects of officials' personal lives were examined, including relations with neighbors, family relations and children's education.[46] The new system has since been adopted in other areas of China.[47] In recent years regular special events have been organized for children to demonstrate their filial piety towards their parents, such as kindergarten children being told on International Women's Day to wash their mother's feet as a sign of respect.[48] Washing the feet of elders is a traditional act of filial piety in Chinese culture.

In 2001 the first ever conference on Confucian filial piety was held in Chengdu. The stated aim of the conference was to "assimilate the quintessence of filial piety, enhance the cohesive force of the Chinese nation, promote social stability and eliminate the negative influence of feudalism in modern life." Participants were reported to have agreed that "the basic principle of morality is to love the motherland and people." The conference was organized by the Federation of Returned Overseas Chinese, the Society for Promoting Cross-Straits Exchanges in Sichuan Province, and the Sichuan Academy of Social Sciences.[49] The first two groups are CCP United Front organizations and the second is under the direct leadership of the Sichuan Propaganda Department. In 2008, China's All Saints Day (*Qingming Jie*), when people traditionally go to visit the graves of their ancestors, was made a national holiday. Previously the government had resisted this, which demonstrates that there are still some limits on the CCP's acceptance and use of traditional culture.[50] However, this is an exception. On the whole the CCP has made strenuous efforts in recent years to promote China's traditional festivals such as the mid-autumn Moon Festival and Chinese New Year as an antidote to Western festivals such as Christmas and Halloween.

Virtue: de

The traditional Chinese notion of virtue (*de*) was strongly promoted by Jiang Zemin in the early 2000s. Jiang first spoke of "ruling with virtue" (*yi de zhi guo*) at the National Propaganda Directors' Annual Meeting in January 2001. Jiang's emphasis on virtue was a warning to Party officials and local leaders to be honest and upright and it was part of efforts to weed out widespread corruption.[51] It did not mean, as some commentators speculated at the time, that the CCP was abandoning "rule of law." As a result of the controversy which surrounded Jiang's original statement, at the 2002 16th Party Congress he emphasized that

> Ruling the country by law and ruling the country by virtue compliment each other. It is necessary to establish a socialist ideological and ethical system compatible with the socialist market economy and the socialist legal standard and consistent with the traditional virtues of the Chinese nation.[52]

His comments can be seen as a critique of widespread corruption and abuse of power within the Chinese political system, couched in terms which mixed traditional Chinese value systems with Chinese socialist terminology.

Prosperous society: xiao kang shehui

At the 2002 16th Party Congress, the new general secretary Hu Jintao promoted the goal of creating a good basic standard of living for all in Chinese society under the rubric *xiao kang* or "prosperous society." The phrase *xiao kang* comes from the Liji or Book of Rites, one of the five classics of Confucianism. It is a metaphor for an idealized society where all have enough for their needs.[53] *Xiao kang* is now a widely used phrase in contemporary political discourse in China.

Harmony: hexie

The concept of "harmony" (*hexie*) was first publicly raised at the Sixth Session of the 16th Central Committee of the CCP, in an article entitled "Resolution on the Main Aspects of the Construction of a Harmonious Socialist Society." The "harmonious society" concept was added into the Chinese Constitution at the 17th Party Congress in 2007. Putting "harmony" in the Constitution was a means to signal that the Party was formally giving up Maoist "class struggle."[54] The Party is currently engaged in a delicate balancing act: it cannot afford to throw out Marxism-Leninism from the Constitution but it is clear its influence has waned considerably. The emphasis on "harmony" also reflects the Hu government's desire to bring more balance into China's economic development by strengthening the social welfare system in urban areas and reducing the tax burden on farmers. The current emphasis on the term is furthermore an acknowledgement of the *lack* of harmony within contemporary Chinese society, and the need for the government to make adjustments in its policies and governance in order to bring about a more harmonious society. The concept of "harmonious society" has had a major impact on Chinese social science writing, and the papers which incorporate this theme are too numerous to list.

Confucius: **Kongzi**

Since 2004 China has set up hundreds of Confucius Institutes around the world in partnership with various foreign universities. Germany has its Goethe Institute, France its Alliance Française, and now China's equivalent is the Confucius Institute. As a figure, Confucius symbolizes China's ancient culture and traditions. Confucius is well known internationally and has immediate associations with China. The choice of this name reflects the goal of the Institutes to help shift foreign public perceptions of China through educational outreach. China is in the process of "re-branding," changing its international image. Confucius Institutes are part of China's new public diplomacy, which follows techniques directly copied from those used by Western countries.

Yellow Emperor: **Huangdi**[55]

The Yellow Emperor is not well known in the Western world, but he is very well known among the Han Chinese diaspora, who are celebrated as the "sons of the Yellow Emperor." Since 1979 the Shaanxi United Front Bureau has hosted annual ceremonies in Shaanxi to celebrate the birth of the Yellow Emperor.[56] Such events stir patriotic sentiment among Mainland and Over-seas Chinese and are also a good tourist draw card. The Yellow Emperor was heavily promoted in the early and mid-Republican period as a symbol of Chinese nationalism. During the early days of the second United Front between the KMT and the CCP, even Mao Zedong had joined in the eulogies to this mythical father of the Chinese nation.[57] From 1949 to 1979, due to the radical politics of the day, there was an interregnum in China's official com-memorations of the Yellow Emperor.

Starting from the early 1980s, the ceremonies have once again been patronized by senior CCP leaders. In 2005 as part of a breakthrough in China–Taiwan relations, senior Taiwanese politician James Soong was taken to pay his respects at the tomb when he visited China for the first time.[58] In 2007, KMT honorary chairman Lien Chan also visited the tomb on his fourth visit to China since 2005, and stated that, "Expressing my greatest respect towards our common ancestor has been my lifetime wish."[59] Further signaling the KMT's willingness to engage in dialogue with the CCP on resolving the Taiwan issue, in 2009 KMT president Ma Ying-jeou paid his respects to the Yellow Emperor at the Martyr's Shrine in Taipei (a venue which, ironically, is a shrine to the KMT's struggle against the CCP). He did so the day before Qingming Festival, the traditional holiday to commemorate the Yellow Emperor.[60]

Respecting the Rites: **mingli;** *honesty and trust:* **chengxin**

Respect for the Rites – the proper behavior between people of different groups and certain ritual acts – was traditionally one of the most fundamental means for propagating Confucian values throughout Chinese society. The notion of *chengxin* (honesty and trust), is also a key concept in Confucian thought.[61] Since 2001 both "respect for the Rites" and "honesty and trust" have also been core values in the "Construction of Moral Education for Chinese Citizens."[62] China's public advertising is dominated by ads promoting awareness of "proper behavior," such as helping children and the elderly. Meanwhile government agencies and local authorities around the country have set up events promoting "honesty and trust."[63] Companies who pass certain consumer tests can apply to the Chinese Consumers Association for a certificate verifying that they are "honest and trustworthy enterprises."[64] Chinese youth are another target group of such messages.[65] These efforts are part of attempts to ameliorate the negative impact of China's market economy and the negative values some associate with it.

Why the CCP now utilizes traditional Chinese concepts

The CCP's selective adoption of concepts and rituals from Chinese tradition reflects the values crisis in contemporary Chinese society. The CCP must step in with a new ideology and new set of values to meet the needs of New, New China, or else risk having that void filled by other potentially hostile forces. Of course Confucianism and aspects of other Chinese traditions are not the only influence in the CCP's revised ideological program; the Chinese masses are now guided with an eclectic mix of values that also include nationalism, consumerism, scientific knowledge, law, competition, and efficiency.[66] It should also be stressed that, unlike the past, the masses are no longer forced to believe official ideology. So long as they do not actively oppose the political status quo or attempt to promote a heterodox value system such as Falungong or multi-party democratization, they are now free to retain their own views.

In choosing to adopt selective concepts from Confucianism, the CCP has been very influenced by the experience of Singapore. In the late 1980s the liberal-leaning general secretary, Zhao Ziyang, was impressed by the "new authoritarianism" which had led to success in Taiwan, Singapore, and South Korea. From the early 1990s Deng Xiaoping promoted Singapore as a model for China.[67] Confucian values were adopted by the Singapore school curriculum in 1982.[68] Singapore was a showcase for proponents of the "Confucian hypothesis," the notion that, much as Protestantism had helped to develop capitalism in Western Europe, Confucianism had an important role in the post-war rise of industrial East Asia.[69] Confucianism as practiced in modern Asia presented a model for an "alternative capitalism."[70] Futurologist Herman Kahn and sociologist Peter Berger, who were so instrumental in promoting the idea that the "East Asian model of capitalism" owed much of its success to Confucianism, are also acknowledged in contemporary Chinese debates on the usefulness of Confucianism in contemporary China.[71] The concepts they developed are now widely accepted, such as Kahn's view that the promotion of Confucian ethics in these societies led to "the creation of dedicated, motivated, responsible, and educated individuals and the advanced sense of commitment, organizational identity, and loyalty to various institutions,"[72] and Peter Berger's conclusion that "a Western-centered perspective [on modernity] is no longer adequate."[73] Such views are extremely attractive to CCP policy-makers who are exploring concepts such as "socialist modernity" and "alternative modernity"[74] as part of resistance to the dominant Western model. Understandably, the Chinese government is extremely antagonistic to the international hegemony of democratization and is looking to find allies in its resistance. According to leading public intellectual Wang Hui,

> in its rejection of Western values, Confucian capitalism enables exponents to embrace the capitalist mode of production and the global capitalist system – phenomena born of Western historical specificity – while adding a layer of cultural nationalism on top. In this context "Confucian capitalism" and the contemporary Chinese socialist reforms are simply two sides of the same coin.[75]

The CCP's acceptance of the need to make adjustments in its contemporary ideology reflects the adjustment in the Party's approach to its mandate to rule which was necessitated by the crisis of 1989. As noted, in 2002 the concept of the CCP as "the Party in power" was enshrined in the Party constitution. The change in terminology reflected a fundamental, albeit subterranean, shift in Chinese politics which has occurred in the last 20 years. Now, more than ever before, CCP leaders are extremely conscious that their right to rule depends on public support. The Party seeks to maintain its dominance in the Chinese political system and it now does so through the introduction of techniques originating in Western democracies such as incessant public opinion polling, molding public opinion through PR campaigns rather than political movements, and the introduction of civics education aimed at building loyalty to the current political model. China's rejection of the Western political model is justified by its leaders in terms of "Chinese tradition" being different and with its own distinct values which are still valid in the contemporary era. Under these terms the CCP's selective introduction of Chinese traditional thought and custom into domestic propaganda can be seen as the Party's antidote to the disease of "peaceful evolution."[76]

Nonetheless the CCP must be somewhat cautious in its utilization of traditional concepts, particularly Confucianism. It faces critics from both the right and left in Chinese politics who oppose the government's promotion of Confucian concepts in modern day China. It also has to be mindful of the cultural sensitivities of non-Han ethnic groups, who resent what they perceive as Han chauvinism. It is notable that in CCP classified and non-classified discussions on ideology "Confucianism" (*Rujia, Rujiao*) is not directly named. Rather the catchphrase "Chinese tradition" is preferred or Confucian concepts such as filial piety are discussed, without linking them to the Ru school. This is ironically similar to the CCP's ongoing avoidance of the term "capitalism" to describe the Chinese economic system, meanwhile implanting many aspects of a capitalist economy.

The CCP's state Confucianism is not the same as the Confucianism espoused by New Confucian purists such as Jiang Qing or Confucian populist Yu Dan. Indeed there is some criticism from New Confucian specialists that the Chinese government is misusing Confucianism for purely pragmatic reasons.[77] There is a risk of further friction from that quarter, some of whom have a strong political agenda. However the depoliticized self-cultivation form of Confucianism as espoused by adherents such as the television personality and mass communications scholar Yu Dan suits the current political needs and is also commercially successful.[78] Yu Dan is insistent on her apoliticism, which in a society like China is, in and of itself, a political statement.

The CCP's utilization of selective aspects of Chinese traditional thought has a further pragmatic use in China's new public diplomacy and as part of attempts to forge a distinctive Chinese approach to international relations. China is uncomfortable with the dominant world order and displays this dissatisfaction through promotion of the "Chinese model" (*Zhongguo moshi*) to other sympathetic countries and through talk of the goal of creating a global "harmonious society." China is on the rise and its leaders know that dominant states must not only have hard power such as military strength, they also need "soft power" which comes from cultural strength.

Furthermore, the CCP's utilization of selective terms from Chinese traditional thought and culture reflects adjustments in the Party's united front work towards Taiwan and the Overseas Chinese. The Party has recognized that Overseas Chinese and many people in Taiwan are attracted by the rituals and language of traditional Chinese culture. By supporting activities which promote traditional Chinese culture the CCP is able to build bridges with these groups which would normally be hostile to communism.

Finally, the CCP's utilization of Confucian terminology in its contemporary ideology reflects its new responsiveness to public opinion and desire to, where possible, be in tune with popular concerns. Many of the ideas on the use of Confucianism and many aspects of Chinese tradition are coming from below and being accepted at the top. The Party is in a transitional phase, experimenting with what is acceptable to people in China and what works well with the existing order. For instance, the movement to introduce Confucian virtues in primary and secondary school developed in late 1989 in Liaoyuan, Jilin Province as a result of the suggestion of a local educator. Parents responded with strong support and the local government approved the experiment by making the textbooks for these courses part of the school curriculum. Soon other areas copied the experiment. In 1993 the

Ministry of Education officially endorsed the "education in Chinese traditional values" on a nationwide level.[79]

Conclusion

The CCP no longer insists that all Chinese citizens must engage in political study as in the past, yet the Party wants to keep other potentially hostile ideologies and interest groups from having an influence in China.

The state-led revival of aspects of Chinese tradition is helpful in drowning out the Western liberal discourse in China. It helps to frame the public discourse in directions friendly to CCP interests. It also serves to stir up patriotism, and antagonism to foreign models. In China's external propaganda it is helping to construct a new image for China and build bridges with Overseas Chinese and Taiwan.

The CCP is determined to take only the best of Confucian and other traditional Chinese thought; it is not engaged in a wholesale adoption of these values. China's state Confucianism is distinctive from, but related to the development of popular, religious, and new Confucianism in contemporary China. Confucian terms are mingled with existing political terms to disguise the fact that the political structure has not fundamentally changed, though the methods of control have been upgraded and modernized.

The CCP's investment in Confucian studies in 1986 and 1992 has had a significant dividend, resulting in a genuine popular interest in an ideology which it is useful for the Party to support. In 2005 the Chinese government made a major investment in Marxism-Leninism research, on a par with its earlier commitment to seeding research on Confucianism. Yet it is hard to believe that this new research project will have the same social impact as Confucian studies in the long run. While Chinese scholars have flocked to receive the bounty from the research agenda to follow their own Marxism-related research projects, there has been only a limited popular response. The government's investment in Marxist-Leninist studies can be seen as an effort to shore up a dying field of study. However the revival of Confucian rhetoric in contemporary China is part of a much larger, ongoing, identity crisis, among Chinese intellectuals as well as coming from the Chinese Party-State, all with a common goal, to explore how China can be both "modern" and "Chinese."

Notes

1   John Makeham, *Lost Soul: "Confucianism" in Contemporary Chinese Academic Discourse* (Cambridge MA and London: the Harvard University Asia Center, 2008), p. 8.
2   Here I follow convention in using the term "Confucianism" to refer to the broad range of thought associated with the Ru school in China. It does not merely refer to the writings of Kongzi as found in the *Analects*, as many key "Confucian" concepts such as filial piety (*xiao*) are not found there, but are still part of what is regarded as "Confucian" Chinese tradition.

3   See Stuart Schramm, *The Thought of Mao Tse-tung* (Cambridge: Cambridge University Press, 1989), p. 72.
4   Hu Jintao, "Speech at the Meeting to Mark the 30th Anniversary of Reform and Opening Up," www.china.org.cn/archive/2009-05/11/content_17753659.htm
5   See Kam Louie, *Critiques on Confucius in Contemporary China* (New York: St. Martin's Press), 1980. It is particularly odd that the CCP is "re-claiming" the Confucian tradition because the very notion of "Confucius" is a construction of the Jesuits, which has been translated back into Chinese modern culture. See Lionel M. Jensen, *Manufacturing Confucianism: Chinese Traditions and Universal Civilization* (Durham NC and London: Duke University Press, 1997).
6   The standard Chinese translation of *zuguo* is "motherland," though "ancestral land" is the actual meaning of the term in Chinese. I have adopted the latter translation as being a more accurate reflection of the connotations this term evokes in Chinese.
7   Mao Tse-tung, "On New Democracy," *Selected Works of Mao Tse-tung*, vol. 2 (Peking: Foreign Languages Press, 1975), p. 369.
8   Zhengyuan Fu, *The Autocratic Tradition in Chinese Politics* (Cambridge: Cambridge University Press, 1993), p. 189.
9   Vsevolod Holubnychy, "Mao Tes-tung's Materialist Dialectics," *China Quarterly* (1964) 19, 3–37.
10 See Guy Alitto, *The Last Confucian: Liang Shuming and the Chinese Dilemma of Modernity* (Berkeley: University of California Press, 1979).
11 "Zhu Muzhi tan duiwai wenhua jiaoliu he xuanchuan gongzuo" (Zhu Muzhi Discusses Cultural Exchanges and Foreign Propaganda Work), *Duiwai baodao cankao*, 1983, no. 9.
12 See Zhong gong Guangzhou shiwei duiwai xuanchuan xiaozu bangongshi, *Shewai renyuan shouze* (A Handbook of Foreign Affairs), Guangzhou: Xinhua shudian, 1985, p. 1.
13 Zhao Pitao, *Waishi gaishuo* (Outline of Foreign Affairs) (Shanghai: Shanghai shehui kexue chubanshe, 1989), p. 198.
14 Tianlong Yu, "The Revival of Confucianism in Chinese Schools: a Historical-Political Review," *Asia Pacific Journal of Education*, 28, 2, June 2008, p. 116. See also Stephen Field, "He Shang and the Plateau of Ultra Stability," *Bulletin of Concerned Asian Scholars*, 23, 3, 1991, pp. 4–13.
15 Fang Keli, "Disandai xin Rujia lueying" (A Sketch of the Third Generation New Confucianisms), *Wenshizhe*, 1989, pp. 45–46.
16 www.kungfutse.com/xhgk.asp
17 Cited in Song Xianlin, "Reconstructing the Confucian Ideal," in John Makeham (ed.) *New Confucianism: A Critical Examination* (London: Palgrave Macmillan, 2003), p. 85.
18 www.qfsq.com/news/view.asp?id=1329
19 Guo Qiyong, "Reflections on the Research of Neo-Confucianism in the Past Two Decades," Chinese Academy of Social Sciences, May 27, 2003, www.cass.net.cn/e_waishiju/InfoShow?Article_Show_Conference_Show_1.asp? p. 3.
20 Han Licheng, "Luoshi de guanjian zaiyu chuangzaoxing de gongzuo," January 26, 1996, in *Shisi Da yilai xuanchuan sixiang gongzuo de lilun yu shixian* (Theory and Practice in Propaganda and Thought Work Since the 14th Party Congress), ed. Zhonggong Zhongyang xuanchuanbu zhengce fagui yanjiushi (Beijing: Xuexi chubanshe, 1997), p. 238.
21 Zhu Houze, interview, December 18, 2007.
22 Zhongguo qingnian bao sixiang lilunbu, "Sulian zhengbian hou Zhongguo de xianshi yingdui yu zhanlue xuanze (Realistic Responses and Strategic Choices for China After the Coup in the Soviet Union) *Zhonggguo qingnian bao* (*China*

Youth Daily) classified supplement, September 9, 1991, republished in *Zhongguo zhichun* (*Chinese Spring*) (January 1992), pp. 35–39.

23 Song Xianlin, "Reconstructing the Confucian Ideal," pp. 91–92.

24 Sebastien Billioud and Joel Thoraval, "Anshen liming or the Religious Dimension of Confucianism," *China Perspectives*, 3, 2008, p. 97.

25 Xuanchuan wenhua zhengce fagui bianweihui, ed., *Xuanchuan wenhua zhengce fagui* (Policies and Regulations on Propaganda and Culture) (Kunming: Yunnan renmin chubanshe, 1999), pp. 63, 64.

26 C. Raja Mohan, "The Confucian Party of China," *Indian Express*, December 19, 2005; Daniel A. Bell, *China's New Confucianism: Politics and Everyday Life in Changing Society* (Princeton NJ: Princeton University Press, 2008), p. 12.

27 Wang Zhongshen, *Duiwai xuanchuan chulun* (Introduction to Foreign Propaganda) (Fuzhou: Fujian renmin chubanshe, 2000), pp. 140–141.

28 The references are too numerous to cite in full, but see for example the scores of essays in Ren Yanjia (ed.) *Zhongguo shehuizhuyi jingshen wenming jianshe baodian* (Collected Writings on Chinese Socialist Spiritual Civilisation Construction) (Beijing: Tuanjie chubanshe, 1999).

29 Interview with senior CCP policy advisor, March 2008. See also www.jjzy.cn/bbs/read.php?tid=23927

30 Interview with propaganda theorist, Beijing, December 2007.

31 *Neibu tongxin* (hereafter *NBTX*), 2006/18, p. 1. 3.

32 *NBTX*, 2005/14, p. 5.

33 "Cultural Icons in Beijing Olympics Opening Ceremony," Xinhua, August 8, 2008, www.china.org.cn/olympic/2008-08/08/content_16167638.htm

34 www.sunofus.com/bbs/redirect.php?tid=42730& goto = lastpost& sid = IBWmK9

35 Qiu Zhi, "Shehuizhuyi hexin jiazhi tixi" (The Core Value System of Socialism), p. 161, and Lin Shangwei, "Lun shehuizhuyi yishixingtai yu dangdai Zhongguo de hexin jiazhi" (On Socialist Ideology and Contemporary China's Core Values), p. 164, both in *Zhongyang gaoceng juece yu guojia zhanlue buju* (An Overview of High Level Central Decisions and National Strategy) (no publisher, 2007), (classified publication).

36 Zhongnanhai lishi wenhua jiangzuo (ed.) *Neibu jiangzuo ji zhuanti baogao* (Internal Talks and Special Reports) (no publisher, 2007).

37 See Li Yuanjiang, ed., *Duiwai xuanchuan jichu* (Basic Foreign Propaganda) (Guangzhou: Guangdong renmin chubanshe, 1987), p. 85; and Wang Zhongshen, *Duiwai xuanchuan chulun* (Introduction to Foreign Propaganda) (Fuzhou: Fujian renmin chubanshe, 2000), pp. 140–141.

38 Chen Junhong, ed., *Jiaqiang he gaijin sixiang zhengzhi gongzuo xuexi duben* (A Reader on Strengthening and Reforming Political Thought Work) (Beijing: Zhonggong zhongyang dangxiao chubanshe, 1999), p. 152.

39 "Filial Sons and Virtuous Wives Honoured in Hebei Province," February 24, 1999, www.people.com.cn/english/199902/24/enc_990224001022_HomeNews.html

40 *NBTX*, 2006/12, p. 16.

41 *NBTX*, 2006/12, p. 17.

42 http://pic.people.com.cn/GB/8767391.html

43 *NBTX*, 2007/15, p. 7.

44 Guo Jujing, *Ershi-si xiao* (The 24 Exemplars), written during the Yuan dynasty, was the classic text known to all Chinese before 1949, and still influential after 1949. This text promoted stories of filial piety, especially of sons to their mothers. After being banned for some years, this book is now widely circulated in China and newspaper reports link it with the Party campaign to promote filial piety. www.nxhao.cn/ns_detail.php?id=10389& nowmenuid = 356& cpath = 0259:& catid = 259

45 Zhang Sennian, "Lun jiating wenming jianshe de zuoyong ji qi neirong" (On the Usefulness of the Construction of Family Morality and its Content) in Ren

Yanjia (ed.) *Zhongguo shehuizhuyi jingshen wenming jianshe baodian* (Collected Writings on Chinese Socialist Spiritual Civilisation Construction) (Beijing: Tuanjie chubanshe, 1999), p. 777.

46   Pan Xiaoqiao, "Should Filial Piety Be a Gauge or Test for Official Promotion?" *Beijing Review*, December 22, 2006, no. 50.

47   Sharon Lee, "Filial Piety Plays a Part in Promotions," *China Daily*, April 9, 2004.

48   "Kids Wash Feet to Show Filial Piety Ahead of Women's Day," China Radio International, March 7, 2007, www.crienglish.com

49   "First Ever Conference on Filial Piety Held in SW China," *People's Daily*, April 3, 2001.

50   "Ching Ming Festival, Once Branded Superstition, Is Revived as Holiday," *South China Morning Post*, April 4, 2008.

51   Wang Binglin, Ding Yun, *Zhiguo zhi dao – Zhongguo gongchandang yide zhi guo de lilun yu shixian* (How to Rule: the CCP's Theories and Implentation on Ruling the Country with Virtue) (Hefei: Anhui jiaoyu chubanshe, 2005).

52   Jiang Zemin, "Report to the 16th National Congress of the CPC, http://english.cpc.people.com.cn/66739/4496615.html

53   Lin Yutang, *The Wisdom of Confucius* (New York: Random House, 1943).

54   Interview with senior Party member, December 2007.

55   www.gwytb.gov.cn:8088/detail.asp?table=Interactions& title = Cross-strait+Interactions+and+Exchanges&m_id = 195

56   See Terence Billeter, "Chinese Nationalism Falls Back on Legendary Ancestor," *Chinese Perspectives*, 18, 1998, p. 45.

57   "Eulogy of the Communist Party," Yao Minjie, and He Bingwu (eds.) *Huangdi jiwenji* (Compilation of Eulogies to the Yellow Emperor) (Xi'an: Sanqin chubanshe, 1996), pp. 43–47, cited by Billeter, p. 46.

58   www.chinadaily.com.cn/english/doc/2005-05/05/content_439646.htm

59   www.gwytb.gov.cn:8088/detail.asp?table=Interactions& title = Cross-strait+Inter actions+and+Exchanges&m_id = 195

60   www.chinadaily.com.cn/china/2009-04/04/content_7649495.htm

61   The following link lists the sections of the *Analects* which refer to *chengxin*: http://zhidao.baidu.com/question/101958348.html

62   For a list of the core values of this project, see this link: www.people.com.cn/GB/shizheng/20011025/590086.html

63   www.people.com.cn/GB/guandian/1033/2094564.html

64   www.people.com.cn/GB/shizheng/8198/30053/index.html; www.tongchuan.gov.cn/structure/zw/ldjhnr_10781_1.htm. Sebastien Billiouid has written in detail on this campaign in "Confucianism, 'Cultural Tradition,' and Official Discourse in China at the Start of the New Century," *Chinese Perspectives*, 3 (2007), pp. 50–65.

65   www.wenming.cn/gzyd/2010-10/13/content_21097783.htm

66   Central Committee of the Chinese Communist Party, "Gongmin daode jianshe shishi gangyao" (Outline of the Construction of Citizen Morality). September 20, 2001. http://cpc.people.com.cn/GB/64184/64186/66690/4494588.html

67   Arif Dirlik, "Confucius in the Borderlands: Global Capital and the Reinvention of Confucius," *Boundary*, 2, 22 (1995), p. 267.

68   Dirlik, p. 239.

69   Tu Wei-ming, *Confucian Traditions in East Asian Modernity: Moral Education and Economic Culture in Japan and the Four Mini-Dragons* (Cambridge MA: Harvard University Press, 1996), pp. 2–3.

70   Dirlik, p. 243.

71   See the authoratative overview of the influence of New Confucianism in Chinese society in the 1980s by Li Qiqian, "A Survey of Confucian Studies in China Today," *Copenhagen Journal of Asian Studies*, 6 (1991), p. 13.

72 Herman Kahn, *World Economic Development: 1979 and Beyond* (New York: Morrow and Quill Paperbacks, 1979), p. 122, cited by Arif Dirlik, p. 244.
73 Peter Berger, "East Asian Development Model?" Unpublished manuscript, 1983, p. 4, cited by Arif Dirlik, p. 245.
74 See "Cultural Diversity, Harmonious Society, and Alternative Modernity: New Media and Social Development," which was part of the high-profile 2007 Beijing Forum at Beijing University. http://ennews.pku.edu.cn/news.php?s=193506823
75 Wang Hui, *China's New Order: Society, Politics and Economy in Transition* (Cambridge MA: Harvard University Press, 2003), p. 162.
76 "Peaceful evolution" is the CCP term for the negative impact of Western society on China. The phrase comes from a speech by then U.S. secretary of state John Foster Dulles in 1955 describing how Western countires could undermine communism through cultral exchange and other contacts.
77 Interview with policy advisor, March 2009.
78 In 2006 Yu Dan gave a series of six talks explaining the *Analects* as part of CCTV's *Lecture Room* (*Baijia jiangtan*) series. The talks were extremely popular, as was the book she published based on those talks, which sold millions of copies.
79 Tianlong Yu, "The Revival of Confucianism in Chinese Schools: A Historical-Political Review," *Asia Pacific Journal of Education*, 28, 2, June 2008, p. 114.

4 "Confu-talk"

The use of Confucian concepts in contemporary Chinese foreign policy

Valérie Niquet

In recent years the propaganda apparatus in the PRC has increasingly been using Confucian key words or notions – what I call *Confu-talk* – in its foreign policy. This Confu-talk constitutes both a tool for internal politics and foreign policy objectives, and forms part of a means to "review, maintain, improve," to use Anne-Marie Brady's characterization, in other words "adapt" the propaganda of the Chinese Party-state, by the exploitation of ancient principles with a strong cultural dimension.[1] It is also part of the effort made by a more assertive China to "consolidate its pre-eminence" both at the hard and soft power level and lies at the base of the rush to establish Confucius Institutes all around the world since 2004.

The emergence of Confu-talk

Confu-talk gradually appeared in official public discourse (articles, official experts' papers, public declarations) from the mid-1990s.[2] These concepts emerged as a way to mend a fraying Chinese society with rising inequalities and poor morals, due in part to the pervasive influence of elite corruption. In that sense, they play the role of a necessary substitute to democratization in a context of growing social demand. They were a convenient response to pop-ular challenges, based on traditional concepts well adapted to traditional weaknesses of Chinese society. The use of these concepts is thus a way to build a new Confucian *contrat social* to replace the breakdown of Maoist egalitarianism and, at the same time, to try to reassure an uneasy interna-tional community confronted with the rise and lack of transparency of China's strategic objectives.

In October 2004, at the fourth plenum of the XVIth Congress, two years after Hu's nomination as the head of the Party, the two principles of the "scientific development point of view" (*kexue fazhan guan*) and "harmonious society" (*hexie shehui*) were adopted as mainstream official slogans. Hu then elaborated on these principles at the Central Party School in 2005.[3] The same speeches have been reiterated every year at different occasions until 2007 and the XVIIth Party Congress, when the building of harmonious society was at the core of Hu Jintao's speech and was officially integrated into the constitution of the Party.[4] The opening ceremony of the Beijing Olympic Games was also an occasion to display these traditional Chinese Confucian values and give them an aura of universality to accompany the rise of a new China and the legitimacy of its own culture and normative system.[56]

The pre-eminence of "harmony"

By using the concept of "harmony" (*hexie*), the Chinese leadership is pursuing complementary objectives. Inside China itself, there is an urgent need to try to answer, at least in words, the challenges of the disintegration of the social order, the fear of rising chaos and lack of "virtue" of the leadership, a result of economic reform policy without a proper system of rule of law independent from the political leadership. In his report to the 17th Party Congress, Hu's insistence on the fight against corruption was in that sense particularly significant.

However, the reference to and the utilization of the concept of harmony as an equivalent to "stability" is also a way to try to mobilize as a support for the regime a supposedly "natural" aspiration of humanity according to a traditional Confucian Chinese's concept of world order. This concept of harmony or harmonious society is built on a mix of traditional popular and, for the leadership, self-serving, Confucian concepts. These include the following:

- *Ren*, a sense of humanity, or benevolence, which refers to man in relation with others, and is now linked to the CCP's insistence on the collective over the individual. It is at the bottom of the criticism of a supposedly more Western "individualistic" conception of human rights.
- *Xiao*, filial piety, is another central component of the Chinese state Confucianism conception of a "natural" order, based on a familiarist and strongly hierarchical organization of social and political relations inside of, and between, states.
- *Li*, or the respect of Rites above rule of law. In today's China, the Party, new guardian of the Rites, guarantees stability and order, which are presented as necessary preconditions for development and common good, and remain above the development of a truly independent legal system.
- *Xin*, trust, is at the core of the filial relationship and is a concept constantly used by China in dealing with "others" either to build trust in a "win-win relation" or as a threat in case of "lack of trust." Any position not in favor of the CCP's interpretation of China's interest is denounced as a lack of trust or a threat to "mutual trust," with all the potential negative consequences regarding trade, diplomatic exchanges and global cooperation as a whole.

The essence of "Chinese characteristics"

The use of notions strongly anchored in Confucian values is also a way for China to try to project a benign image, where influence is claimed to result not from the use of force, but from the power of conviction or seduction, of *wen* over *wu*.[7] Under the imperial system, this power of conviction evolved from the moral superiority (*de*) of the emperor. Today, China's influence should evolve from the moral superiority of the CCP's policy of "reform with Chinese characteristics," with China's economic successes as a testimony of this "moral" superiority, and not from the use of, or the threat to use force. These ideas constitute the basis for the "peaceful reunification strategy" with Taiwan without ruling out, however, the possible use of force in case of a lack of conviction on the part of Taiwan leading to a possible declaration of independence.

This "peaceful" discourse claims, however, to be an answer to the "hegemonic" Western model. It is also well adapted to China's real capabilities, and part of an asymmetric strategy of the "weak" (China) against the strong, where the weak, for the time being at least, has no capability to match its adversary or impose its own vision of the world by force, and must rely on the power of conviction.

The use of Confucian values by China is thus part of an indirect way to impose a new world order after the Cold War, supposedly based on the respect of the new "Rites" of international rules and the UN, where China is playing an increasingly active role, and oppose any disruption of these "Rites" today in favor of China's interests.[8] Confucian values are also a way for China to put forward the pacifist characteristics of the Chinese civilization, the world of *wen*, opposed to the outside aggressivity of the world of *wu*.

Confucian values and soft power

This "pacifist" or non-military power strategy translates into the recent appropriation by the Chinese propaganda apparatus of the concept of soft power mixed with the more traditional Confucian values of the peaceful, moral and cultural influence of the rightful emperor or political leader. This is a way to build a new Chinese model of international relations based, in a self-serving way, on balance, dialogue, trust and the official rejection of hegemony or interference.

This new model of benevolent power "in harmony" with natural aspirations to filial relationships, in a hierarchal framework, fits with China's hope to see its pre-eminence recognized, at least in Asia, in the traditional sphere of influence of Chinese/Confucian culture. In Asia, these principles translate Beijing's wish to recreate the idealized "harmonious" tributary system of the past, a world order on the scale of Asia, based on an accepted but mostly loose allegiance to the emperor of China, disrupted only by the chaos brought by the irruption of Western powers in the middle of the nineteenth century.

More recently, in 2008 CASS (the Chinese Academy of Social Sciences) published its annual report introducing a new concept called the "peace dove strategy" where, in a "harmonious" organization, the United Nations and the UN Charter are the head, Asia is the body, Apec and Asem the two wings and Africa, Latin America, etc. are the tail of the peace dove.[9] In that scheme representing the world as envisioned by China, China itself is not mentioned as, following traditional Confucian principles, it *is* the world (*Tianxia*).

An answer to the China threat theory

The use of pacifist Confucian values in propaganda is also of course mostly an answer to the China threat theory. In 2006, for instance *People's Daily* published a paper called "China Threat Fear Countered by Culture." The paper was related to the opening of new Confucius Institutes, a way to "dissolve misconceptions about China development as a threat by making its traditional value system known to the world." In other words, "when people know China better, they will find out that harmony is an essential part of China's tradition, and a country that values harmony poses no threat to the world."[10] In military circles, at international conferences organized by the Academy of Military Science, as a kind of adjustment of propaganda work, harmony and the "traditional pacifism" of Chinese civilization gradually took pre-eminence over the more classic Chinese military strategy principle of "win without war" inspired by the works of Sun Zi, China's most famous strategist.[11]

The use of Confucian values and the opening of Confucius Institutes are part of this strategy of "benign influence" and answer to the necessity to rather artificially build soft power instruments whose aim, as a propaganda tool, is "to wrench misunderstanding and hostility."[12] Moreover, Beijing's interest in developing its soft power, and the building of soft power instruments in "harmony" with Confucian peaceful foreign policy principles, is also a way for China to reposition itself on the ideological scale vis-à-vis Japan, perceived as a global leader in terms of soft power.

The building of a new, benign, political image

China, in spite of its economic reforms, remains mostly, in terms of organization, a Leninist state. However, at the ideological level, the use of consensual Confucian principles is a way to erase the outside world's awareness of this reality. As part of a classical united front strategy, regarding Taiwan particularly and relations with the KMT, Confucianism is also a way to "normalize" the regime, to minimize its very political specificity. Moreover, in terms of image and perception, by using selective Confucian principles, the Chinese leadership can create a sense of China's leaders as "moderates," benign and powerful reformers, the "new Mandarins"; as opposed to the chaotic and violent system of rule by crisis and permanent revolution culminating in the chaos of the Cultural Revolution with its bizarre anti-Confucius/anti-Lin Biao campaign (*pi lin pi kong*) (which lasted from 1973 to 1974 to counter the re-emergence of Deng Xiaoping and attack Zhou Enlai).

To further the contrast, and the use of common popular understandings of Chinese history, while Mao Zedong referred to Qin Shi Huangdi, China's first emperor famous among many other things for the destruction of all books including Confucian classics, the new leadership has chosen to stress harmony and the figure of Confucius. This is also a strategy to evade the looming issue of political reforms.

China's recent stress on Confucian "Asian" values, as opposed to "Western" values is also a way for the CCP government, in a more proactive way, to build a counter-model with two dimensions: one of nationalist cultural affirmation as this model is supposed to be the ultimate result of a 5,000-year long history where external influence is usually minimized; as well as a tool of foreign policy where the new "Beijing consensus" based on the values of "trust," non-interference and "harmony" is opposed to a Western *modus operandi* supposedly based on interference, competition, use of force and forced moral superiority.[13]

By presenting this counter-model to the world, the CCP can reassert itself to the Chinese people as the savior or rehabilitator of a traditional Chinese model for a long time obliterated by the dominant West. Beyond China and purely ideological issues, the issue at stake is also the capacity of the PRC to gradually impose its own set of values on the international arena.

This current of thought and the stress on the specificity of Asian values minimizes the differences between states, history and political systems in Asia to build a kind of supposedly harmonious and exotic Asian universalism with Chinese characteristics (*Tianxia zhuyi*) or at least an extended regionalism, where the role of state and collectivities are supposed to play a dominant role as opposed to the Western stress on individuals. In that sense, and particularly when mainland China is in fact dominated by individualism and there has been a dramatic reduction of the role of the state in social issues, the exploitation of traditional Confucian values, with their echo of the past, also helps to rebuild morale at the individual level. This has, paradoxically, taken the form of the appropriation, in an accultured society looking for its lost roots, of a Westernized, limited conception of "Confucian values" mixed with the aspiration of the new rich to the outward sign of "gentility with Chinese characteristics."[14] Alongside a stronger feeling of national identity encompassing Chinese both inside and outside the Chinese mainland, this has led to the emergence of a "national studies fever" (*guoxue re*) in recent years.[15]

References to traditional Confucian values is thus a way for China, in a kind of "reversed Orientalism" both to "unify" internally with references to a very simplified vision of a national culture close to the concept of *caractère national* very much in favor in modern Europe up to the Second World War, and to "influence" externally in a supposedly "non-aggressive" manner, another proclaimed traditional, or Confucian, "Chinese characteristic."[16]

The neo-Confucianists

The use of Confucian values and the building of a counter-model culminate with political thinkers like Jiang Qing whose paper, *Zhengzhi ruxue* (Political

Confucianism) belongs to a long line of thought starting in China in 1919, as a reaction to the May Fourth movement.[17] According to the neo-Confucianists, "Confucianism is a set of values that makes us Chinese." In that sense it constitutes an integral part of the effort to build a specific China model against the Western model, China here playing the symbolic role of the "other" defined only by its "otherness" in relation with the West.

After the May Fourth movement in 1919, the neo-Confucianists emerged, opposed to Marxist thinkers or writers like Lu Xun, with the will to defend the principle of a revolution based on Chinese culture and the rehabilitation of authentic, humanist, Confucian principles unlike the corrupt and immobile system of state Confucianism. This current of thought was maintained in Hong Kong and Taiwan after 1949 with the opening in Hong Kong of the *Xin Ya Shuyuan*, and reappeared in the PRC after the reforms in the 1980s. This movement echoed what had been going on outside China, both in the Chinese cultural sphere, particularly in Singapore, and in the United States around Chinese scholars at Harvard University, in particular Du Weiming.[18]

In 1984, the Confucius Foundation was established in Jinan around Liang Shuming (1893–1988), one of the "fathers" of the neo-Confucianist movement, with his first book published in 1917.[19] In 1986 a new research project on neo-Confucianism was launched at Beijing University. The first corpus, in six volumes, of neo-Confucianist thought was published in 1996. These initiatives are also part of a new interest for *guoxue*, and patriotic education, with the establishment of a *guoxue yanjiu suo* at Beijing University in 2004 and the edition of the "official" portrait" of Confucius in 2006.[20]

In 2004, two years after Hu Jintao came to power, this movement accelerated and translated into official propaganda. The Central Party School established the Confucian classics as part of its curriculum, harmony (*hexie*) became the new mantra and, last but not least, Qu Fu, the birthplace of Confucius, officially celebrates Confucius' anniversary as part of its efforts to put itself on the map and attract foreign investment.

The role of Confucius Institutes

It is in this context that one must look at the opening of Confucius Institutes. Confucius Institutes are part of efforts to modernize China's propaganda apparatus by, in a very Chinese way, going back to the past. Confucius Institutes play many roles. According to the official website, "Confucius Institutes can be established in various ways, with the flexibility to respond to the specific circumstances and requirements found in different countries."[21] However, in spite of this pragmatism and apparent diversity, Confucius Institutes are all institutionally linked to the National Office for Teaching Chinese as a Foreign Language of the Ministry of Eucation, the *Hanban*. The institutes are part of the vast range of organizations which, co-ordinated by the Central Propaganda Department of the CCP, play an interface role in China's official communication with the outside world.

The importance of the role attributed to the diffusion of the Chinese language in China's contemporary foreign propaganda is reflected in the number and diversity of the ministries and administrative institutions involved in managing the Confucius Institutes. There are 12 such institutions, from the Ministry of Education to the Information Office of the State Council (its alternative name is the Office of Foreign Propaganda), and the National Development and Reform Commission, through organizations dealing with Finance, Overseas Chinese, Foreign Affairs, Foreign Trade, Culture and all the media organizations.[22]

The Hanban is officially involved in all decisions and responsibilities concerning the opening of Confucius Institutes, well above the normal bilateral links established between universities, Chinese and foreign. Hanban decides where and when to open Confucius institutes "in countries or cities where the head office believes there is a need." It publishes and "disseminates" Chinese language books and teaching materials and, more globally, "communication products" like films and TV programs.[23]

Confucius Institutes were born out of the new financial capabilities of the Chinese State. An increasing part of these new riches is going to the renewed "outside propaganda" (*waixuan*) effort of the CCP. In 2009, 45 billion yuan was dedicated to international propaganda in order to "spread" soft power through the development of specific media programs, the creation of a Chinese equivalent of CNN (or Al Jezeera), and the rapid expansion of Confucius Institutes so as to "make China heard in international affairs."[24]

The amount of seed financing for Confucius Institutes is apparently around US$100,000, a rather imprecise "round sum" but most certainly significant, particularly for increasingly cash-starved universities worldwide.[25] This amount can be rather liberally used to cover the "initial operations" of a Confucius Institute, including the renovation of buildings and the recruitment of teachers and personnel.[26]

Officially, the Confucius Institutes' role and objectives are to "improve understanding of China in every country of the world" (*cengjing shijie geguo dui zhongguo de liaojie*). In that sense, they are part of the external communication strategy of China and the CCP. They must "help to build a deeper friendship through better understanding and contribute to the construction of a harmonious world." However, there is also a strong flavor of the Five Principles of Peaceful Coexistence mixed with this Confu-talk in the stress on "mutual respect, friendly negotiations and mutual benefit" as the principles to follow when establishing a Confucius Institute. It is also specified that "Confucius Institutes will not contravene the laws and Regulations of China" and "shall not be involved in any activities not consistent with the missions of Confucius Institutes," which are "to help bring about global peace and harmony."[27]

The Institutes make a direct link between cultural, civilizational, and economic might, in order to construct the image of the new, emerging and irresistible Chinese power. The Chinese ambassador to Zimbabwe emphasized this element when he declared at the opening ceremony of the new Confucius Institute in that country, "Chinese language is the door to an ancient culture with one of the world's fastest growing economies of the 21st century." These two characteristics, particularly in the African context where China is very active, contribute to legitimate China's role as a "model" or a new kind of "elder brother."

Officially, the models for Confucius Institute are the French Alliance Française, the British Council, or Germany's Goethe Institute. By referencing these institutions, China positions itself as just one "normalized" power among others. Priority in the curricula of many Confucius Institutes is given to Chinese language studies and the promotion of friendship with other countries through the development of business and government exchanges.

In order to achieve these aims, Chinese authorities, through the Hanban, give teacher training materials, set up the teaching curriculum, promote Chinese teaching materials, Chinese movies, TV programs, etc., all with the objective of extending China's "influence." A further objective of the Confucius Institutes is to support on-campus degree programs including research centers to fuel research work in the field of Chinese studies. Hanban's requirement that the activities of the Confucius Institutes fit within Chinese law (which has very broad notions of what constitutes a threat to state security), imply that such research will only fall within politically correct boudaries.

The first Confucius Institute was opened in Seoul in November 2004 following the opening of a "prototype" in Tashkent in April 2004. By October 2010 there were 322 Institutes and 369 "Confucius Classrooms" operating in 96 countries in the world.[28] According to Chinese reports, the sheer number of newly opened Confucius Institutes testifies to the new irresistible influence of China in a world "begging for the opening of Confucius Institutes."[29] But in some cases at least, many of the Institutes remain mostly empty shells unless they answer to a strong strategic priority or are invested in by the host institution.

In spite of these limitations, the opening of Confucius Institutes is also described as having a "strong appeal" to both "scholars and government officials" who bow to Chinese culture and civilization by "joining with ordinary People to learn Chinese language." Such statements are used as a rebuttal to the criticism against the principles and organization of Confucius Institutes in some Western academic circles.

A broad diversity of establishments

It is interesting to observe the establishment of Confucius Institutes following different patterns and local situations. In Asia, Confucius Institutes opened within the traditional sphere of the influence of Confucian culture and followed the improvement of relations with different countries in the region. This is the case for South Korea where the first Institute was opened, or in Japan.

There are also many Confucius Institutes in Southeast Asia, where Chinese communities are traditionally important and can play a role in that movement alongside economic interests for a rapidly developing China. However, it is interesting to note that while many Confucius Institutes have been established in Thailand, traditionally open to relations with China and with a very "Thailandized" Chinese community, there is only one in Indonesia where suspicion of China's influence is traditionally higher.

At another level, the opening of Confucius Institutes also serves the purpose to confirm or strengthen China's political links with other governments. But when traditional party-to-party links remain as a strong channel, there is no need for Confucius Institutes, as is the case with North Korea. Relations with these two countries remain in the hands of the external relations department of the CCP, in charge of relations with "brother countries," whereas Confucius Institutes are linked to the Propaganda Department.

Confucius Institutes are also a way to build new positions in the void left by other powers, former colonial or ideological powers, after the end of the Cold War, while renewing older alliances. This is particularly the case in Africa where Confucius Institutes opened in South Africa, the most important economic partner of China and a major power in Africa; in Kenya; but also in Rwanda, Zimbabwe, and Sudan, where the opening of Confucius Institutes goes along with a very strong Chinese influence on the ground.

China's objective in Africa is to offer, along "non-ideological lines" a new model of development, a form of South–South relations based on harmony and trust building against Western interference and insistence on loan-conditionality. These principles, under the new clothes of the Confucius Institute with a strong emphasis on Chinese superior culture and growing influence and legitimacy are not so far away from the more traditional Five Principles of Peaceful Coexistence, which were and remain the basis for South–South cooperation. There is indeed no real change of policy in this approach, but new tools, adapted to the ideological evolution of the post-Cold War world, to implement these policy objectives of alliance or friendship building.

The case is of course different for the opening of Confucius Institutes in the US and Europe where universities have a stronger autonomy. For host institutions in the West, and particularly in the United States or Australia, the discourse is often on the defensive, stressing the fact that Confucius Institutes are strictly apolitical, opened only, for instance, to "facilitate mutual understanding between the people of China and the people of the United States."[30] However, the sheer number of Confucius Institutes in the US and in Europe allows China to develop a discourse on the new pre-eminence of the Chinese language, as a further testimony to the power and at least economic attractiveness of China. This positioning plays a significant role in the perception of balance of power in Asia, particularly vis-à-vis Japan. Consequently, the Japanese Embassy to France for instance, is now regularly complaining about the fact that far less pupils study Japanese in high schools in France than

Chinese.[31] If Japan's soft power has been a stimulus for China's will to expand its own cultural influence through the building of Confucius Institutes, in a reverse influence in the context of power rivalry in Asia, Tokyo is now supporting a "tenfold boost of Japanese language centers to counter the spread of Chinese language and culture abroad."[32]

However, in developed countries, Confucius Institutes have also been somewhat "taken advantage of" by host universities or institutions. On most websites of Confucius Institutes opened in the United States, the stress is put on language teaching, business opportunities and tourism, and in some specific cases, on the link to services rendered to the local Chinese community. In the West, Confucius Institutes are established as more equal joint ventures between Chinese and foreign universities, often in order to consolidate older links of cooperation.

However, for some smaller universities, Confucius Institutes are also a way to promote and advertise their "internationalization" and try to seduce business circles and potential donors. In these cases, Confucius Institutes are presented as part of the development of networks with China, "the fastest growing economy in the world."[33] Such universities, on their websites, tend to underscore the fact that they have been "selected" by China through the Hanban, as a way to distinguish themselves and build an image of excellence in a very competitive educational community. This reflects the image that the CCP Propaganda Department and the Hanban would like to project, of high level Western institutions and individuals "begging" for the opening of Confucius Institutes.

The case of France

Forty-eight Confucius Institutes have been opened in Europe in the last few years. In terms of political influence in Europe, China has apparently decided to put its stress on opening new Confucius Institutes in what are perceived to be the most influential countries in the EU: France, Germany and Great Britain, an open admission of the Institutes' diplomatic role. In Eastern Europe, eight institutes have been opened in Russia, another most important "strategic partner of China."

In France, eight Confucius Institutes have been established since 2005, which is less than Great Britain (14), though on a par with Germany. This is despite China's "traditional links" with France, where many senior politicians have been proud to be considered a "friend of China." France is a friend, however, who has proved unable to win for China the lifting of the arms embargo imposed by the EU since 1989, an important goal for Beijing.

The first Confucius Institute was established in Poitiers in 2005, with the strong support of Jean-Pierre Raffarin, former prime minister and senator of the Vienne *département*, where Poitiers is situated, and a "old friend" of China.[34] The Institute, which moved to new buildings on the campus of Poitiers University in 2009, receives strong support, including financial, from the region, the *département* and the city of Poitiers. It is also sponsored by the Chinese telecommunication company ZTE, established inside the high technology business park of the Futuroscope, a project also closely and personally followed by Prime Minister Jean-Pierre Raffarin.

The Confucius Institute of Poitiers is thus a good example of an integration model between politics at the highest level in relation with China, local political interests and business incentives. Eager to expand its presence in France, interested in the advantage of being at the technological pole of the Futuroscope in terms of potential transfers, ZTE could only accept the proposal made by a French prime minister to support the local Confucius Institute.[35] To my knowledge, this is the only case where a Confucius Institute in France is financed by Chinese enterprise money.

Since then, four other Confucius Institutes have been established in France with different objectives. In Rennes, the Institut Confucius de Bretagne is part of the hope of the region to establish closer business links with a booming Chinese economy and thus build its own legitimacy as a dynamic economic zone, ready to attract new enterprises and businesses. The stress is also put on a specific program devised for entrepreneurs with an ambition to do business with China.

The Confucius Institute in Rennes is strongly supported by regional and local authorities and is an illustration of the new stress put on "decentralized cooperation" between local entities, in the case of Rennes, between Brittany in France, and Shandong province in China.

In Paris, the situation is somewhat different as the Confucius Institutes have to compete with old established "Oriental studies" centers in the capital.[36] In 2002, a Chinese cultural center was established in order to promote Chinese culture and most certainly with the hope to emulate – and challenge – the Maison de la Culture du Japon established in 1997 at Quai Branly in Paris. A Confucius Institute is now part of this Chinese cultural center with new buildings added in 2008.

Another case is the Paris VII University Confucius Institute, established alongside, but with no institutional connections to, the much older Département des Langues et Civilisations Orientales of the university.[37] In this case, significantly, the Chinese language and civilization department of the university tends to be suspicious and rather dismissive of the Confucius Institute both for its lack of academic credentials and ambitions and, not surprisingly, for the money and help received in order to establish the Confucius Institute inside a chronically financially deprived state higher education system.

At the opposite extreme, on its website, the Paris VII Confucius Institute stresses the fact that the Institute is "close to" the LCAO Department of the university in the hope of increasing its own legitimacy. However, whatever their locations in France, Confucius Institutes put the stress mostly on traditional culture in a non-challenging way and business aspects. Chinese cuisine, tea, traditional medicine, Taichi (but *not* Falungong and other politically unacceptable forms of Chinese religion), and Chinese language constitute the curricula alongside business courses.

All of the Institutes have a strong incentive, in order to make money, to tap into the French *formation permanente* system whereby it is compulsory for business enterprises and unemployment agencies to financially participate in the *formation permanente* of the employees or unemployed, in whatever sector the employee may wish to go, including learning Chinese language and business practices. So in France at least, China's foreign policy goals have the potential to match quite neatly with local needs.

Conclusion

To conclude, the Confucius Institutes, and the international promotion of Confucian values, are the two most visible elements of China's ideological soft-power building and a new strategy for foreign propaganda. Inside China itself they are also part of a new "pride building" project promoting Chinese culture, which is aimed against the growing influence of Western and Japanese "soft culture" on the emergence of new behavior and political norms in Chinese society.

Nonetheless, particularly outside China, these new efforts remain limited to the top down, in the absence of any real cultural and ideological attraction to CCP-led China. China's financial capabilities to make such investments do indeed remain the essential factor in the expansion of Confucius Institutes, as well as the attractiveness of a booming Chinese economy. Without these factors, the rush to open new Confucius Institutes could be less impressive, as well as the rush to study the Chinese language.[38]

In terms of efficiency, one can only wonder about the degree of adherence to this new China model, in a rather opportunist game of balance of power where China offers new opportunities and a renewed margin of maneuver, particularly to developing countries. As in other fields, the global economic crisis will test the ability of the Chinese system to maintain its newfound capability to "influence," but so far it has not been found wanting.

Notes

1 For a thorough discussion of the use of key Confucian concepts and terminology, see Anne-Marie Brady, *Marketing Dictatorship, Propaganda and Thought Work in Contemporary China* (Lanham MD: Rowman and Littlefield, 2007) and Anne-Marie Brady, "Making the News Fit to Print," *China Economic Quarterly*, March 2009, pp. 47–51, and Brady's chapter on Confucianism in contemporary ideology, Chapter 3 in this volume.

2 The official adoption of concepts like "harmonious society" has been the result of a gradual endorsement and introduction in CCP "thought work" of traditional Confucian concepts since the mid-1980s. The China Confucius Research Institute (*Zhonghua kongzi Yanjiu suo*) was established under the auspices of the Central Propaganda Department in 1985. In 1996 a large scale research project on Confucius was launched by the same department, followed by the "CCP spiritual civilization construction project" and the introduction of traditional Confucian terminology in the propaganda work. See Anne-Marie Brady, "State Confucianism,

Chineseness, and Tradition in CCP Propaganda" and Tian Longyu, "The Revival of Confucianism in Chinese Schools: A Historical Political Review," *Asia Pacific Journal of Education*, 28, 2, June 2008.

3   "Hu Jintao Calls for the Task of Bringing Society Together Harmoniously to be Accomplished Thoroughly and Energetically," in Gudrun Wacker and Matthis Kaiser, "Sustainability Chinese Style: The Concept of Harmonious Society", *SWP Research*, RP6, August 2008. See also: "Building Harmonious Society First Task," *China Daily*, February 22, 2005.

4   "President Hu Speaks on National Development," *China Daily*, June 25, 2007.

5   Daniel Bell, "New Chinese Beliefs Draw on Old," www.taipeitimes.com/news, July 9, 2008.

6   During the 60th anniversary ceremony however, more "orthodox" Marxist slogans like "Socialism is good" and "With the Communist Party the future is bright" were very much on display as well as old legalist and imperial revival slogans in favor at the end of the Empire and in Meiji Japan like "Rich and strong" (*Fu Qiang*). These slogans, however, were not translated on the official English language CCTV program, as they were contrary to the calls for "harmony". One could conclude that the remnants of communist ideology are kept strictly for internal consumption and a completely new strategy of communication based on traditional Confucian principles has been built both for internal consumption and for foreign and Overseas Chinese consumption.

7   For a discussion on the concepts of *wen* and *wu* in imperial China see for instance Alastair Iain Johnston, *Cultural Realism, Strategic Culture and Grand Strategy in Chinese History* (Princeton NJ: Princeton University Press, 1998) and Valérie Niquet, *Les fondements de la stratégie chinoise* (Paris: Editions Economica, 1998).

8   China remains wary of any reform of the United Nations Security Council that could result in a proportional reduction of its own influence, particularly vis-à-vis Japan or India, its two Asian neighbors and potential strategic challengers.

9   "Chinese Think Tank Initiates Peace Dove Strategy," *People's Daily online*, January 29, 2008.

10   "China Threat Fear Countered by Culture," *People's Daily online*, January 29, 2008.

11   Sun Zi is the author of the *Sun Zi Bingfa*, "The Art of War of Sun Zi," written during the Warring States period.

12   Feng Huiyun, *Chinese Strategic Culture and Foreign Policy Decision Making* (New York: Routledge, 2007).

13   In his keynote speech at the sixtieth anniversary of the PRC on October 1, 2009, President Hu Jintao made once again this reference to the 5,000-year-old history of China.

14   This reminds us of the the building of new "Chinatowns" or "old China streets," mimicking the ones found in the West.

15   Sheila Melvin, "Modern Gloss on China Golden Age," www.newyorktimes.com, March 3, 2009.

16   Anne Cheng, "Le retour des valeurs confucéennes face à l'universalité des Droits de l'Homme," unpublished paper presented at the 2009 Total University workshop on China. This phenomenon reminds us of what was going on in Meiji Japan with the "invented tradition of a modernized version of the ethic of the old bushi class" in C. Douglas Lummis, "Ruth Benedict: Obituary for Japanese Culture," *Japan Focus*, 19 July, 2009.

17   Leon Vandermeersch and Umberto Bresciani, "Reinventing Confucianism," *China Perspectives*, no. 4-5, January-February 2003. In a rather provocative way, Jiang Qing proposed to recreate a religious cult of Confucius: "Confucianism Will Never Become a Religion," *China Daily*, June 1, 2006.

18 Anne Cheng, "Le retour des valeurs confucéennes," and *Histoire de la pensée chinoise* (Paris: Seuil, 1997); John Delury, "The Ancient Sources of Modern Doctrine," www.hoover.org/publications/policyreview, April-May 2008.

19 Guy Alitto, *Liang Shuming and the Chinese Dilemma of Modernity* (Berkeley: University of California Press, 1979).

20 "Official Image of Confucius Sparks Debate Among Scholars," *People's Daily online* September 26, 2006.

21 www.english.hanban.org

22 Ibid.

23 Ibid.

24 Nicolas Becquelin, "China's New Propaganda Machine," *Wall Street Journal Asia*, January 30, 2009.

25 *Le Figaro*, March 30, 2008 and Tom Hyland, "Confucius Says Universities at Risk in Link up with Chinese Government," www.theage.com.au, November 8, 2007.

26 www.english.hanban.org

27 Xu Keqian, deputy director of North Carolina University Confucius Institute, "An Introduction to Confucius Institutes in Modern China," http://ncsu.edu/oia/confucius/

28 www.hanban.org/confuciousinstitutes/node_10961.htm

29 China is never described as being on the "demanding" side. "Booming Confucius Institutes Enhance China's Soft Power," www.chinaview.cn, November 12, 2008.

30 Indianapolis University Confucius Institute Presentation at: http://.iupui.edu/china/

31 In France, there is compulsory study of at least two foreign languages in middle school with the possibility of a third one at high school (lycée) level.

32 *Kyodonews*, April 17, 2008.

33 See for instance: www.kennesaw.edu/confuciusinstitute/

34 Jean-Pierre Raffarin regularly organizes conferences on China, either in Poitiers, in Paris or in Beijing. He is also one of the sponsors of the Comité France–China, a business organization supporting increased relations between France and China. He has his own blog in Chinese : http://blog.ifeng.com

35 See: "Le Chinois ZTE entend imposer sa marque en France et vise 10% du marché," http://comparatel.fr/news/, May 31, 2009.

36 The Ecole des Langues Orientales was founded by Napoleon and led to a very strong school of sinologists at the end of the nineteenth century.

37 www.confucius.univ.paris7.fr and interview with François Jullien, former director of the Département des Langues et Civilisations Orientales, University of Paris VII.

38 Lu Yiyi, "Blind Spots in China Soft Power," *Straits Times*, July 9, 2007; Joshua Kurlantzick, *Charm Offensive* (New Haven CT: Yale University Press, 2007).

5 Linguistic engineering in Hu Jintao's China

The case of the 'Maintain Advancedness' campaign

Ji Fengyuan

Linguistic engineering is the attempt to affect people's attitudes and beliefs by manipulating the language that they hear, speak, read, and write. It takes a 'pluralistic' form in democratic societies, where governments, political parties, lobby-groups, advertisers, religious groups and social movements promote words, slogans and discourses to advance their often divergent goals. And it has taken a totalitarian form under many Marxist dictatorships, which have used it as a tool in their attempts to create new, revolutionary human beings capable of creating a communist future.

Linguistic engineering took an exceptionally radical form in Mao Zedong's China, for Mao saw the Chinese people as 'a blank sheet of paper' on which he could write the most beautiful characters and paint the most beautiful pictures.[1] He wrote his characters and painted his pictures with many instruments, and the most precise of them was undoubtedly the Chinese Communist Party's massive programme of linguistic engineering. This programme required people to make revolutionary verbal formulae part of their daily lives by seasoning their speech and writing with officially approved slogans, phrases and revolutionary scripts that gave 'correct' linguistic form to 'correct' thought. It was based on the assumption that, with constant repetition, the revolutionary words would penetrate people's minds, engendering revolutionary beliefs and values. The whole process was centrally controlled, with the formulae being approved by Party leaders and disseminated by the Central Propaganda Department, the New China News Agency and other Party-controlled organizations. The media and the Party then taught these formulae to the whole population, whose individual members were expected not only to use them but to make sure that their family, friends, and colleagues used them. The Chinese people as a whole were cast in the role of language police.[2]

China's great programme of linguistic engineering was at its most intense during the ten-year Cultural Revolution that began in 1966. However, within a couple of years of Mao's death in 1976, the Communist Party had abandoned his policies of constant revolutionary upheaval, along with the totalitarian goal of creating new, revolutionary human beings.[3] With totalitarian transformation of consciousness no longer an objective, there was no need to apply policies of linguistic engineering to the entire population. Moreover, under the guidance of Deng Xiaoping, the Reform Era saw changes in Chinese society that weakened the Party's control of people's lives and made the wholesale implementation of linguistic engineering impossible. From the 1980s decollectivization and the rise of township and village enterprises undermined the cadres' domination of the rural economy and rural society, and at the same time large numbers of peasants were able to ignore the Party's ban on migration to the cities, where they eventually formed a huge 'floating population' outside the Party's control. In the cities themselves, the rise of private, collective and foreign-owned enterprises took most people out of state sector employment, removing them from the Party-controlled work units (*danwei*) that had regulated their existence. Most people also bought their own apartments instead of living in state-owned housing allocated by their work units.[4] Taken collectively, these changes destroyed the institutional structures though which the Party had controlled people's everyday lives, making it impossible for it to enforce rigorous controls on people's language even if it wanted to. As a result, a de facto private sphere began to emerge, and on many topics new discourses uncontrolled by the state began to proliferate. China might still have had an authoritarian government, but it no longer had a totalitarian one.

However, linguistic engineering is not confined to totalitarian societies, and it persists in attenuated forms in Reform Era China. It has two main aspects. First, the Party still promotes its message through extensive 'thought work',[5] and as part of that project it seeks to influence the linguistic construction of politically important issues. It devises specific linguistic formulae that express key elements of current policy, and these formulae are used in Party documents, in intra-party discussions and in the media. From there, they pass into the political vocabulary of ordinary Chinese. To pick just the most obvious example, Deng Xiaoping's carefully devised formulae ('Practice is the sole criterion of truth', 'Seek truth from facts', 'Development is the ultimate truth', 'Socialism with Chinese characteristics', and 'Socialist market economy') displaced the formulae of revolutionary Maoism and became the focal points of new political discourses during the post-1978 Reform Era. These formulae have passed into general use both inside the Party and outside it, and they impose a framework on debate that has made it very difficult for conservatives with Maoist sympathies to argue that China's move towards a market economy is 'travelling the capitalist road' rather than 'constructing a socialist market economy'.[6]

The second aspect of linguistic engineering in the Reform Era is that, while it has been greatly relaxed outside the Party, it continues in something like its original form in specific intra-Party contexts. Why should this be the case? First, while the power structures that supported tight controls over language amongst the general population have collapsed, the structures that can be used to enforce Mao-style linguistic engineering within the Party remain intact. Second, while the Party no longer aims at transforming the consciousness of the entire population, it remains committed to ensuring that its own members have the correct ideology, or at least that they know what the correct ideology is and are prepared to comply with it. Third, by making all Party members recite political formulae that express the current Party line, the Party suppresses disagreements within its ranks and maintains a show of Party unity. Party members who disagree with the dominant discourse can try to work around it or reinterpret it, they can question particular policies associated with it, and they can sometimes attack it obliquely. However, they risk their own political futures if they challenge the discourse directly. Moreover, in particular official contexts (during a political campaign, for example) they can be forced to participate in it.

In this essay, I am going to explore the operation of linguistic engineering within the Chinese Communist Party itself, taking as my focus the manipulation of language by current Party chairman Hu Jintao during the great 'Maintain Advancedness' campaign that was trialled during 2004, then ran from January 2005 until July 2006. In particular, I am going to show how Hu used carefully devised linguistic formulae during the campaign to consolidate his ascendancy within the Party, to promote his reform agenda, to strengthen Party discipline, and to help revive idealism and a sense of mission amongst government cadres.

The full title of the Maintain Advancedness campaign was the 'Educational Campaign to Maintain the Advanced Nature of the Chinese Communist Party' (*Baochi gongchandangyuan xianjinxing jiaoyuhuodong*). Despite its claim to be merely 'educational', it was an updated version of a traditional rectification campaign. Moreover, like its predecessors it signified the outcome of a power struggle over how to deal with current issues and define the correct Party line.

The problems that the Maintain Advancedness campaign was intended to address were a by-product of the policies of Hu's immediate predecessors, Deng Xiaoping and Jiang Zemin. From 1978, their reforms had created a vibrant private sector that was the engine of astonishing economic growth. However, the benefits of privatization and growth were unevenly distributed, and serious problems emerged:

- Huge gaps opened up between the rich and the poor, between the cities and the countryside, and between the coastal regions and the country's vast interior.
- Corruption spread, as Party members used their positions within the Party-state to ensure that they were not left behind when it came to new opportunities for wealth-making.
- There was an avalanche of protests in rural areas against corrupt, self-serving and exploitative cadres.
- There was a growing lack of clarity about the Communist Party's role in a society that was based increasingly on a market economy, and doubts began to emerge about its relevance.
- The Party centre had difficulty in implementing reforms at a lower level because local officials sometimes lacked ideological commitment, because

they were reluctant to introduced changes that would reduce their revenue, and because they often put personal and regional interests ahead of Party policy.
• The Party's failure to address these problems adequately was undermining its support and endangering its legitimacy.

Hu and his colleagues tried to address these difficulties through policies advanced under two banners: the campaign to create a 'harmonious society' (*hexie shehui*), announced in February 2005 as an attempt to redress inequalities, injustices and grievances through well co-ordinated development; and the campaign to build a 'new socialist countryside' (*shehuizhuyi xin-nongcun*), announced in February 2006 as an attempt to reduce rural–urban disparities.[7] However, in Hu's analysis, new policies were only part of the solution, for the Party itself was deeply implicated in the problems that had emerged. The Party therefore had to be rectified if it was going to regain its idealism, improve its image and become an effective instrument of reform. Such a rectification would also give Hu an opportunity to consolidate his dominance and ensure that he left a substantial theoretical legacy – a matter of some importance to an accomplished theoretician who had been president of the Party's theoretical powerhouse, the Central Party School, from 1993 to December 2002.

Because the Chinese Communist Party has always claimed to be based on correct theory, all additions to its theoretical tradition must appear, at last nominally, to grow out of the existing body of doctrine. Hu achieved this consistency by claiming to base his theory on the doctrine of his predecessors, Mao Zedong, Deng Xiaoping and Jiang Zemin. Indeed, he took as his start-ing point Jiang's own claim to theoretical importance, the doctrine of the 'Three Represents' (*sange daibiao*), which had been ratified by the 16th Peo-ple's Congress in 2002. The doctrine asserted that 'The Party must always represent the developmental trend of China's advanced productive forces, the orientation of its advanced culture, and the fundamental interests of the overwhelming majority of the people.'[8] From Jiang's point of view, the phrase 'the overwhelming majority of the people' was crucial: it was so general that it could be taken to include, not only the workers and peasants, but China's new class of capitalists. And, since a Party that represented the interests of capitalists could certainly welcome them as members, they could now be recruited into the Party to consolidate their loyalty and 'indoctrinate them with the Party orthodoxy'.[9]

Hu made his own theoretical breakthrough by basing his doctrine (nomin-ally) on the Three Represents, then putting his own gloss on the phrase 'the fundamental interests of the overwhelming majority of the people'. If the Party took these words seriously, he implied, it could not continue to promote growth through policies that enriched the few but neglected 'the interests of the overwhelming majority of the people'.[10] He thereby turned Jiang's theory into a critique of Jiang's policies – policies that had disproportionately benefited capitalists, corrupt officials and a few great cities, leaving most people far behind.

The Maintain Advancedness campaign was Hu's instrument for rectifying the Party that had implemented Jiang's policies – his instrument for turning it into a purified and disciplined organization that would correct its errors by implementing his policies, working tirelessly for the people's benefit and helping to distribute the benefits of economic growth more widely. At every stage, Hu carefully legitimated both the campaign and his own theoretical views by linking them to the Communist Party's ideological heritage. He did this by ensuring that all Party members learned and used carefully crafted linguistic formulae that established the link. These formulae were given prominence in the central Party document that launched the campaign. They were then reproduced in Party documents issued at lower levels, in articles published in the official media, and in speeches by Party leaders ranging from Hu himself right down to local Party secretaries. Finally, we shall see, the formulae had to be repeated in the 'self-examinations' that each individual Party member was required to write in the course of the campaign.

The central formula used to introduce the campaign, repeated countless times with only minor variations, announced the campaign's guiding ideologies by declaring that it was intended

> to bring about deeper understanding of Deng's theory and the important thought of the Three Represents, to understand the spirit of the 16th Party Congress and the spirit of the 3rd and 4th plenums [of the 16th Central Committee] and to raise the understanding of strengthening the Party's ruling capacity.[11]

To most non-Chinese, this formula listing the campaign's guiding theoretical influences is at best opaque, but to Chinese Party members it was an unmistakeable signal that Hu Jintao was now the Party's supreme ideologist. They all knew that it was at the third Plenum of the 16th Central Committee that Hu had elaborated the doctrine of 'balanced' economic development that would overcome the deficiencies of Jiang's approach; that it was at the fourth Plenum that he had explained his 'people-centred scientific development concept of coordination and stability' (with its implication that Jiang's focus on breakneck development was neither people-centred nor scientific); and that it was at the fourth Plenum that Hu had emphasised that the Party must strengthen its ability to govern so that it could implement his reforms at all levels. All Party members knew that when Hu told the Party that it would have to change in order to 'maintain its progressiveness' he was telling it to make both its theory and its practice conform to the new Party line that he had established. They found it perfectly natural that, as heir to the Party's tradition of linguistic engineering, he should drive the point home by making Party members recite a formula that listed the Central Committee plenums that had authoritatively endorsed his thought.

After being launched in January 2005, the Maintain Advancedness campaign fell into three phases. For its first six months, it focused on high-ranking Party officials; for its second six months, it targeted urban Party members; and for its third, it was directed at rural Party members. However, unlike the great campaigns of the Mao era, it did not involve the mobilization of the whole society, for the Party now had neither the desire to organize such campaigns nor the organizational structures required to keep them under control. It invited people outside the Party to submit criticisms and suggestions, but the campaign was not an attempt to transform *their* consciousness. Its purpose was to transform the consciousness of *Party members*, including those who had lost contact with the Party organization through processes of social and economic change.

The Chinese Communist Party has always been careful to support its message with appropriate non-verbal contexts. Since the Maintain Advancedness campaign was intended to revive Party members' sense of mission and sacrifice, the campaign's organizers decided to evoke the idealism of the past by promoting 'revolutionary tourism' – getting Party members to visit the graves of revolutionary heroes and make the long journey to revolutionary bases like Yan'an. Hu and other Party leaders led the way by travelling to these areas, and according to some estimates there were 100,000,000 visits to these sites in 2005.[12] The Party also organized its members into watching 'Red movies' that recalled the heroism of revolutionary times; it asked them to renew the oath that they took when they joined the Party; and it encouraged them to celebrate the day on which they joined the Party as a 'Red birthday'. Finally, the Party gave great publicity to model Party members and arranged for them to visit many Party branches so that others could learn from them. All these activities reinforced what the campaign was saying in words. In effect, the Party was involving its members in ideologically loaded *experiences* that were part of the same discourse as the ideologically loaded *verbal formulae* that everyone had to use.

The campaign, in the classic Maoist tradition, was controlled by the Party leadership through a central 'Leading Group' set up by the Standing Committee of the Politburo. This Leading Group distributed instructions and central Party documents to lesser leading groups headed by the Party secretaries at every level of the hierarchy, right down to the Party's 3.3 million local branches. It also distributed the instructions and documents to official national media outlets, such as the *People's Daily* and Xinhua News Agency, which published key excerpts and provided detailed commentary under the guidance of the central Leading Group. This commentary was then copied and adapted to local circumstances by the lower-level official media. At all levels, the commentary was scrutinized carefully to ensure that it conformed to the correct line.

A crucial point, from the perspective of this chapter, is that the official line not only had a specific *content* but was expressed in carefully chosen *words* that were adopted throughout the Party and media hierarchies. These prescribed linguistic forms were modelled by the official documents, by the speeches of Party leaders, by the press, and by the media. Ordinary Party members adopted them because there was no alternative language in which to discuss the issues raised by the campaign, and because an attempt to invent one would rightly have been taken as a rejection of the Party's authority in the realm of political language. And it was these formulae, starting with the central slogan 'Maintain Advancedness', that identified the issues, limited the debate, and structured the discourse of the campaign. So both political content and linguistic form were vital.

It is clear that the required uniformity of content and language was achieved through what we might call 'the great downward copying process'. The process began with the 'originals' – key documents and instructions approved by the Party's highest leaders. Both the content and language of these originals were then copied by successive levels of the Party hierarchy right down to Party secretaries in the local branches, who in turn made sure that they were copied by Party members at the grassroots. This downward copying process was based on the model set by Mao Zedong's original (and far more brutal) Party rectification campaign in Yan'an in the 1940s, and Yan'an precedents influenced other matters as well. Both campaigns began with the study of ideological texts and Party documents, both moved on to verbal and written forms of criticism and self-criticism, and both culminated in confessions of shortcomings and resolutions for self-reform. In the case of the Maintain Advancedness campaign, all Party members were given a substantial book containing prescribed texts that had to be mastered. The texts consisted of five collective Party documents and three documents attributed to each of the Party's four great leaders – Mao Zedong, Deng Xiaoping, Jiang Zemin and Hu Jintao himself. With the assistance of speeches by current Party leaders, editorials in the official press and supplementary reading materials compiled by local Party committees, Party members had to spend a minimum of 40 hours studying the documents, linking them to the purpose of the campaign. They were expected to know the key formulae used in the documents, and to be able to use those formulae correctly. The formulae included the following:

- *'The Two Musts'* (liangge wubi).[13] This formula, promulgated by Chairman Mao in 1949, was used by Hu to remind cadres how to go about their work: 'We must be sure to make cadres continue to preserve a work style of humility, circumspection, free from arrogance and rashness, and we must be sure to make cadres continue to preserve a work style of hard work and struggle.'
- *'The Eight Upholds and the Eight Opposes'* (bage jianchi bage fandui).[14] This was a numerical moral formula dating to 2001 that listed maxims or slogans designed to improve the Party's 'working style' – the way in which cadres carried out their jobs. Cadres were expected to link all these maxims to the campaign. We can classify the maxims, relating them to the themes of the campaign, as follows:

a. The first maxims told Party members to 'Uphold emancipating the mind' and warned them to 'Oppose sticking to old ways, not progressing'. This echoed Deng Xiaoping's slogan 'Emancipate the mind', which had been at the heart of the movement towards greater intellectual openness during the early years of the Reform Era. The maxims implicitly enlisted Deng in support of Hu's demand that people get rid of old ways and emancipate their minds from all ideas inimical to the Maintain Advancedness campaign.

b. Hu was determined to make the Party act with the welfare of ordinary people in mind, instead of submitting to the dictates of bureaucratic imperatives. In this respect, three maxims were especially useful, one telling cadres that they had to 'Uphold close ties with the masses', and two others warning them that they had to 'Oppose formalism and bureaucratism' and 'Oppose making arbitrary decisions and taking peremptory actions'.

c. Hu had attacked corruption, lavish lifestyles and cronyism. Three slogans therefore instructed cadres to 'Uphold hard struggle', 'Uphold appointing people on their merits' and 'Uphold what is upright and just, honest and clean'. These Three Upholds were complemented by Three Opposes – 'Oppose hedonism and pleasure seeking', 'Oppose malpractice in appointing people', and 'Oppose seeking personal gains from using power'.

d. Finally, because no reform was possible if Party members failed to carry out instructions, cadres were enjoined to 'Uphold combining theory [as interpreted by Hu] with [their own] practice', to 'Uphold the principle of democratic centralism', to 'Uphold Party discipline', and at the same time to 'Oppose liberalism' – a doctrine that would have allowed individuals to debate the Party line.

Having studied the prescribed texts associated with the campaign, Party members had to apply to *themselves* and to their *colleagues* the principles that they had absorbed. This process was centred on a hand-written self-evaluation, at least 2,000 words in length, in which all Party members had to examine their own attitudes and behaviour in the light of the campaign's principles. Before writing the self-examination, they had to solicit comment and criticism from their colleagues. Those who had dealings with the general public had to seek criticism from 'the masses' as well. All these criticisms had to be incorporated into the self-examination when it was written up. Of course, most cadres were careful not to put themselves in a bad light needlessly, and they no doubt toned down some of the criticisms that they received. However, it was unwise simply to ignore criticism, because all cadres were aware that their superiors had been instructed to make their own inquiries. And even if one's colleagues and the masses offered nothing but praise, cadres knew that they would have to invent some plausible criticisms themselves so as not to appear to be refusing to cooperate with the campaign.

The materials distributed with the campaign included detailed instructions for writing up the self-examination. Cadres had to measure themselves by the standard set in the Party constitution, and they had to assess their world view, values, work and way of life from the perspective of the Two Musts and the Eight Upholds and the Eight Opposes. All criticisms had to consist of the following parts:

1 An examination of one's thought, work and way of life since the 16th Party Congress, which had endorsed the principles underlying the campaign.
2 A summary of the main problems and shortcomings revealed by the self-examination.
3 An analysis of the ideological roots of the problems and shortcomings revealed by the self-examination.
4 The measures to be taken to ensure improvement.
5 The way forward in the future.

While the instructions said that 'It is not possible to have a set standard and uniform style' in writing up the self-analysis, this was belied in practice. Official Party websites included model self-examinations to help Party members do what was required, in both form and substance. In addition, numerous unofficial websites produced generic 'one size fits all' self-examinations, as well as variants tailored to the requirements of cadres holding particular positions. With 70 million Party members pondering their past failures to 'Maintain Advancedness', these websites proved extremely popular. During the campaign, the Xin Lang website, which featured model self-examinations for download, was reputed to have scored more 'hits' than any other website – of any variety – in the country. It goes without saying that Party members who used these websites had to adapt the most helpful model self-examinations to their own circumstances. All cadres had to discuss their self-examinations with their superiors, and a self-examination that did not match the person who had allegedly written it would rightly be taken as a sign of insincerity.

All the model self-examinations not only had appropriate political content, but they were written using officially prescribed linguistic formulae. For example, they seem invariably to have included the formula that the self-examination process had been conducted under the guidance of 'Marxism–Leninism–Mao Zedong Thought, Deng Xiaoping's theory and the important thought of the Three Represents'. They invariably made it clear that the author of the self-examination had studied the book of readings devised for the campaign, and they asserted that the author had considered his or her behaviour against the standard set by the Party constitution, the Two Musts, the Eight Upholds, the Eight Opposes, and often Hu Jintao's speech setting out the 'Six Upholds' – a series of basic requirements for Party members.[15] All self-analyses had to follow this formula as a sign that their authors accepted the Party's official ideology, that they respected the Party's constitution and that they acknowledged the authority of the texts that everyone involved in the campaign had been required to study.

Once the model self-analyses got beyond their introductions, they were tailored to each Party member's particular situation. However, they remained heavily formulaic, combining and recombining standard political words and phrases. The following are representative examples of verbal formulae taken from the model self-criticisms on official and unofficial websites. They recur in self-criticism after self-criticism, and in every case they incorporate the wording of official Party documents:

- 'I have a wrong attitude towards political study … I lack a deep understanding of the core meaning and scientific essence of Marxism–Leninism– Mao Zedong Thought, Deng Xiaoping's theory and the important thought of the Three Represents' (This was a standard formula for confessing doctrinal mistakes. Most of its terminology is taken from the Party's constitution).
- 'I didn't pay enough attention to establishing a scientific world view, outlook on life, and values.' (This confession repeats a formula linked to Hu's Scientific Development Concept and it reiterates the campaign's instruction that all Party members had to scrutinize their world view and values.)
- 'I need to strengthen my political ideals and always remember the oath that I took when I joined the Party.' (This incorporates the words of official documents that advised Party members to strengthen their political ideals and renew the oath that they took when they joined the Party.)
- 'I will help to build a Party serving the interests of the people.' (This formula echoes Jiang Zemin's 'Third Represent', which states that the Party represents 'the fundamental interests of the overwhelming majority of the Chinese people'; it echoes Hu's Scientific Development Concept with its emphasis on 'taking people as the basis' and 'putting people first'; and it echoes Mao's essay 'Serve the People', which everyone had to study precisely because it gave a Maoist pedigree to Hu's concept.)

What are we to make of this almost complete reliance on officially prescribed formulaic language? To most Westerners, it seems shallow and insincere, but most Chinese see it very differently. The formulae are the Party's standard language of moral-political analysis in the Hu Jintao era, and its members have learned to use them as easily and naturally as a physician uses the technical jargon of modern medicine. For them, use of the formulae signifies their sincerity and their loyalty to the Party line, and they know that a refusal to use them would be a challenge to the Party's authority.

Why does the Party still go to the trouble of standardizing its language? I have already suggested that one reason is that linguistic uniformity enables it to impose unity on its members by making them all use the same words to repeat the current Party line. However, two other reasons are equally important. The first is that the Party is heir to the Chinese tradition of rote learning as a method of acquiring knowledge and imparting virtue. Children in imperial China were made to chant moral maxims word for word, and candidates for imperial office had to learn Confucian texts by heart.[16] It was assumed that the repetition of correct words with a correct message would in time produce correct thought. This assumption was reinforced by the Party's ideological inheritance from the Soviet Union and it underpinned the policies of linguistic engineering in the Mao era.[17] It also underlies the attempts to use linguistic engineering to rectify the attitudes of Party members today.

A second reason for the standardization of language is that the Party remains formally committed to the view that Marxism–Leninism–Mao Zedong Thought is a science, which like other sciences requires standardized terminology to avoid confusion and ambiguity. In practice, of course, Chinese political language is both generalized and ambiguous, and the advantages of standardized language are less scientific than political. In particular, by saying that their doctrine of 'socialism with Chinese characteristics' is a scientific theory that has inspired China's economic policies, China's leaders are able to claim full credit for the country's astonishing economic growth. This enables them to parry the suggestion that China has succeeded only because it has abandoned socialist policies for capitalist ones, and to argue that Communist Party rule and their own version of socialist theory are the recipe for future success.

The Party's continued commitment to linguistic engineering within its own ranks is clear. It is also clear that the Party's leaders believe that linguistic engineering helps it to get its message across and persuade people that the message is correct. Are the leaders justified in thinking that linguistic engineering has these effects? Let us approach the question by asking first whether linguistic engineering helps people to *remember what they have learned* during political campaigns. There are, in fact, good theoretical reasons for believing that it does. Because the official formulae are used constantly, they are difficult to forget. And because they are used as building blocks for the campaign's wider discourse, they are linked systematically to the whole of that discourse. This is important, because it means that the formulae act as the easily recalled nuclei of mental schemas – clusters of interconnected concepts and beliefs linked together in wider associative networks. Cognitive psychologists have demonstrated that details embedded in such schemas are much easier to recall than facts that are isolated or disorganized.[18] So by assisting the formation of schemas, well-entrenched linguistic formulae stabilize the knowledge built around them. That is why, over 40 years later, those who participated in the Cultural Revolution can still remember its linguistic formulae, together with much of the knowledge linked to them. And that is why party members whom I interviewed in late 2008, over two years after the Maintain Advancedness campaign, could still easily remember both the campaign's formulae and the concepts and beliefs associated with them. Constant repetition, stable linguistic form and schematic structuring of knowledge are excellent aids to recall.

There are also good theoretical reasons to believe that linguistic engineering assists *persuasion* through activating a variety of 'primitive affective and associational processes'.[19] For example, when nearly all people use the same language to say the same thing, this produces powerful modelling, reference group and validity effects that make it difficult for any individual to retain an independent opinion.[20] Similarly, when people repeat verbal formulae with an evaluative content, this tends to sway their attitudes through higher order conditioning;[21] when they are rewarded with approval for saying 'correct' things in the 'correct' way, processes of operant conditioning encourage them to believe what they say;[22] and when they willingly repeat formulae that commit them to certain principles, most experience unpleasant cognitive dissonance if they flout those principles.[23] The forms of linguistic engineering employed in the Maintain Advancedness campaign were well calculated to activate all these mechanisms, so there are good theoretical reasons to believe that they had at least some effect on attitudes. However, the *strength* of that effect varies with the circumstances. It is easy to persuade people to accept attitudes that are compatible with many of their existing values, especially if the new attitudes tap their idealism, appeal to their self-interest, or consolidate their identification with a group. On this basis, the campaign no doubt influenced the attitudes of a fair number of cadres. At the same time, it is difficult to persuade people to adopt attitudes that will require them to give up wealth, privilege or self-respect, so the campaign was more likely to make corrupt cadres fear discovery and punishment than to touch their hearts.[24]

Even in the unlikely event that the Maintain Advancedness campaign did little or nothing to change attitudes, it must still be rated as at least a partial success from the Party's point of view. It resulted in the expulsion of 44,738 Party members, the rectification of 156,000 'weak or non-functional' local Party organizations, the establishment of 130,000 new Party organizations, and the provision of intensive training to over 2.9 million Party leaders.[25] Many cadres were shocked at its intensive and sometimes punitive nature. By the time it ended very few remained unclear about the type of performance expected of them and very few retained the misconception that in the Reform Era ideological matters were no longer regarded as crucial. As a massive exercise in linguistic engineering, the campaign also strengthened Party discipline because the 'great downward copying process' and the self-criticisms forced every member of the Party to acknowledge that the Party's leaders had the authority to determine theoretical matters, to distinguish good conduct from bad, and to tell everyone what to say and how to say it.

There is something very impressive about a campaign that makes some 70 million people read the same official documents, use the same criteria to analyse their attitudes and work performance, and produce written self-criticisms using the same officially authorized verbal formulae. And all those who participated in the campaign know that their self-examinations remain on file, with records of comments by their co-workers and superiors, to be used by the Party either to advance their careers or to block their future progress. This demonstration of the Party's power over its members will not easily be forgotten. Control of language, control of ideas, and control over people's lives enhance the power of all rulers.

Notes

1   Mao Tsetung, 'Introducing a co-operative', in *Selected Readings from the Works of Mao Tsetung*, Beijing: Foreign Languages Press, 1971, p. 500.
2   For a detailed analysis of linguistic engineering in the Mao era, see Ji Fengyuan, *Linguistic Engineering: Language and Politics in Mao's China*, Honolulu: University of Hawai'i Press, 2004.
3   Ji, *Linguistic Engineering*, pp. 305–17.
4   For a concise summary of these changes, see Susan Shirk, *China: Fragile Superpower*, Oxford and New York: Oxford University Press, paperback edition 2008, pp. 29, 278 n.82.
5   On thought work and propaganda in the Reform era, see Anne-Marie Brady, *Marketing Dictatorship: Propaganda and Thought Work in Contemporary China*, Lanham, MD: Rowman & Littlefield, 2008.
6   For excellent discussions of these debates, see Wei-Wei Zhang, *Ideology and Economic Reform under Deng Xiaoping 1978–1993*, London and New York: Kegan Paul International, 1996; and Richard Baum, *Burying Mao: Chinese Politics in the Age of Deng Xiaoping*, Princeton, NJ: Princeton University Press, 1994).
7   'Building harmonious society crucial to China's progress: Hu', *People's Daily Online*, 27 June 2005, reporting Hu's speech announcing the policy on 19 February 2005 (accessed 27 February 2009); 'China issues policies to launch "new socialist countryside" construction', *People's Daily Online*, 21 February 2006, reporting the release of the Central Committee and State Council document announcing the policy (accessed 27 February 2009).
8   Jiang Zemin, 'Zai qingzhu zhongguogongchandang chengli bashizhounian dahuishangde jianghua', speech at the celebration of the eightieth anniversary of the founding of the Chinese Communist Party (2001), reprinted in *Zhonggongzhongyang baochi gongchandangyuan xianjinxingjiaoyu duben* (Readings for Education to Maintain the Advanced Nature of the Communist Party), Beijing: Dangjianduwu chubanshe, 2004, p. 162.
9   Jia Hepeng, 'The Three Represents campaign: reform the Party or indoctrinate the capitalists?' *Cato Journal*, vol. 24, no. 3, Fall 2004.
10 For discussion of the early stages of the campaign, see Joseph Fewsmith, 'CCP launches Campaign to Maintain the Advanced Nature of Party Members', *China Leadership Monitor*, no. 13, Winter 2005, p. 2.
11 Zhonggongzhongyang (CCP Central Committee), 'Guanyu zaidangnei kaizhan baochi gongchangdanyuan xianjinxing jiaoyu huodong detongzhi' (CCP opinions on Party-wide education to maintain Party members' Advanced Nature), in *Duben* (Readings), pp. 111–12.
12 Gao Haishen and Zhou Zhengguo, 'Lun Hongse Lüyou de xingqi jiqi shenceng yuanyin' (On the deep reason for the rise of popularity of Red Tourism), *Lilun Qianyan* (Theory Front), no. 21, 2006, available at www.cntheory.com, filed under date 28 July 2008. Accessed 16 March 2009.
13 'Liangge wubi' (The Two Musts), quoted in *Duben* (Readings), p. 116.
14 'Bage jianchi bage fandui' (The Eight Upholds and the Eight Opposes), quoted in *Duben* (Readings), p. 116.
15 Quoted in *Duben* (Readings), pp. 57–59.

16   Jonathan Unger, *Education under Mao: Class and Competition in Canton Schools, 1960–1980*, New York, Columbia University Press, 1982, pp. 68–70; Anita Chan, Richard Madsen and Jonathan Unger, *Chen Village: The Recent History of a Peasant Community in Mao's China*, Berkeley: University of California Press, 1984, p. 76. See also Ji, *Linguistic Engineering*, pp. 41–44.

17   Ji, *Linguistic Engineering*, chapter 2 and elsewhere.

18   See the classic study by G. H. Bower, M. C. Clark, A. M. Lesgold and D. Winzenz, 'Hierarchical retrieval schemes in recall of categorical world lists', *Journal of Verbal Learning and Verbal Behaviour*, vol. 8 (1969), pp. 323–43. For excellent discussions of other research, see J. R. Anderson's *The Architecture of Cognition*, Cambridge, MA: Harvard University Press, 1983, pp. 86–125, 171–214; and the same author's *Cognitive Psychology and Its Implications*, 4th edn, New York: W. H. Freeman, 1995, pp. 150–54, 180–87, 200–203, 211–13, 220–29.

19   Richard E. Petty and John T. Cacioppo, *Communication and Persuasion: Central and Peripheral Routes to Attitude Change*, New York: Springer-Verlag, 1986, p. 9.

20   On modelling effects, see A. Bandura, 'Analysis of modeling processes', in *Psychological Modeling: Conflicting Theories*, ed. A. Bandura, Chicago: Aldine-Atherton; on reference group effects, see D. Bem, *Beliefs, Attitudes and Human Affairs*, Belmont, CA: Brooks/Cole, 1970, pp. 79–88; and on the validity effect, see L. E. Boehm, 'The validity effect: a search for mediating variables', *Personality and Social Psychology Bulletin*, vol. 20, 1994, pp. 285–93.

21   For a summary of the research, see R. M. Perloff, *The Dynamics of Persuasion*, Hillsdale, NJ: Lawrence Erlbaum, 1993, pp. 63–69.

22   W. A. Scott, 'Attitude change through the reward of verbal behaviour', *Journal of Abnormal and Social Psychology*, vol. 55, 1957, pp. 72–75; R. N. Bostrom, J. W. Vlandis and M. E. Rosenbaum, 'Grades as reinforcing contingencies and attitude change', *Journal of Educational Psychology*, vol. 52, 1961, 112–15.

23   The seminal work is L. Festinger, *A Theory of Cognitive Dissonance*, Stanford, CA: Stanford University Press, 1957. Perloff, *Dynamics*, ch. 10, has an excellent summary of subsequent research.

24   For a discussion of the circumstances under which linguistic engineering worked and those under which it failed during the Mao era, see Ji, *Linguistic Engineering*, pp. 285–314.

25   David Shambaugh, *China's Communist Party: Atrophy and Adaptation*, Washington, DC: Woodrow Wilson Center Press, 2008, p. 130.

Part II
New methods of control

6 From control to management

The CCP's "reforms of the cultural structure"

Nicolai Volland

Since the mid-1990s, the Chinese media sector has been transformed rapidly under the impact of market forces, a process that has accelerated since 2000. Many observers have explained these developments in terms of a dichotomy between politics and economic trends: the media are torn between the "Party line" and the "bottom line," with a conspicuous increase in the power of market forces – forces which eventually might overcome the residual resistance and free the Chinese media from the overpowering control of the Party-state.[1] The amazing increase in the breadth of information available to Chinese media audiences is generally quoted as evidence for such an inevitable development.

More recent research has pointed out that the logical conclusion from the marketization of the Chinese media may have been premature.[2] The Chinese media remain engaged in a prolonged tug-of-war in which the Party-state retains a degree of overall control over a public sphere that has been described, in Samuel Huntington's terms, as "praetorian."[3] Other observers have pointed out the proactive role of the Party-state in initiatives such as the conglomeration of Chinese media companies since the late 1990s; increased economic pressure in the larger concerns has sometimes resulted not in more leeway for chief editors and program directors, but has rather contributed to taming some of the more rebellious media voices, a seemingly paradoxical outcome.[4] The Party-state, driven by the CCP's determination to retain its grip on the channels of ideological persuasion, has – more or less successfully – reformed its propaganda apparatus and adapted it to the requirements of a modernizing economy and a globalizing society.[5]

This chapter seeks a different explanation of the marketization process in the Chinese media sector since the 1990s and the political implications of this process. I propose to view developments such as commercialization and conglomeration of Chinese newspapers, TV stations, and publishing houses in the broader context of what has come to be called "reforms of the cultural structure" (*wenhua tizhi gaige*). Developments that closely parallel those witnessed in the media sector in the narrower sense have fundamentally transformed the Chinese cultural sphere – theater companies, art troupes, museums, etc. – in short, the entire sphere that has traditionally been the portfolio of the CCP Propaganda Department. The goal of these reforms has been to turn around notoriously unproductive and overstaffed work units, and make them into revenue providers (i.e., cash cows) for the local bureaucracies in charge of them.[6] More importantly, the cultural reforms must be regarded as a strategy to reassert the Party's control over a sector that has, since the mid-1980s, seen broad inroads from private and sometimes unruly service providers.[7] The revival of the state-led Chinese cultural industries has become more marked in the wake of the global financial crisis of 2008.[8]

I argue thus that the logic of cultural reforms implies that there is no contradiction between marketization and political control; the CCP-led transformation of the cultural sector (including the media sector) is not paradoxical at all. To the contrary, the goal of cultural reforms is to replace a principally bureaucratic approach to control with more flexible forms of management, and in this way to reassert the Party-state's influence in the cultural sphere through means such as ownership or majority control of financially successful or self-supporting companies that will then contain and edge out of the market smaller, more unruly players in the public sphere. The reforms of the cultural structure thus aim at replacing bureaucratic-administrative control with economic-financial control, and to render both the media themselves and the Party's control more effective.

On the following pages I will trace the origins of the cultural reforms policy and clarify its bureaucratic intentions. I will show that the aim of the reforms is not to liberalize or open up this sector, but rather to strengthen Party controls and to further isolate the cultural sector from external influences. I will conclude with a note of caution: while the cultural reforms were designed to tame a sector that had caused the Party-state and its agents more than a few headaches in the past, the reforms remain work-in-progress, and players at all levels are learning to adapt. Evidence from a variety of subsectors, including the media, shows that the CCP has been only partly successful, as basic level players adjust to the new rules and learn to use them to their own advantage and to pursue their own agendas – agendas that may be at odds with those of the Party-state.

Reforms of the cultural structure

In the late 1990s, the Chinese government introduced a broad set of "reforms of the cultural structure" (*wenhua tizhi gaige*).[9] As the name suggests, these reforms were conceived in analogy to the well-known reform packages for the economy (*jingji tizhi gaige*) and politics (*zhengzhi tishi gaige*) that have transformed China in the past three decades. Whereas political reforms stalled in the 1980s, economic reforms have proceeded at a sustained pace and have catapulted the Chinese economy onto the world stage. Their success thus predestined the economic reforms to serve as a model for the cultural reform package that was launched in the late 1990s.[10]

The "cultural reforms" target work units such as theater companies, art troupes, and museums, but also publishing houses, journals, and media enterprises.[11] The primary goal of the reforms is to transform these units from state-run, subsidized bureaucracies into professionally managed and market-oriented companies; the importance of creative industries and the potential for commercial value of the entertainment business figures prominently in the discussions surrounding the cultural reforms. At the same time, the new companies shall not only be financially self-sufficient, but also generate income for their owners, the local governments in general, and the cash-starved propaganda authorities at the provincial and municipal levels in particular. In a global context, the Party has recognized that "creative industries" are a major building bloc in a knowledge economy and may be key to China's "going out" strategy, in the nation's effort to consolidate its industrial footprint in the modern international economic arena.[12] Finally, Party documents reveal the political logic behind the reform effort: the cultural reforms are designed to enhance the position of the Party-state across the cultural sector, where successful private companies and entrepreneurs had made considerable inroads, often in the gray area between legality and illegality, in the course of the 1990s.[13]

A turning point for the cultural reform policy was 2004, when their implementation began on a national level. To reflect these changes, a new bureau was set up in the CCP Propaganda Department, the policy-making body in charge of the entire culture sector.[14] Rather than strengthening the Department's relatively powerless Literature and Art Bureau, the leadership of the propaganda sector decided to set up a new Cultural Reform Office (*Wenhua tizhi gaige bangongshi*). Under the Cultural Reform Office, three suboffices were created, in charge of "industry development" (*shiye fazhan chu*), "research" (*diaoyan chu*), and "liaison" (*lianluo chu*). This structure reveals that the new Cultural Reform Office is perceived as a think tank that develops strategies in close coordination with industry representatives across the country. Its independent status as a bureau (*ju*) level unit within the Propaganda Department, with its own staff, makes clear the importance attributed to the issue of cultural reforms.

The vice-head of the Propaganda Department in charge of cultural reforms is Ouyang Jian. Ouyang's career is interesting and helps to shed light on the development of the cultural reform project as a whole.[15] He joined the Propaganda Department relatively recently, in December 2004. After serving 11 months as deputy secretary of the Department's secretariat – ostensibly a period of apprenticeship that allowed him to familiarize himself with his new environment – he was appointed vice-head in November 2005. Born in 1957, Ouyang must be considered a relatively junior cadre. He spent his early career in Yunnan, in his home region of Dali (Ouyang belongs to the Bai minority group). Holding an M.A. degree in economics, he was publishing widely on economic conditions in Yunnan province in the late 1990s, when he captured the attention of his superiors. In 2001, Ouyang was appointed Party secretary of the neighboring district of Lijiang. Lijiang had suffered major damage during a severe earthquake in early 1998 and the city was still under reconstruction when Ouyang arrived. He quickly recognized the potential of Lijiang's unique Naxi cultural heritage for the development of tourism, practically the only potential source of revenue and economic opportunity in this otherwise remote backwater. Ouyang lobbied hard and got Lijiang approved as one of nine officially assigned national trial sites (*shiyan di*) for cultural reform. (This was not a small achievement in itself, as Lijiang was the only medium-size city on the list that was announced in June 2003. The other trial sites were the provinces and province-level cities of Beijing, Shanghai, Chongqing, Guangdong, and Zhejiang, as well as the cities of Shenzhen, Shenyang, and Xi'an.)[16] On the ground, Ouyang targeted the existing cultural work units and transformed them into modern companies. He ordered a revamp of the local museum, brought in outside investors from Shenzhen to transform the municipal nationalities song and dance ensemble into a modern performance company, privatized the local cinema, and merged the administrative bureaus in charge of culture, broadcasting, and press and publication into one unified directly under the city government.[17] These initiatives quickly paid off and when the central government introduced longer national holidays three times a year to promote domestic tourism, Lijiang was catapulted into the top range of destinations for both Chinese and foreign visitors. The region's economy boomed and Lijiang was elevated to the rank of a district-level city (*shi*; Lijiang was formerly just a district *qu*) under Ouyang's tenure.[18]

In recognition of Ouyang's success in turning around the local economy, in particular his efforts on Lijiang's cultural economy, the Party leadership decided to "helicopter" him to Beijing, bypassing the usual term at the provincial level. In the Propaganda Department, Ouyang was placed in charge of rolling out nationwide the very policies of "cultural reform" that he had been pioneering at the local level. It is remarkable that the leadership in Beijing decided to bring in outside talent, rather than a career cadre with decades of experience within the Party's propaganda bureaucracy. Apparently, the Party's top leaders were not only impressed by Ouyang's performance in Lijiang, but also saw the need to shake up existing structures and promote new approaches. It is likely that the failure of previous efforts to jumpstart the process of cultural reform (such as the establishment of the Culture Industry Bureau in the Ministry of Culture in 1998) made the leadership in Beijing inclined to elevate a newcomer with fresh ideas and a proven track record to a position with significant influence, to roll out the cultural reform policies on a nationwide basis.

Reimagining culture

Since the introduction of economic reforms in the 1980s, the Chinese government has carefully differentiated between "commercial work units" (*qiye danwei*) and "non-commercial work units" (*shiye danwei*).[19] The latter indicates those work units that do not primarily serve the purposes of material value creation – such as the manufacturing and service industries – but rather are entrusted with serving the needs of "spiritual civilization" (*jingshen wenming*) activities within the Chinese political field. Schools, publishing houses, newspapers, TV stations, performance groups, museums and the like, were all originally exempt from the pressures of economic reform. They continued to receive subsidies that insulated them at least partly from market pressures; in return, non-commercial work units were to serve the Party line with much less leverage over their own priorities than was the case for commercial work units. Non-commercial work units were expected to carry out unpopular policies that explicitly served propagandistic purposes. In return, they were guaranteed a minimum level of subsidies; subsidies of commercial work units, in contrast, were rapidly abolished in most sectors.

Once economic reforms deepened in the 1990s, however, the distinction between commercial and non-commercial work units created problems on several levels:

- the exemption from market pressures meant that the work units in question were also exempt from pressures to improve efficiency and responsiveness; many non-commercial units thus remained slow-moving and bureaucratic, sometimes hardly capable of carrying out their assigned tasks;
- the ban on commercial activity created opportunities for shadow players working on the fringes of the industry and in hard-to-define gray areas (the so-called "second channel" of private entrepreneurs in the publishing industry is a prime example);[20]
- the private entertainment industry was not only a strain on the official state-owned work units (loss of business, departure of good personnel) but also created control problems that proved troubling on the political level;[21]
- international pressure has intensified since China's entry into the WTO in 2001; while the accession protocols explicitly restrict competition in all areas dominated by non-commercial work units (most ostensibly the media), foreign pressure to open markets remains high and manifests itself in indirect ways;
- the imbalance between commercial and non-commercial work units has created a significant income deficit within the official administration at both central and local levels; while bureaus in charge of industry and commerce have ample opportunities to cash in (both legally and illegally) on the ongoing boom, the cultural and propaganda bureaucracies have remained a notoriously cash-strapped sector within the administration – and were therefore, until recently, considered unattractive appointments that most cadres would try to avoid;
- taken together, the cleavage between commercial and non-commercial work units has resulted in serious control deficits that, in the long term, have the potential to endanger the Party-state's grip on the ideological front, which has been a crucial pillar of CCP power since the very day of its founding.

The reforms of the cultural structure are designed to address these problems. The attempt to prevent the marketization and commercialization of culture through differentiation between commercial and non-commercial work units has proven a failure; in the face of widespread commercial inroads by non-state players and semi-legal commercial experiments by the state-sanctioned work units, the barrier has in fact already broken down to a considerable degree.[22] As a consequence, the Party decided to legalize the transformation of non-commercial work units into commercial work units (*qiye danwei*) on a trial basis.[23] The situation in the cultural sector seems indeed to resemble closely the situation at the onset of the economic and political reforms two decades earlier: the growth of alternative power structures and market elements outside the state controlled system that were eroding the (already low) effectiveness of the state-owned agricultural and industrial sector, and were posing a threat to the control capabilities of the central state. Then as now, the CCP decided to react with a flexible approach, to quietly acknowledge many of the "wild" structures that had already grown, to co-opt them wherever possible, and otherwise to make itself the spearhead of the movement, so as to control its direction.

According to this logic, a limited number of commercially operating cultural work units under state supervision is thus more desirable than a large number of small private players nestled in the fringes and gray areas of the sector where they are difficult to control. The targeted development of state-invested enterprises in the cultural sector, working with full bureaucratic backing and reaping all the benefits provided by the markets, would likely produce additional sources of income and enhance the control capacities of the Party-state.

From the relevant documents on cultural reform it becomes clear that the commercialization of the cultural sector was driven not only by economic considerations, but that political rationales also played a major role in the decision-making process:

> We must fully understand the importance and urgency of the reform of the cultural structure from the vantage point of implementing a scientific outlook in an all-round way and constructing a socialist harmonious society, from the vantage point of *consolidating the leading position of Marxism in the ideological field*, and from the vantage point of *strengthening the Party's ability to govern*; we must strengthen the sense of responsibility and mission, grasp the important strategic moment, deepen reform, accelerate development, and inject strong vigor into the construction of an advanced socialist culture.[24]

The passage above clearly locates the reform initiatives in the cultural field within the larger drive of the CCP to retain strong overall control of the social and political processes of the PRC, a task that has been identified as particularly urgent in the face of increasing social tensions. What is at stake is the long-term consolidation of the CCP's rule, and it is imperative to guard against all kinds of challenges to the Party's institutional security – what the document calls "strengthening the Party's ability to govern" (*jiaqiang dang de zhizheng nengli*, a major slogan of the Hu Jintao era). It is in this context that the document speaks of "cultural security" (*wenhua anquan*),[25] a concept that hints at the existence of threats to the existing institutional structure that arise from cultural sources, both within the country and from abroad:

> The principles and demands of reform of the cultural structure are: upholding the forward looking orientation of advanced socialist culture, upholding the leading position of Marxism in the ideological field and *guaranteeing our national cultural security*; upholding the persistence in practice and courageous innovation, establishing a new perspective on cultural development; upholding the *dominant position of social effects* and pursuing the realization of a unity of social effects and economic effects; upholding the harmonious development of the cultural cause and cultural industries; and upholding [the principles of] varied treatment, differentiated leadership, measured progress, and gradual advance.[26]

The language in this high-level document – the six-fold repetition of the verb "upholding" (*jianchi*) – marks its importance: similar language appears in numerous CCP policy documents, referring back to Deng Xiaoping's infamous "four cardinal principles" (*si xiang jiben yuanze*) that had been promulgated in spring 1979 and were designed to establish clearly recognizable limits for the process of economic reform and political reform. In a similar vein, the document establishes the borderlines for the reforms of the cultural structure and defines the proper context for this reform push. At the same time, the vocabulary deployed by the document has defensive undertones: the very need to "uphold" and "strengthen" the Party's grip over the cultural sector implies that the CCP's control in this realm has been effectively undermined by actual development over the past two decades. The cultural reform package is thus designed to reverse this trend.

Commercialization of the cultural sector can thus be turned into an opportunity to rebuild the Party-state's control over media, publishing houses, and the arts and entertainment sectors – something that has become increasingly difficult with the growth of the sector in recent years. The forms of management envisioned in the project of controlled commercialization through cultural reforms are conceived as a more sophisticated and effective approach to securing political control.

Implementation

Controlled commercialization of enterprises in the cultural sector began in trial locations and trial industries in the late 1990s, but has since been rolled out on a national basis. The following section presents three examples that illustrate the modes and effects of reforms of the cultural sector.

Newspaper conglomerates

The formation of newspaper conglomerates since 1996 remains the best-researched example of reforms in the cultural sector, and it was here where experiments with new business structures began.[27] The newspaper sector has been under tight control ever since 1949, and no new, private players have emerged in this market. The position of the traditional Party press had nonetheless come under pressure by the mid-1990s, as more entrepreneurial papers from South China, such as *Southern Weekend* (*Nanfang zhoumo*) and *Southern Metropolitan Daily* (*Nanfang dushibao*), as well as popular morning and evening papers, attracted an ever increasing amount of readers, thus eroding the advertising basis and the revenue stream of the political press. At the same time, other sources of information such as TV and the Internet were adding pressure on the Party press, as subscription numbers tumbled.[28]

The first newspaper conglomerate was formed in 1996 around the *Guangzhou Daily* (*Guangzhou ribao*). Virtually all Chinese newspapers have since joined local newspaper conglomerates. The merging process has usually followed a pattern that can be summed up as "let commercial papers nourish the Party papers" (*shangbao yang dangbao*), an arrangement in which one politically important but economically weak paper forms the core of the conglomerate, in which it is supported by the more economically successful papers. A case in point is the Wen-Hsin newspaper conglomerate in Shanghai that was formed to give a new lease of life to the ailing *Wenhuibao*. The latter, a paper with a long tradition targeting a chiefly intellectual readership, had seen a plunge in circulation figures in the 1990s; on its own, the paper needed a constant stream of subsidies from the central government. *Xinmin Evening News* (*Xinmin wanbao*), in contrast, with a daily circulation of over a million copies, focuses on lighter content and is highly successful, producing significant bonuses. Under the new arrangement, the losses of *Wenhuibao* will be covered by *Xinmin wanbao*; the two papers retain separate editorial offices but will merge their accounting departments. The need for subsidies from Beijing no longer exists, and *Xinmin wanbao* is supposed to inject fresh lifeblood into the management of *Wenhuibao*.

However the Wen-Hsin Newspaper Conglomerate is often quoted as a prominent failure of the conglomeration strategy. While the pairing of relatively successful partners such as in Guangzhou has worked out well, staff and management at Xinmin were annoyed at having to support *Wenhuibao*, paying for the losses produced by their "partner." More importantly, it was *Wenhuibao* that was given the leading position in the venture (as is apparent from the name of the new conglomerate), and not the much larger Xinmin. This arrangement makes clear the priorities of the central government and the overall considerations of the reform strategy: while the cultural reforms are supposed to make the enterprises in question self-sufficient and to generate revenues for local governments, it is the political objective that overrules other priorities. Conglomeration in the newspaper sector is intended to create clearer structures of authority and place market-oriented newspapers such as Xinmin under the direct control of their more politically minded partners.

The strategy of conglomeration – the creation of larger players with more muscle to compete in an increasingly crowded cultural marketplace – has been an experience that was crucial in the formulation of the cultural reform policies for other segments of the cultural sector. Professionally managed, incorporated companies which balance economic and political prerogatives have since appeared in numerous other areas.

The publishing industry

Since the late 1990s, the Chinese publishing industry has been notorious for the discrepancy between the monopoly officially granted to state-owned publishing houses and the influence of private sector companies. Under the guise of "publishing consulting companies" or "design studios," private entrepreneurs, most of them with roots in the booming book retail business, have made major inroads into the market.[29] With superior market knowledge and rapidly rising salaries, they have been able to attract better talent than many state-owned publishing houses and have, within a few years, outgrown the gray area that had nurtured them. As of 2005, according to estimates of industry insiders, private publishers were controlling as much as 50 percent of the book market due to superior design and marketing skills and a strong position in the distribution chain.[30] The so-called "second channel" was on the brink of becoming the *de facto* first channel, or the preferred mode of publishing in the PRC. The Propaganda Department and the General Administration of Press and Publication were alarmed by the failure of the state-owned publishing behemoths to regain a competitive edge in the market without great incentives.

The solution was very similar to the newspaper and television sectors: conglomeration. The formation of local publishing conglomerates meant not only economies of scale, but also a thorough reshuffle of the internal structures of the publishing houses involved and the introduction of more effective bonus systems. Equipped with access to new sources of cash, management with more experience in a market economy, and an overall stress on orientation towards consumers, the publishing conglomerates have been given the green light to take on their private competitors. By summer 2007, the private sector was feeling the pressure of the new conglomerates that were learning quickly and adopting many of the strategies that had led the private publishers to success. With their easy access to bank loans, financial muscle, and bureaucratic backing, some of the new conglomerates were able to negotiate contracts with leading authors, who had previously preferred to work with private publishers, but were now lured back by the better conditions offered by the state-owned sector.[31]

The conglomeration in the publishing sector, however, does not seem to have edged the private entrepreneurs out of the market – the obvious goal of the Propaganda Department and its strategy of cultural reform. Rather, both the state-owned and the private sector players are accommodating themselves to the new situation, searching for mutually beneficial engagements. The Party-state's strategy to reassert control through commercial means seems to have been only partly successful in this case, as the new structures are twisted to serve needs other than those they were originally designed to. It remains to be seen if these structures will eventually increase or decrease the Party-state's reach.[32]

Film distribution

The last case study here concerns the Kunming Film Distribution Company, a provincial level experiment that was successful enough to be declared a model and that has consequently been given wide publicity.[33] The Chinese cinema industry at the turn of the century faced a crisis as audience visits dropped. Most viewers preferred watching cheap VCDs and DVDs (mostly illegal copies available on street markets) in the privacy of their homes over the expensive and antiquated public cinemas.[34] In early 2004, four of the eight cinemas of Kunming, a provincial capital of 2 million people, had suspended screenings; only one multiplex built with Hong Kong capital was operating at a profit. In this situation, the provincial government declared the state-owned Kunming Film Company (*Kunming dianying gongsi*) a test site for the cultural reform policies that were rapidly gathering pace.

Problems at the company included high debt levels, a bloated staff list of mostly elderly workers, high pension obligations, antiquated equipment, and a general shortage of capital. Under the guidance of the municipal leading group in charge of cultural reforms (*Kunming shi wenhua tizhi gaige he wenhua chanye fazhan lingdao xiaozu*), the company was restructured; excess staff were laid off and compensated, and the company received injections of new capital. The centerpiece of the reform was a management and staff buy-out: while the management purchased 42 percent of shares in the new company, staff received 57 percent. Shares were distributed according to seniority and length of work at the company. In September 2004, the new company was inaugurated: the Kunming Film Ltd. (*Kunming yingye youxian zeren gongsi*). The company started work under new leadership and a leaner structure that allowed for more direct control of the seven cinemas falling under its management. The reforms generally followed the precedents established over the last decade in the course of reforms of state-owned companies (*qiye danwei*).

Several factors indicate that the reform of the Kunming Film Company was a pilot project that was designed to promote the new policy of cultural reforms. First, that the entire process took only six months to approve and carry out demonstrates the involvement of the municipal Party and government authorities and their determination to make the reform a success. Second, the management buy-out and privatization of a state-owned non-commercial work unit (*shiye danwei*) was technically illegal at the time it occurred. Only in April 2005, almost a year after the restructuring of the Kunming Film Company, was investment of private capital in non-commercial work units formally approved by the State Council.[35] Kunming's move ahead would have been impossible without strong backing from the provincial leadership.

The restructured company set out to revive the ailing film screening business in the city by overhauling the available facilities, developing sideline businesses such as gastronomy and video rental to develop the cinemas into comprehensive entertainment venues, planning for multiplexes, re-evaluating the inherited property,[36] and trying to attract foreign investment. With a leaner, recentralized structure and a business model aiming at profitability, the main objective of the cultural reform process seems to be to re-establish the authority of the Party-state in a sector that, out of neglect, had allowed private interests (in this case the sellers of pirated DVDs and rental shops) to establish alternative business structures that were hard for the cultural bureaucracy to control. Furthermore, the new company would generate cash income, all the while providing the municipal propaganda organs with easy access as a central node to control entertainment content. The restructuring of the Kunming Film Company thus seems to be in line with the observations for other sectors of the cultural industry, namely, a focus on central players, approaches to restructuring borrowed from the economic reforms in other sectors, and an overall goal of enhancing the Party-state's control capacities while making the new enterprises economically profitable.

The strategies of restructuring explored in the three examples above point out the directions in which reforms of the cultural sector could and would proceed. Many of these strategies were picked up once the cultural reforms moved beyond the trial stage, and were rolled out on a nationwide scale. The reform process accelerated significantly after 2005, and received additional impetus in the wake of the global financial crisis when, in late 2008, the government announced a stimulus program of 4 trillion RMB. The overwhelming majority of the stimulus went to state-owned companies, who were given access to vast sums of bank credit under greatly relaxed lending conditions. Like many other sectors – infrastructure and real estate in particular – many recently revamped companies in the cultural sector jumped at the opportunity and embarked on ambitious expansion programs, fired by new capital. Private sector companies, in contrast, were usually denied additional credit lines, which put them into an inferior position in the market place. The financial crisis thus seems to have accelerated the state-led expansion of the cultural industries that was set in motion by the cultural reforms.[37]

Conclusion

In this chapter I have proposed to re-evaluate recent developments in the Chinese media sector and the Party-state's propaganda apparatus from the perspective of the cultural reform drive that was launched in 2003. The cultural reforms, covering not just the media in the more narrow sense, but also publishing houses, museums, performance groups, and other entertainment businesses, have overhauled the business structure of these enterprises, allowing them to transit from non-commercial to commercial forms of management. This does not mean, however, that commercialization is in itself the chief objective of the cultural reform process. The reinvigoration of the cultural businesses may be desirable from the point of view of cadres within the sector, who may be the first beneficiaries of the privatization that is often at the core of the reform measures. The revamped enterprises may also prove to be more effective in capturing market share and supplying their audience with cultural products of the "mainstream" kind (*zhuxuanlü*), that are desirable for the Party. As this chapter has shown, however, the foremost concern of the CCP's decision to allow the overall commercialization of cultural enterprises is to reassert its control over the sector, to re-establish the Party-state's grip of the domain of culture and ideology. In the otherwise marketized setting of the PRC economy, large segments of the market for culture and entertainment goods had been captured since the early 1990s by private players operating on the semi-legal fringes of the cultural field. These hard-to-control entrepreneurs were calling into question the Party-state's claim to overall control of the field of ideology, a claim that ever since the breakdown of the Soviet Union in 1991 has possessed special sensitivity.[38] The cultural reform process is designed to edge these players out of the market and to reaffirm the Party's control through more direct management of a smaller number of enterprises – management, however, that takes the form of controlling majority shares, appointments of senior managers, and access to markets and financing, rather than political directives and orders that can be more easily ignored and circumvented. Management is thus replacing more direct forms of control and intervention into the media; the forms of management that are created, however, are aimed at enhancing the Party-state's influence in the media sector.

Evidence regarding the success of the Party-state's move to re-establish control in the cultural field remains mixed. While some private players admit that the new, cash-rich behemoths are giving them a hard time, new forms of arrangements continue to appear. As this chapter indicates, the adaptability of the private sector and in some cases, the emergence of structures that benefit both the private and the public sector, do all raise questions about the Party's ability to secure control of the cultural sector in the long term. It appears that the cultural sector is rapidly developing the same complex corporate structures that have appeared in other sectors of the Chinese national economy over the last decade. These structures may allow a modicum of compliance with the interests of the central state, yet their very complexity actually may increase the leverage of the various players involved to pursue their particular interests. It remains to be seen if these outcomes will eventually work for or against the CCP's original intentions in initiating the process of cultural reform.

Notes

1 Yuezhi Zhao, *Media, Market, and Democaracy in China: Between the Party Line and the Bottom Line* (Urbana: University of Illinois Press, 1998).
2 For an overview of the substantial body of this research see Barrett McCormick, "Recent Trends in Mainland China's Media: Political Implications of Commercialization," *Issues and Studies* 38.4–39.1 (2003), pp. 175–215.
3 Daniel C. Lynch, *After the Propaganda State: Media, Politics, and 'Thought Work' in Reformed China*, (Stanford, CA: Stanford University Press, 1999).
4 Chin-Chuan Lee, Zhou He, and Yu Huang, "'Chinese Party Publicity Inc.' Conglomerated: The Case of the Shenzhen Press Group," *Media, Culture and Society* 28.4 (2006), pp. 581–602. See also the contributions in Chin-Chuan Lee (ed.), *Chinese Media, Global Contexts* (London: Routledge, 2003).
5 Anne-Marie Brady, *Marketing Dictatorship: Propaganda and Thought Work in Contemporary China* (Lanham, MD: Rowman and Littlefield, 2008).
6 For discussions of these processes, albeit from quite different interpretive angles, see Michael Keane, *Created in China: The Great New Leap Forward* (London: Routledge, 2007); and Shuyu Kong, *Consuming Culture: Best Sellers and the Commercialization of Literary Production in Contemporary China* (Stanford, CA: Stanford University Press, 2005), esp. ch. 3.
7 For a brief discussion that places the cultural reforms in the context of capitalistic development see Yuezhi Zhao, *Communication in China: Political Economy, Power, and Conflict* (Lanham, MD: Rowman and Littlefield, 2008), pp. 108–14.
8 The phenomenon of "advances of the state sector, retreat of the private sector" (*guo jin min tui*) is only beginning to receive attention from observers. Compare Patrick Chovanec, "Guo Jin, Min Tui," at http://chovanec.wordpress.com/2010/08/30/guo-jin-min-tui-%E5%9B%BD%E8%BF%9B%E6%B0%91%E9%80%80/ (accessed January 29, 2011).
9 The CCP started debating efficiency problems in institutions throughout the propaganda sector from 1992. See Brady, *Marketing Dictatorship*, pp. 110 15. The policy proposals that emerged from these debates, however, remained piecemeal and made little impact on the industrial landscape of the culture sector. Similarly, the creation in 1998 of a Culture Industry Bureau under the Ministry of Culture (see Zhao, *Communication in China*, p. 23), a government body with little actual decision-making power, did not have much impact. This began to change only with the designation of trial sites (selected provinces and cities, see below) that were given permission to experiment with new policy approaches, and which, as so often in Chinese politics, became the true pioneers of new initiatives that were later rolled out nationwide. "Cultural Reforms" were officially proposed at the CCP's 16th Party Congress in 2002 and have become a major buzzword in politics since then.
10 Evidence from case studies shows that administrators charged with implementing the cultural reform policies do often refer to established practices from the economic reform process. See below.
11 For selected cases see Keane, *Created in China*, ch. 11. A much broader picture emerges from the annual blue books on culture (*Wenhua lanpi shu*). Jiang Lansheng, Xie Shengwu (ed.), *2001–2002 nian: Zhongguo wenhua chanye fazhan baogao* (Beijing: Shehui kexue wenxian chubanshe, 2002). The blue book has thereafter been published on an annual basis (quoted hereafter as *Wenhua lanpishu*). Local blue books have recently appeared. See, for example, Ai Shuqin, Qu Wei (ed.), *Heilongjiang wenhua lanpishu, 2005–2006 nian: Wenhua chanye fazhan baogao* (Haerbin: Heilongjiang renmin chubanshe, 2006); Yang Chunguang, *2007 Ningxia wenhua lanpishu* (Yinchuan: Ningxia renmin chubanshe, 2007); Peng Lixun, *Chengshi wenhua chuangxin yu hexie wenhua jianshe: 2007 nian Shenzhen*

wenhua lanpishu (Beijing: Zhongguo shehui kexue chubanshe, 2007); Hou Shuiping (ed.), *Sichuan wenhua chanye fazhan baogao: 2006* (Beijing: Shehui kexue wenxian chubanshe, 2006); Zhang Qunzheng (ed.), *2003 nian Hebei wenhua chanye fazhan baogao* (Shijiazhuang: Hebei renmin chubanshe, 2004).

12   Compare Keane, *Created in China*, p. 156f.

13   Especially "Zhonggong zhongyang, Guowuyuan guanyu shenhua wenhua tizhi gaige ruogan yijian" (dated January 12, 2006). See http://news.xinhuanet.com/politics/2006-01/12/content_4044535.htm (accessed March 31, 2008).

14   Compare my "In Search of the Propaganda Department: Decentralization, Transparency and the Internet in China," in Barrett McCormick and Zhou Yongming (eds.), New Media and Citizenship in China, forthcoming.

15   Ibid.

16   "Lijiang wenhua tizhi gaige qi pa zhanfang," *Guangming ribao*, October 18, 2005, via www.yn.gov.cn/yunnan,china/72626041549488128/20051018/1012914.html (accessed March 31, 2008).

17   See Gao Sheng, "Lijiang shi wenhua tizhi gaige shidian gongzuo qingkuang," in Zhang Xiaoming, Hu Huilin, and Zhang Jiangang (eds.), *2006 nian: Zhongguo wenhua chanye fazhan baogao* (*Wenhua lanpi shu*) (Beijing: Shehui kexue wenxian chubanshe, 2006), pp. 291–300. Interestingly, the new culture bureau unifies all the traditional areas of concern of the Party's propaganda department; the overlap can be thus be interpreted as stressing the renewed role of the propaganda authorities in driving the process of cultural reform.

18   Lijiang remains a closely watched example of successful cultural reform. The work report ("Lijiang shi wenhua tizhi gaige shidian gongzuo qingkuang") was officially approved by the State Council and distributed as a successful example of cultural reforms.

19   See Zhao, *Communication in China*, p. 77.

20   See Kong, *Consuming Literature*, ch. 3.

21   In the publishing industry, for instance, the sale of book numbers (ISBNs) is a perennial problem against which the government has fought for almost two decades, mostly in vain.

22   The willingness of many publishing houses to sell their book numbers to increase their cash flow is a case in point.

23   Two State Council documents spelled out the rules for cultural reforms: "Wenhua tizhi gaige shidian zhong zhichi wenhua chanye fazhan de guiding" and "Wenhua tizhi gaige shidian zhong jingyingxing wenhua shiye danwei zhuanzhi wei qiye de guiding (shixing)" (both dated December 31, 2003). See http://cnci.gov.cn/news/media/20071031/news_10303_p7.htm (accessed March 31, 2008).

24   "Zhonggong zhongyang, Guowuyuan guanyu shenhua wenhua tizhi gaige de ruogan yijian" (dated January 12, 2006), via http://news.xinhuanet.com/politics/2006-01/12/content_4044535.htm (accessed April 9, 2009) (emphasis added).

25   For similar language see Jin Bingliang, "Zhongguo chuban chanyehua jincheng yu guojia wenhua anquan," *Chuban kexue* 2004.5, available at http://www.cbkx.com/2004-5/634.shtml (accessed March 31, 2004).

26   "Zhonggong zhongyang, Guowuyuan guanyu shenhua wenhua tizhi gaige de ruogan yijian" (emphasis added).

27   Since there are numerous detailed studies on the conglomeration of the news sector, the following discussion is limited to those aspects directly relevant for the cultural reform policies in general. For more details see Yuezhi Zhao, "From Commercialization to Conglomeration: The Transformation of the Chinese Press within the Orbit of the Party-State," in *Journal of Communication* 50.2 (2000), pp. 3–26; Lee, Zhou, and Yu, "'Chinese Party Publicity Inc.' Conglomerated"; Zhang Yuliang, *Bianqian zhong de Zhongguo dalu baoye zhidu tuxiang* (Taipei: Jingdian wenhua, 2006); Bai Ruoyun, "Media Commercialization, Entertainment,

and the Party-State: The Political Economy of Contemporary Chinese Television Entertainment Culture," *Global Media Journal* 4.6 (2005), http://lass.calumet.purdue.edu/cca/gmj/sp05/graduatesp05/gmj-sp05gradinv-bai.htm (accessed June 2, 2006). For a summary of experiences and statistics on conglomeration in the news sector see *Zhongguo xinwen nianjian*, 2004, pp. 79–111.

28 The decline is readily visible from the annual statistical yearbooks (*Zhongguo xinwen nianjian*); it has been dramatic in most cases.

29 The following discussion focuses on aspects of relevance for the cultural reform process as a whole. For details see Nicolai Volland, "Voices from the Prairie Tribe: Business, Politics, and Literature in China's Second-Channel Publishing Industry," paper presented at the School of Oriental and African Studies, London, October 5, 2006; and Kong, *Consuming Literature*, ch. 3.

30 Interviews conducted in Beijing and Shanghai, July 2006 and May 2007.

31 A case in point is the Shanghai Century Publishing Group. For an account from the management's perspective see Chen Xin, *Zhongguo chuban chanye lungao* (Shanghai: Fudan daxue chubanshe, 2006), esp. pp. 285–94, 398–428.

32 In at least one case, a triangular structure has emerged, in which a state-owned publishing house and a private entrepreneur have partnered with a foreign investor to form a highly successful company. Foreign investment in the cultural sector remains strictly controlled and, in the publishing sector, prohibited. The company in case thus seems to be an indicator that the reforms of the publishing industry may have increased undesired results. Based on interviews in Beijing and Shanghai, May 2007.

33 The following discussion is based on Wang Yanan and Chen Tianliang, "Gaige: Kunming yingye de niepan," *Wenhua lanpishu* 2006, pp. 313–22. The commercialization of the Chinese film industry has received a considerable amount of scrutiny. For more details see Ying Zhu and Stanley Rosen (eds.), *Art, Politics, and Commerce in Chinese Cinema* (Hong Kong: Hong Kong University Press, 2010), and the studies therein.

34 Compare Shujen Wang, "Piracy and the DVD/VCD Market: Contradictions and Paradoxes," in Zhu and Rosen, *Art, Politics, and Commerce in Chinese Cinema*, pp. 71–83.

35 "Guowuyuan guanyu fei gongyou ziben jinru wenhua chanye de ruogan jueding" (dated April 13, 2005), quoted in Wang Yanan, " Kunming yingye de niepan," p. 321.

36 Real estate speculation may have been one crucial motive involved in the restructuring of the company, although the available evidence on this point is insufficient.

37 The phenomenon of "advances of the state sector, retreat of the private sector" (see note 8 above) is a recent trend that awaits further exploration. It is also unclear if the rapid expansion of the public players in the cultural sector is sustainable in the long term, or if overambitious expansion projects and ill-considered lending practices will create future burdens that may turn into liabilities for the companies that were only recently turned around.

38 On the impact of the collapse of the Soviet Union on discussions within the CCP, see David Shambaugh, *China's Communist Party: Atrophy and Adaptation* (Washington, D.C.: Woodrow Wilson Center Press, 2008), pp. 42–53.

7 Sword and pen

The propaganda system of the People's Liberation Army

Wang Juntao and Anne-Marie Brady

One of the key themes of interest to researchers looking at the People's Liberation Army (PLA) is the topic of civil–military relations.[1] In the context of Chinese politics, this means the relationship between the Chinese Communist Party (CCP), the Chinese state, and the PLA. There is little disagreement among most scholars that the state has limited authority over the CCP and the PLA; however, the relationship between the CCP and the PLA has been a matter of some debate in recent years. Although most commentators accept that up until the 1990s the PLA was a Party army, recently some have claimed that the modernization of the PLA has introduced an element of limited pro-fessionalism which has changed the traditional relationship described above.[2] However in this chapter we argue that the relationship between the CCP, the Chinese state and the PLA is actually still relatively unchanged. The PLA is still dominated by the CCP, but the means to control it have become somewhat more sophisticated than in the past.

The main mechanism by which the ruling core of the CCP controls the PLA is the PLA propaganda system. In conventional terms, the PLA propa-ganda system consists of the operations of propaganda units, their docu-ments, activities, organizations, and regulations. However, the scope of the PLA propaganda system is actually much broader: it consists of a compre-hensive synergy of institutions, mechanisms, and operations through which the CCP circulates its political messages, mobilizes its followers, and con-vinces the armed forces to support the Party message. The propaganda system of the PLA is a sub-set of the CCP system for managing the public sphere in China and China's foreign propaganda. Like its civilian counterpart, the PLA propaganda system is extremely complex. It includes four major sub-systems and many other minor sub-systems.

This chapter will focus on a number of aspects of civil–military relations in contemporary China, including: the role of political thought work in the PLA and its relationship to military professionalism; the evolution of the PLA's propaganda system in recent years; the structure and mechanisms of the PLA propaganda system; the PLA propaganda system's response to the changing social environment in China; and the role that the PLA propaganda system plays in Chinese politics.

Civil–military relations in China

Many political analysts have been interested in researching the relationship between the CCP, the Chinese state, and the PLA. It is one of the most important features of the CCP political regime. In his 1957 text *The Soldier and the State* Samuel Huntington put forward a model of an idealized relationship between the military and the civil sector, whereby the military is a professionalized force, separate from domestic politics.[3] Following this framework, in a 1991 article David Shambaugh noted that in the Chinese political context, civil–military relations are actually Party–military relations.[4] However, in a later article, Ellis Joffe refined that analysis by proposing that there are actually three patterns within Party–military relations: Party control, symbiosis, and professionalism.[5] According to Shambaugh, although Joffe's argument of a symbiosis with professionalism still constitutes the Party–military relationship, evidence in recent years shows that professionalism is slowly developing such that the Party–military relationship has transformed into a civil–military relationship. Some experts speculate that this trend may become a factor in China's eventual democratization.[6]

Such an observation is incorrect. If we look at the agenda of the State Council and the National People's Congress (NPC), it is clear that neither the State Council nor the NPC have authority over the PLA. Apart from voting on proposals for funding the PLA, neither body has ever discussed any substantial issues regarding the PLA. PLA-related items appear more often on the NPC agenda, but this does not mean that it has authority over the military. Joffe proposes a pattern of Party–military relations as "integration at the top" and "separation at the bottom."[7] Although this describes the facts regarding Chinese civil–military relations, it does not explain the dynamic interaction between the military and the Party – especially at the very top level of Chinese politics, the Standing Committee of the Politburo. It should be noted that the role of military leaders in the Party has varied over time. For example, during the Cultural Revolution, Marshal Lin Biao had much more power than did Liu Huaqing in the 1990s; Lin Biao and Peng Dehuai, both ministers of the National Defense Department, had substantial authority, while Zhang Aiping and Geng Biao were little more than symbolic leaders in China's military affairs.[8]

Current approaches for analyzing the PLA fail to explain the chains of command between the military and the government. The problem is due to an over-emphasis on institutions. Shambaugh observes that the concept of a "military corps" is not appropriate for understanding Chinese military traditions; however, he believes the concept of institutions can be attached to Chinese political reality.[9] Yet examining institutions is often not the correct approach to understand the dynamics of dramatic political change in China.

There are three features that must be understood in China's current Party–military relations: first, the military is always isolated from the Party as an institution, but is controlled directly by the Party's ruling core; second, in moments of crisis the Party–military relationship is adjusted to meet political demands by the CCP ruling core; third, even at the best of times (for example, when there are no political threats from within or without the Party), the ruling core still maintains institutional ambiguity within the Party–military relationship.

In the post-Deng era, despite increased legalization and bureaucratization there has been no fundamental change to these features. Rather, the central leaders of recent times, Jiang Zemin and Hu Jintao, who both lack a military background but still wished to control and use the Chinese military, have been able to manipulate the existing institutions to maintain their personal power. Although the Party–military relationship has been formally institutionalized in order to legitimize CCP control of the military, the new era leadership core has been careful to coordinate the entire institutional system (Party-state and military). This enables the core leadership to exclude any potential rivals for power from taking control of the military.

One important factor in ensuring the success of this strategy is the very personalized, but never institutionalized, relationship between the CCP and the Central Military Commission (CMC). The CCP needs absolute control over the military and seeks to ensure its loyalty both to the CCP as a whole, and its most senior figure. The second most important factor in the CCP's control of the PLA is the PLA propaganda system. These two factors are linked as the most senior figure in Chinese politics, the general secretary of the CCP, is also in charge of guiding propaganda and thought work in China. By investigating the PLA propaganda system we can better understand China's Party–military relationship and its evolution.

A brief history of the PLA propaganda system

The role of the CCP and the PLA propaganda system has not changed significantly since the PLA was established; however, its officially stated principles, agenda, institutions, methods, and working mechanisms have varied over time. The CCP's propaganda and thought work towards the military emerged before the establishment of its own armed forces, as the CCP's earliest military experience came from its political work with the National Army (*guomin jun*). With help from the Soviet Union, the CCP was involved in Sun Yat-sen's effort to establish the National Army from 1924 to 1927. Sun embraced the Soviet military model and as part of that, introduced political work into this new military force. Political commissars were embedded within the army and a political department was also established to assist the commissars' work. The political commissars and the political department made up a political work system that paralleled the military command system in the army. The Guomindang army later continued the Soviet model of having full-time political staff subordinate to military officers.[10]

In 1927 the Guomindang purged the CCP from its military. In response, during the Nanchang Uprising on August 1, 1927, the CCP founded its own armed force. Soon after the uprising a special committee (including both political commissars and the Political Department) was set up by the CCP to coordinate various parts of this military force. A further important CCP military force was formed when Mao Zedong tried to establish a new kind of army – totally different from that of a professional army – during the Autumn Uprising launched on September 7, 1927. The CCP took the lead in this army and established Party branches in all its companies. However, during the early years of the first Chinese Civil War (1927–37) the CCP and its military leaders disputed the role of the Party and its relationship to the army's military command system.

Mao's idea to establish a new kind of army first gained wider acceptance at the Gutian meeting in 1929. From this date the Red Army in the Soviet areas under Mao's leadership would consist of a special team of political campaigners that conducted not only military tasks, but also propagated CCP ideas, educated the masses, established local governments, and helped to expand CCP organizations into new locations. The Party dominated the military at all levels, with political commissars and political departments working in parallel to the military command. At the National Conference on Political Work in the Red Army in 1934 these ideas were accepted by the entire CCP military. It was here that the CCP leadership announced for the first time that political work was the "life blood" (*shengmingxian*) of the CCP army.[11] This term is still used to describe propaganda and thought work.

At the 1934 conference it was proposed that all political commissars should study military affairs and be skillful in military action and field combat. This became the means to guarantee the dominant influence of the CCP and its commissars over the army. In most military units from the Anti-Japanese War through to the end of the Second Civil War, political commissars possessed slightly less military ability than military commanders of the same rank. However, in this period the latter had no grounds on lack of professionalism to challenge the Party and its political work system.[12]

Thus there are four models of Party–military relations in the CCP army: the professional military model as in the Western world, the Soviet model, the traditional Chinese army model, and Mao Zedong's model. Although CCP work in the army was occasionally interrupted, Mao's model became the guiding influence on the PLA – particularly after he consolidated his rule over the Party in the mid-1940s. From then on the CCP had absolute authority over the PLA. Within army units the Party committee, through discussions led by the Party secretary, had the final say on all issues. In the early years after the CCP came to power in China the PLA had a very important role in constructing government and establishing social stability. The PLA has evolved into a special organization not only engaged in military activities, but with a role in political, economic, social, cultural, educational, medical, disaster relief, and environmental matters.[13]

After 1949 there was considerable discussion as to how the PLA could become more professionalized. Some proposed returning to the Soviet model;

but this suggestion met with resistance from PLA military officers.[14] In the late 1950s, Mao decided to break away completely from Soviet influence and develop further his own model for Party–military relations.[15] Consequently, there was a dramatic increase in political work within the PLA, a change which eventually affected the whole nation. PLA political commissars compiled the handbook *Quotations from Mao Zedong* (popularly known as the Little Red Book) as a quick reference for PLA soldiers' political study. The text was mass-produced and became essential reading during the Cultural Revolution. Throughout the 1960s the PLA propaganda system played an essential part in targeting Mao's rivals within the civilian propaganda system and helped to launch and sustain the Cultural Revolution. When all Party and government organs were severely weakened as a result of the policies of the Cultural Revolution, the PLA was charged with maintaining CCP rule and Mao's domination over the country. Later the PLA was crucial in reasserting political order. PLA officers took many important posts in various civil sectors. In this period political work became the PLA's central task, overriding military and other professional issues. Although many PLA officers withdrew from their civil sector postings when the state structure was restored in the late 1960s, the PLA still maintained its social influence through many activities. According to Mao, the PLA served as a good school for training Party cadres and citizens to become qualified members of an ideal society.[16]

In the second half of the 1970s, Deng Xiaoping, with support from the PLA leadership, gradually became the dominant figure within the CCP. In 1977, senior military leader Ye Jianying urged Hua Guofeng to have Deng returned to the political stage. During Deng's debate with Mao's followers on the "criterion for truth," a PLA newspaper editorial served as a powerful force in helping Deng win the fight.[17] This was yet another example of the potential of the PLA propaganda system to rival the propaganda system targeted at Chinese civilians and to become involved in leadership struggles.

Knowing this, when Deng seized power in the CCP at the end of the 1970s he immediately reformed the PLA in order to ensure support at every step of his reform and openness policy and squeeze out any potential rivals. Under the leadership of Deng and his reform-oriented colleagues, both the CCP and the whole country underwent the transformation from a totalitarian regime to a new society in which the Party withdrew from many civil sectors. Deng believed that peace was the dominant trend in the world and development should be the central issue for China. Consequently the political and military role of the PLA shrank significantly as its size and budget were reduced. Deng did, however, continue to use the PLA to support his position against his senior peers who opposed the new reform policies.[18]

During the 1980s, Deng did not make many military demands on the PLA; however, he needed to continue the political work within the PLA propaganda system in order to ensure new policies were accepted within the military and to secure his leadership within the CCP and over Chinese society. Thus, while the Party withdrew from Chinese society, its influence was maintained and even strengthened within the PLA. In 1987, the General Political Department of the PLA promulgated the "Resolution of the Central Military Commission of the Chinese Communist Party on Army Political Work in the New Period."[19] This document summarized Deng's ideas about Party and political work within the PLA. The working agenda focused on promoting the notion that downsizing the PLA would help China's economic development.[20]

In 1989 the PLA came to another turning point in its history. When students and citizens demonstrated in major cities, many Party members and government officials sympathized with the protesters. Senior leaders regarded the Chinese armed forces as the last bastion to defend their rule and called upon the PLA to crush the civilian demonstration. Although some officers and soldiers were initially confused and hesitant to act, political work successfully mobilized units to action. During the crisis unit Party committees made decisions and directed the military action of commanders of all ranks.[21] The PLA central command only accepted orders and instructions from Deng, who had no other title in the CCP except chairman of the CCP CMC. In this way, Deng and his supporters were able to override the authority of other senior officials such as the Party general secretary Zhao Ziyang, who supported the protest movement.

In November 1989 Deng Xiaoping stepped down as chairman of the Party CMC and was succeeded by Jiang Zemin, who had been appointed Party general secretary just before the June 4 crackdown. The decision to appoint Jiang as *both* general secretary *and* chairman of the CMC, was a move to re-centralize power, after more than a decade of decentralization. Deng and others in the post-June 4 leadership believed that too much decentralization had led to factionalism and the events of 1989. In 1990 Jiang was also made president of the PRC, a role that had previously been merely ceremonial, but which Jiang utilized in order to better manage China's high-level foreign interactions.

The post-1989 leadership stepped up political work in the PLA and reintroduced some tried and true methods such as political indoctrination, in contrast to the softer approach adopted in the 1980s.[22] The role of the Soviet military in the coups which led to the break-up of the Soviet Union in 1991 was a stark reminder to CCP leaders of the necessity of this task. Throughout the 1990s, under Jiang Zemin's leadership, the PLA was reorganized, reorientated, and received year-on-year budget increases in order to upgrade military technology as well as cover the ever-growing costs of PLA retirees' retirement funds. Despite predictions that raising professionalism would weaken the PLA propaganda system, it was actually rebuilt and strengthened by this transformation.

Jiang's ideas on PLA political work unfolded in three stages.[23] In the first phase from 1989 to 1992, following the breakup of the Soviet Union, the 1991 Gulf War, and as China's economic reform expanded in the early 1990s, Jiang warned that the stability of the army was critical for China's overall stability, and he reconfirmed that the Party held absolute leadership over the PLA.

During this period, Jiang sought to develop a means to better control the army.[24]

In the second phase, from 1993 to 1999, China faced serious political and economic challenges. These challenges also influenced military work and the effectiveness of political thought work directed at the military. Jiang developed new ideas and methods to manage the army using regulations and norms. He also focused his attention on political thought work; on how to control the thinking of military officers and soldiers in the new era.[25] In 1999, Jiang issued one of his most important political documents, "The Resolution on Problems in PLA Ideological and Political Work under Reform and Opening Up and the Development of a Socialist Market System." Jiang stated that the multi-polar system, globalization, the revolution in military technology and strategy, and the increase of local conflicts, would all bring new challenges to China's national security.[26] From 2000 Jiang's approach to dealing with the new challenges the PLA faced were embodied in a series of official documents and regulations that defined and framed the new role of political work within the PLA.[27] According to Jiang the CCP had two main concerns with the PLA: one was how to win a limited high-tech war in the information era; the other was how to maintain the PLA's political orientation and quality.[28]

The third phase of Jiang's approach to political work in the PLA began in 2002, when Jiang began to transfer some of his political power to Hu Jintao. Hu was made general party secretary in 2002, and state president in 2003, but had to wait until September 2004 before Jiang stepped down from his role as chairman of the Party CMC and February 2005 till he resigned from the state CMC. Even after 2004, Jiang still tried to maintain his powerful position in politics and within the PLA. Before he left power one of his measures was to highlight his theoretical contribution to the military in all guiding documents for the army's future development. The other was to enhance political work in the PLA by having the PLA take orders from the CMC, but with the CMC still personally connected to Jiang through his associates within that body. Reflecting these complex relationships, after 2004 Hu continued to issue many new policy statements on PLA thought work which emphasized Jiang's contribution.

The organizational structure of the PLA propaganda system

Various institutions within the PLA are involved in propaganda and thought work: the Party committee system, the commissar system, the political department system, the discipline inspection system, the Military Youth League, and the General Military Congress.[29] The following section outlines the various functions of these institutions.

The Party committee system

The CCP establishes its ruling infrastructure throughout all military units: the branch committee at the company level; the primary committee at the battalion level; and the Party committee at the regiment level and above. These organs are either elected in the Party congress of the military units, or appointed by superior Party committees. Party congresses are held every five years. Congress participants are elected by Party members both directly and indirectly. Committees hold meetings every quarter at the regiment and brigade level, every half year at the division and corps level, and annually at the district level. The committee selects a standing committee to represent it, and to perform its duty and authority when the committee is not holding a meeting.[30] In principle, the committees make collective decisions on all issues. However, the agenda, discussion, and criteria are determined by superior committees and the Party CMC. All officers and soldiers understand that the CCP has absolute authority over the PLA. Officers implement Party decisions and manage routine Party affairs as part of their duties. They received orders either from the Party committee (if they were committee members) or at Party member meetings. The Party committee designs the plan and schemes for propaganda and thought work, and coordinates and supervises propaganda and thought work activities via PLA sectors and officers. In addition, in all committees, there is a standing member especially in charge of propaganda and thought work. The Party committees are effective because they are in charge of determining the system of promotion for officers and soldiers.

Commissars

The CCP copied the commissar system from the Soviet model when they worked in the National Army. However, eventually their commissar system became more powerful than those under the Soviet or Guomindang system. In the PLA, commissars are set up in all units at the company level and above and called by different names at different levels: political worker (*zhengzhi gongzuoyuan*) at the platoon level, political director (*zhidaoyuan*) at the company level, political director (*jiaodaoyuan*) at the battalion level, and political commissar (*zhengwei*) at the regiment level and higher. Commissars are appointed by superior Party committees.[31] The commissars are in charge of political work, which in China's political context is very broad, including taking charge of discipline and inspection in military courts (though in some fields they do not have full authority to make decisions). However, their most important task is to ensure the Party's leadership over the army and to manage the political thinking of all officers and soldiers. In general, commissars and military commanders are of the same rank but work in different fields. Both must implement decisions made by the Party committee, and both have to obey orders from commissars and military commanders at superior levels. However, the figure holding real power is usually the secretary of the Party committee who can manage the Party committee's agenda. In practice, commissars are usually the secretaries in the Party committees below the district level, while commanders of districts take the posts at their level. From interviews, conflict between commissars and military officers is usually based not on differences between their duties, but more likely due to personal issues. No military commander may challenge the PLA's political work, while all commissars must respect military work. Throughout history, the military ability of PLA commissars was the same as military commanders. In the contemporary period, this is less significant, since there are few opportunities to prove the military ability of the current commanders.

Political department

The political department is another pivotal institution to ensure the Party's political management of the PLA and the minds of its members. The political department system is only present at the regiment level and above and supervises PLA propaganda and thought work activities. It operates in parallel to the General Staff Department and is directly under the leadership of the CMC. There are political departments set up in all units from the brigade level through to the district level. At the regiment level, it is called the political section.

The political department is led by the Party committee, political commissars, and the senior leadership. This organ helps commissars manage political work in their military units. Its duties include providing input into judicial decisions in the military court. Political departments prepare the thought work schedules, draft documents, and organize political education events. On military campuses, the political department is in charge of managing all cultural and educational activities.

Discipline Inspection Commission (DIC)

The Discipline Inspection Commission educates officers and soldiers on Party ideology, state policies, national law, and regulations in the PLA. The DIC is established in all units at the regiment level and above. It is elected by the Party Congress. In its regular work, the DIC follows the Party committee at the same level and superior DICs.

Other organizations

The Chinese Youth League (CYL), General Military Congress, and all officers are also part of the propaganda system in the PLA. The CCP has a CYL organ in all its units in the PRC state system. In the PLA, the CYL is organized in parallel to the CCP: committees at the regiment level and above, general branches at the battalion level, and branches at the company level. Committees and lower branches are selected either at Party congresses or at general meetings of CYL members. The CYL is always directed by the CCP at the corresponding level.

The CCP also has a General Military Congress at the brigade level and below. The Congress is not a professional military organization, but an annual meeting with attendants elected by soldiers and officers, and as such, the CCP describes it as a democratic body. All PLA soldiers and officers are members. In principle, the Congress discusses and decides on all political, economic, and military issues; however, they are in fact directed by Party channels and the Congress serves as a rubber stamp body. Nevertheless, the Congress does provide a forum for soldiers and officers to express some critical views or make suggestions. The CCP often uses the Congress to discuss how to implement Party resolutions in the military, and at the same time, educate its officers and soldiers about these resolutions.

Most officers in the PLA are CCP members and all have an obligation to promote Party decisions and policies. The CCP appoints specific thought work tasks to each officer Party member. Although these activities are not necessarily related to their military duties, their seniority and status helps the CCP to engage in thought work throughout the PLA.

The military media, culture, education, and publishing sector

The PLA has its own media, culture, education, and publishing sector. This includes newspapers, radio stations, television channels, and a PLA-only intranet, as well as sites which are open to the public; song and dance troupes, military schools, and a number of publishing houses. The themes and topics of the PLA news media are not determined by journalists, but by Party committees. Reading the *Liberation Army Daily* is a major part of political study in the PLA.

The chairman of the CMC

The critical link to understanding the CCP–PLA relationship is an examination of the role of the chairman of the Party and state CMC. While the CMC chairman is appointed or elected separately by the NPC and the CCP Central Committee, the single nominee never faces competition or challenge because the candidate is always the most powerful statesman in both the CCP and the PLA. After the election, the CMC chairman performs duties alone, with decisions made outside the authority of both the CCP and the NPC. The CMC chairman determines the themes of the PLA propaganda system.

However, in some special cases, the real CMC chairman is not always the person formally posted. Between the end of Hua Guofeng's term of office and until the early period of Jiang Zemin's time in power, it was actually Deng Xiaoping who was in control of the CMC chairmanship. In other words, the person who controls the CMC chairman is actually the most powerful person in China. Many experts believe Jiang currently holds this role. Usually, such a person is a former CMC chairman, who appoints a small group of deputies to control the key posts in PLA's operations. Even when that person retires, the deputies continue to follow him and help him to control the PLA. Until he assigns his own personnel, the formal chair of the CMC cannot really control PLA operations.

Because the connection between the CCP and the PLA is neither fully institutionalized nor stable, and because the power structure at the top of the CMC is uncertain, it is the most powerful person in China who has complete authority. He can use the PLA to interfere with power struggles within the CCP; he can also use the CCP to control the PLA. Because that person is usually the most powerful person in the CCP, he normally arranges a successor group to ensure his influence even though he has no formal title in the CCP. Thus it is the personal relationship, not the institutions, that determines the real authority in China's power operation. As the power operation of the CMC is not transparent, neither institutionalization nor professionalism can challenge the person in power. In the current CMC, Jiang Zemin maintains influence through his key allies Guo Boxiong (vice chairman of the CMC) and You Xigui (director of the Central Guard Bureau).

The agenda and methodology of the PLA propaganda system

Examining the agenda of the PLA propaganda system is a useful means to better understand the CCP–PLA relationship. The work of the PLA propaganda system is even more complex than that of the civilian propaganda system. First, it must maintain the CCP and its ruling core's control over the military; second, it must maintain the PLA's positive reputation in Chinese society; and third, it helps the CCP maintain control over Chinese society. In this section the PLA propaganda system agenda will be discussed in two parts: (1) propaganda and thought work directed at the military; (2) PLA propaganda and thought work activities directed at Chinese society.

Based on the experience of the Chinese Civil War, the Anti-Japanese War, the Korean War, and the skirmishes against India, Vietnam, and the former Soviet Union, PLA officers believe that soldiers' mental state, will, courage, and spirit is a major part of military capability. Although the PLA was comparatively less equipped and trained than their rivals in most of their conflicts, they seldom lost battles because they were already mentally adjusted to meeting the challenge. Each company and military unit has their own exhibition hall to honor their heroes, record their triumphs, and display the prizes of war as lessons for educating new soldiers. It is believed that propaganda and thought work can enhance military power by assisting military training, discipline, and overall performance. This leaves military officers free to concentrate on professional matters.

The processes of recruitment and demobilization also require propaganda and thought work. On entering the army, new soldiers undergo intensive training. Political thought work is instrumental in getting them used to their new life. New recruits often have conflicts with officers and other soldiers during military training, field operations, and daily military life. This is especially so as a result of the one-child policy that has resulted in a generation of so-called "little emperors." Although there were some effective methods to maintain good relations between soldiers developed during the Civil War, these are not sufficient to deal with the "little emperors." The contemporary PLA propaganda system has developed special methods to handle such problems such as daily thought work, which can be likened to the religious services held in Western armies. Political education trains soldiers to be politically qualified to serve the CCP.[32]

Similarly, there are many old soldiers and officers who are demobilized every year. Many of them lose discipline once outside military life. Political thought work helps solve these problems too. The PLA propaganda system has developed training programs to teach demobilized army personnel useful skills and knowledge and prevent them from becoming a source of resistance to the Party-state.[33]

Another important activity of the PLA propaganda system is managing culture and education on military campuses. During the Civil War, the PLA was like a family for many soldiers who felt like orphans in a dysfunctional society. Such a tradition extended into peace time, whereby the PLA established various cultural and athletics facilities for soldiers. The PLA uses these facilities to carry out propaganda education. There are two kinds of education in the PLA: primary and vocational. The PLA requires all units to do their best to eliminate illiteracy, which is still very common in the poorer parts of China where many PLA soldiers are drawn from. Primary, secondary, and tertiary education is available in the PLA. PLA educational programs are also part of propaganda and thought work. All textbooks and materials are edited and approved by the PLA political department.

The most important theme of PLA political education is on the ideology of the leadership.[34] Before the 1990s, the prevailing ideologies were Marxism–Leninism and Mao Zedong Thought. After Deng's death, Deng Xiaoping Theory was added to this list of ideologies. By the end of the 1990s, the Three Represents Theory was also added. Because the latter was proposed by Jiang Zemin, the real reason for including it was to ensure Jiang's position in the PLA. This helped affirm him as one of the PLA founders and everlasting mentors – allowing his influence to continue to steer the PLA even after his formal retirement. In recent years, Hu Jintao's ideas on harmonious society and scientific development have also been added to the list of theories to be studied. Education with the names of leaders attached fosters loyalty to those leaders, increasing the likelihood that any challenges to the existing leadership, whether from within the Party or from Chinese society, will face resistance from the PLA.

PLA political education also emphasizes the role of the PLA in Chinese society. The first point is that the PLA is the CCP's army and hence absolutely led by it. The PLA must always follow instructions and orders from the CCP. The notion of nationalization (or the state being in control) of the PLA is defined as a wrong concept that contradicts the leadership of the CCP. Such education makes any resistance and opposition to the CCP futile in the minds of common soldiers and officers. The second guiding point is that the PLA is the people's army and should therefore serve the people's interest. This education underlines the fact that while the PLA is a special force serving the CCP's political interests; at the same time the PLA, by providing help to the Chinese people in times of difficulty, can help to uphold a positive view of the CCP within Chinese society.[35]

A further method utilized to maintain the PLA's loyalty to the Party is regular education about the latest political policy, law, or political situation. When the CCP makes a new policy or promulgates new documents, the PLA immediately delivers a formal notice requiring all officers and soldiers to learn, discuss, and follow the new developments. In most cases PLA propaganda cadres reinterpret the latest policies to fit the PLA situation either by concentrating on issues relevant to the PLA and therefore more easily understood by soldiers, or by solving existing problems. Information on the latest national crises is also important to the PLA. Thus "situation education" is another regular form of political thought work in the PLA. Most "situation education" is based on official guidance evaluating the current situation, analyzing important issues, and with proposals to resolve difficult problems. Such crisis management allows the PLA to follow and defend the CCP during politically complex situations.[36]

As the military is an organization with concentrated power, the political loyalty of its elite is the most important factor of control for the CCP. The CCP makes group study a routine part of work within PLA Party committees. In group study, all core members sit together periodically to study important policy documents and speeches, exchange views and understandings, discuss how to apply policy to their work, and make work plans. These meetings are designed to bring the personal opinions of all the core members towards consensus on important issues. Group study is supervised by the Party secretary, who in turn reports to a superior committee. Through this mechanism, the CCP can manipulate the entire military unit to follow its ideas and policies.[37]

Political thought education used to be a very popular mechanism in CCP politics; however, in the post-Mao era, due to the decline of state control in many areas, the CCP has withdrawn it from certain sectors of society. In the PLA, however, it remains very important. On January 1, 2007, a new document entitled "Outline for the Ideological and Political Education of PLA" was promulgated, in which political thought education was defined as the basic approach for the CCP in leading the army, and the key to ensuring the PLA fulfill its duty. PLA political thought work normally takes between 42 and 66 days per year, and is implemented through group study, unit meetings, conferences, class lectures, ritual ceremonies, military campus culture, and inspirational activities.[38] The practice of daily thought work was developed by the CCP during the Civil War. This method ensures all officers and Party members take care of the political thoughts of their subordinates.[39]

Science, cultural, and vocational education

The original purpose for science, cultural, and vocational education was to help soldiers find jobs after they left military service. However, since such programs are usually run by the political work system, commissars and political departments combine such education with political thought work by integrating both into textbooks, lectures, exercises, and group studies.[40] All military campuses have cultural centers and recreational facilities operated by their political departments, who decide the schedules and activities. These include lectures, competitions, parties, conferences, concerts, dances, shows, and clubs, all of which are held for the purpose of both entertaining soldiers, and also educating them with political thought.[41]

Contemporary challenges to political thought work activities

In the post-Deng era, with the rise of modernization and professionalism in the PLA, political thought work and the PLA propaganda system have not been weakened as expected by some experts,[42] but actually institutionally strengthened. However, political work has been adjusted in response to significant changes in both society and the military. Although political work faces various challenges, these do not arise from modernization or professionalism in the military, but rather from changes in society owing to the dramatic changes in CCP policy since the post-Mao era. The first problem is ideology. During the pre-reform era, the CCP built up the PLA to establish communist society in China and the world. Despite many evolutions of their ideological concepts, the CCP's basic principles have been maintained, namely: absolute Party leadership over Chinese society. In the current period popular dissatisfaction with government corruption, social disparities, and political immorality are all potential challenges to the continued justification of CCP dominance of the political and military system. Moreover, in an era of information communication technology, it is impossible for the PLA leadership to monopolize information channels and block soldiers from learning about the real problems China faces.[43] Economic change has also had an impact on the level of interest of soldiers and officers in serving in the PLA. Budget cuts, price increases, the rise of the Chinese middle class and the *nouveau riche*, all make it difficult to maintain the military's advantage over other careers. Economic reform and personnel reform in the state sector, which traditionally absorbed many demobilized soldiers, is also causing trouble for veterans when they return to civilian life. Unlike in the past, many demobilized soldiers now find it difficult to get a job when they finish their service. For soldiers and low-ranking officers, domestic family issues are also a concern. Many long-serving soldiers find it hard to find a wife (though the dedicated PLA channel, CCTV-7, now has a soldiers' dating show to help fix this particular problem). Married soldiers frequently have concerns about the quality of their children's education, medical care, and housing while on base.[44] In addition, various ideologies, opinions, and new perspectives frequently appear on military bases. Concepts such as materialism and individualism are direct challenges to the PLA propaganda agenda. Hence, in order to successfully dominate and manage the thinking of soldiers and officers, PLA propaganda and thought work must challenge and eliminate these threats. In recent times modernization has lifted the education level of PLA personnel, giving them greater ability to understand theories and analyze problems independently.[45]

The PLA has constantly adjusted its propaganda and thought work in response to these new challenges. In the 1980s, because the CCP considered reforming the PLA under a new model of disarmament and modernization, the PLA and the PLA propaganda system experienced difficult times. As a result, the role of the CCP within the Chinese state, the reputation of political work within the PLA, and the function of the PLA propaganda system were under constant scrutiny. Political conflict in 1989 proved the importance of the PLA's political loyalty and pivotal role in maintaining the regime. During the Jiang era, the CMC introduced a set of regulations to confirm and regularize political work within a modernized, professionalized military. In the current era, Hu Jintao has worked even harder to improve thought work and the PLA propaganda system.

Re-orientating content

The first problem that the PLA has solved in maintaining the PLA propaganda system has been updating its content. Not only do contradictions exist between the theories of Marxism–Leninism–Maoism, modern social science knowledge, and current CCP policy, but there are also problems of reality being inconsistent with CCP ideology. Following the modernization of the military, officers and soldiers enjoy better education compared to that of the old infantry. Moreover the military system can no longer completely isolate soldiers and officers from the rest of society. As a result, PLA propaganda cannot avoid confrontation with competing discourses.

Hence the PLA has reformed the content of its propaganda and thought work to reflect the changing times. The PLA has a tradition of gathering information on ideas that are popular amongst its soldiers and officers. Since the Jiang era, the PLA has had a rule requiring all Party committees to hold periodical meetings and to research new thought trends and problems on military campuses.[46] Based on such information, at the company level, Party branches develop arguments targeted towards negative thinking among soldiers and officers. Following discussion, model responses are developed, and political commissars and Party members are mobilized to circulate those responses amongst military units.

For those above the regiment level, the PLA holds workshop meetings whereby political commissars and Party activists exchange ideas and research problems. Every year, the PLA holds a nationwide propaganda conference to reward excellence and share experiences. When new documents are published, the PLA political work system holds workshop meetings to research how to learn and propagate those documents effectively. In developing their propaganda to deal with current issues, political commissars and officers in political departments try to introduce new theories into their products. For example, in news and reports, they have introduced theories from fields such as ethnic studies, the social sciences, engineering, and the natural sciences. The PLA also has its own social science research network. The PLA assigns research tasks to its own institutes, or contracts out projects to civil sector institutes. These research projects investigate current problems, discuss solutions, create new theoretical approaches, and develop and distribute propaganda publications on relevant issues.

Upgrading methods

PLA leaders have upgraded thought work with new technology and methodology. For the PLA, the most significant challenge has been from multimedia and information technology (such as the Internet). Their utilization of this technology has served as an important means for improvement in PLA thought work. From the late 1980s, modern information communication technologies (such as radio, TV, audio recordings, VCD and DVD formats) gained popularity in China. The PLA has been unable to isolate soldiers and officers from these audio-visual products. In the 1990s, the PLA began to use multimedia in propaganda and thought work. In 2000, the GPD and General Logistics Department joined to promulgate the policy of "furthering cultural construction at army grass roots." They provided three years' worth of funds to establish cultural facilities in all of the PLA's brigades, regiments, battalions, and companies, which would encourage military personnel to stick to base when seeking cultural activities. In 2002 upgraded cultural centers were established in more than 95 percent of brigades and regiments. These all have home theater systems and karaoke.[47]

In March 1999, the GPD decided to establish a Propaganda-Education Online Network for the entire military. This project was completed by December 1999.[48] Within six months, the network had successfully stored hundreds of thousands of books and four major newspapers (*Peoples Daily, Army Liberation Daily, Guangming Daily,* and *China Youth Daily*). The network operates between 7:50 a.m. and 9:00 p.m. every day.[49] Within a year, the network had extended to 90 percent of all corps and 85 percent of brigades;[50] only six months later it had been extended to almost all brigades.[51] In October 2005, the PLA opened the Political Work Online Network for the Entire Army (PWONEA). This intranet has six functions: instruction, news resources, propaganda-education, training, entertainment, and communication. It has 44 channels, 382 columns, 2,530 sub-columns, 53 large databases, over a thousand publications, and 700,000 images.[52] PWONEA is effectively a virtual political work facility and virtual political working team.[53] Aided by such facilities, PLA propaganda and thought work has become much more effective, with the capability to work on every single individual in the military.

The PWONEA is the PLA's own set of information channels by which soldiers and officers receive information and news of current events both domestic and foreign – all presented in a narrative favorable to the CCP. The PLA propaganda system works as an interpreter to help soldiers and officers understand current affairs, involving not only political commissars and military officers, but also inviting other experts and leading professionals to affirm the Party line. For most soldiers and officers, these professionals and experts make convincing educators. Despite all the challenges it faces, the PLA propaganda system maintains its unbeatable hegemony on military campuses.

Military–civil/Party–people relations

Mao once said that the PLA was the Party's trump card to defeat its enemies.[54] He also stressed that government came out of the barrel of a gun.[55] Thus, the PLA's role in the CCP regime is not only to win wars, but also to work as a special team to launch various campaigns on behalf of the CCP.[56] Although the PLA's civil influence appears to have declined relative to the Mao era, it remains a final and effective means to maintain the CCP's rule over China. Accordingly, the PLA engages in various thought work activities to exert influence upon civilian society. There are two goals in this: first, to improve army–people relations, and second, to facilitate the political interests of the CCP.

Public relations work

During the Civil War era (1927–37, 1945–49) the CCP and the PLA formed a broad front to fight against the ruling Guomindang and its army. As part of their political work, PLA propagandists developed skills and tactics in public relations (PR) with great success. In the late Civil War period, they convinced many liberal intellectuals to support the CCP. For a long time after 1949 the CCP did not require the PLA to engage in PR work to such an extent as in the past. However, when China reformed its institutions and opened its doors to the world in the 1990s, PLA PR work became necessary again. The PLA also needed PR work to improve its reputation after the June 4, 1989 crackdown. Although PLA-directed PR work towards the Chinese people is separate from that of the CCP, the outcome is the same: working to serve CCP interests. The following activities amongst the civilian population can all be regarded as part of the PLA's PR work on behalf of the CCP.

Enforcing the law and policy of government

Although the PLA has always played an important role in maintaining social order and enforcing state authority in China, it has been more frequently involved in recent times. In late 2006, the CMC promulgated the State Preparatory Scheme on Public Emergencies (*guojia tufa gonggong shijian zongti yingji yuan*). Under this rule, the PLA is authorized to take any necessary action to respond to emerging threats to government authority and political stability. However, it can only do so if the provincial Party secretary directs it to intervene, a further demonstration that the PLA is still a Party army. In crisis situations the PLA propaganda system serves as the authoritative voice of policy when local government and the Party lose control of the situation. The PLA played a crucial role in quelling disturbances in Tibetan areas in 2008 and Urumqi in 2009.

Political speeches

During the Cultural Revolution, the *Liberation Army Daily* was used as an important channel of communication when local Party organizations and the state machine were destroyed by rioting. Since then, the PLA has always been a leading outlet to announce important messages from the ruling core. For example, the speeches of high ranking officers appear in the media during Party sessions or the National Congress, and at important events supporting the state, Party, and ruling core.

Emergency aid force

The PLA's reputation among the Chinese people was severely damaged as a result of its role in the crackdown on the popular protests of 1989 in Beijing. By 1991, the PLA's image began to improve significantly after its activities to provide aid to people caught in natural disasters were more widely promoted. The PLA disaster relief teams have excellent equipment, discipline, and coordination. Party propaganda specialists have long argued that, properly handled, natural disasters can be utilized as a means of raising government approval ratings. In August 1998 severe floods along the Yangzi River prompted a major propaganda campaign: promoting national unity in the face of danger, selfless courage, and the spirit of struggle. This campaign was a necessary distraction at a time of major restructuring in the state-owned enterprises sector that led to massive unemployment nationwide. According to a 2004 National Defense White Paper, the PLA participated in more than 120 rescue actions and reduced losses of more than 10 billion yuan over the 2002–2004 period. Soldiers and officers numbering 240, 000 were dispatched into action, saving 230,000 people. During the 2003 SARS crisis, PLA hospitals took charge of many cases.[57] The PLA also had a crucial role in disaster relief after the 2008 Sichuan earthquake. When the PLA delivers aid to people in trouble, the PES propagates CCP political messages at the same time.

Construction force

The PLA used to maintain dozens of divisions of construction forces that took on difficult projects such as building roads and railways in remote areas. Although most of those divisions were transferred to civil sectors of the state after the 1980s, the PLA continues to maintain special construction forces. If necessary, they are called to take on special construction tasks. The PLA uses them to support civil projects, such as helping people build houses, schools, roads, ports, and other facilities to improve their living conditions. Between 2002 and 2004, the PLA completed more than 490 construction projects at the provincial and national level. When the PLA is deployed for these construction projects, their officers and soldiers also propagate CCP ideology.

Production force

According to Mao, the PLA was also a production team. Before 1949, many PLA military units produced food in order to reduce their burden on society. During the Civil War, the PLA required all units to help villagers with food production. Such traditions have remained in place in the contemporary period. According to a document jointly issued by the General Staff Department and the General Political Department, on average, each soldier and officer has to perform "volunteer" work for the civil sector for no less than eight days per year.

Social services

Over its long history, the PLA was isolated from the civil sector in China, and so it had to develop its own independent system of service facilities for soldiers and officers. In many areas, their facilities tend to be the best equipped. The PLA passes on the advantages of such service facilities to people living nearby. Services cover all aspects of daily life. Between 2002 and 2004, the PLA trained more than 100,000 civilian technicians in broadcasting weather reports, map design, water services, and hospital work. PLA soldiers and officers always request that those they assist acknowledge the CCP for providing those services.

Supporting civilian governments and caring for the people

One of the long-standing concepts of CCP rule is the notion of "supporting the army and caring for the people" (*yong jun ai min*). From the army's perspective, this concept is expressed as "support the government, love the people" (*yong zheng ai min*). This concept requires the army to demonstrate care and love for the Chinese people. It has been a convention since the Civil War years. Routine operations include sending PLA representatives to visit their local areas and deliver services and gifts to the local people during holidays, festivities or other special events. In reciprocation, local governments hold welcome conferences or meetings in which both sides exchange warm sentiments. On these occasions the PLA representatives always promote CCP political messages.

Military–civilian community-building

As discussed in previous chapters, moral education on "spiritual civilization" is one of the central ideological messages directed at the Chinese masses. Activities organized on this theme have become the major means for the PLA to exert influence over Chinese society.[58] The PLA works with local administrations to develop a so-called "civilized community" in their area. This program has become known as "military–civilian spiritual civilization construction." Here the concept of spiritual civilization includes both moral and political functions. There are two major occasions when the PLA initiates activities under the name of co-construction. One is during annual public events such as Children's Day and commemorations to remember the end of World War II.[59] During these times, PLA troops join with local governments around their neighborhood to hold themed activities. The other occasion is during moments in which the CCP announces important policies or during special events, whereby PLA troops send their representatives discuss those policies and events with local people. Other activities for the co-construction of a civilized community include special training programs for disaffected youth, and maintaining community security.

National defense education

According to the National Defense Law, the PLA is tasked with educating citizens (in particular youth) about national defense and military training. Other civilian units assist with arranging these activities.[60] The national defense education curriculum comprises not only military and defense knowledge, but also the CCP line on national defense, the international situation, foreign relations, foreign policy, PLA construction plans, regime security, and other political issues.[61] After the 1989 student demonstrations, the CCP initiated military training programs for newly enrolled students. During the 1990s, military training also expanded into the national education program for high school students. Such military training programs are considered by the CCP as a strategic measure to maintain political security.[62]

Reservist and militia forces

In the Chinese military system, the PLA includes an active army, as well as a reservist force and militia. The PLA is in charge of military training and political work for reservists and militia as a necessary part of its propaganda and thought work.[63]

Veteran education

In order to maintain readiness amongst veterans for a military callup, they are enrolled and connected to the PLA through the reservist and militia system.[64] PLA propaganda and thought work therefore also extends to these veterans.

Conclusion

In order to reveal the true face of Chinese politics we need to focus on the actual working mechanisms of the Party-state system and their consequences in the Chinese political context. Examining non-crucial institutions may lead to inappropriately comparing the Chinese situation with that of Western democracies. The above analysis of the PLA propaganda system reveals how, despite military modernization and the rise of professionalism, PLA political work has not weakened in recent years. In fact, since the late 1980s, the PLA has strengthened Party control over its soldiers and officers. Such efforts have succeeded with little resistance from military commanders. With an appropriate agenda designed by the CCP, political work is made to appear favorable to the military. Nonetheless, the PLA has adjusted propaganda and thought work in response to changes in the makeup of army personnel and the military and social environment. The Party's efforts to upgrade propaganda content, introduce new technologies, and develop new methodologies, have been remarkably successful in dealing with the challenges that have emerged since the reform era.

The role of the PLA at both the state and society level has not changed; it remains the pivotal mechanism to ensure the CCP's rule over China, despite acting through more subtle channels than in the past. Utilizing refined institutional mechanisms and operational tactics, the ruling core of the CCP has no problem in controlling the PLA, through which it extends its control over the whole of Chinese society. The CCP's relationship with the PLA and the continued importance of the PLA propaganda system as an instrument for ensuring the PLA remains a Party army, illustrate very clearly that in China, carrot and stick approaches to social control and one-party dominance go hand in hand.

This chapter has revealed some new features of post-1989 politics in China and some of the reasons why – despite economic reform, increasing transparency, and modernization – the CCP has managed to strengthen its power in Chinese society. CCP manipulation of institutions and tactics has not only successfully dealt with problems arising from an open market economic system, a free society, and competing ideologies, but has also made China appear to be embracing liberal politics, leading some to believe China will eventually become a democratic society. However, the CCP continues to retain firm control over the two crucial means to securing its rule: the PLA and the propaganda system. The more crucial an institution is to maintaining the CCP's authority, the more tightly the latter controls it. It is an approach which bodes well for China's ongoing political stability.

Notes

1 Dennis J. Blasko, *The Chinese Army Today* (New York: Routledge, 2006), pp. 171–81; David Shambaugh, *Modernizing China's Army: Progress, Problems, and Prospects*, (Berkeley: University of California Press, 2004), pp. 1–55; June Teufel Dreyer, "Recent Developments in the Chinese Military," in *A Military History of China*, ed. David A. Graff and Robin Higham (Boulder, CO: Westview Press, 2002), pp. 285–302; You Ji, "Jiang Zemin's Command of the Military," *The China Journal*, no. 45 (January 2001), pp. 131–38; Thomas A. Bickford, "Regularization and the Chinese People's Liberation Army: An Assessment of Change," *Asian Survey*, vol. 40, no. 3 (May-June, 2000), pp. 456–74; David Shambaugh, "The People's Liberation Army and The People's Republic at 50: Reform at Last," *The China Quarterly*, no. 159 (September 1999), pp. 660–72; David Shambaugh, "China's Military in Transition: Politics, Professionalism, Procurement, and Power Projection," in David Shambaugh and Richard H. Yang (eds.), *China's Military in Transition* (Oxford: Oxford University Press, 1997); Ellis Joffe, "Party-Army Relations in China: Retrospect and Prospect," *China Quarterly*, no. 146 (June 1996), pp. 299–314; June Teufel Dreyer, "The New Officers Corps: Implications for the Future", *China Quarterly*, no. 146 (June 1996), pp. 314–36; Tai Ming Cheung, "Guarding China's Domestic Front Line: The People's Armed Police and China's Stability," *The China Quarterly*, no. 146 (June, 1996), pp. 525–47; Jeremy T. Paltiel, "PLA Allegiance on Parade: Civil-Military Relations in Transition," *The China Quarterly*, no. 143 (September 1995), pp. 784–800; David Shambaugh, "The Soldier and the State in China: The Political Work System in the People's Liberation Army," *The China Quarterly*, no. 127 (September 1991), pp. 527–68; Ellis Joffe, *The Chinese Army after Mao* (Cambridge, MA: Harvard University Press, 1987).
2 David Shambaugh, *Modernizing China's Military: Progress, Problems, and Prospects* (Berkeley: University of California Press, 2004), pp.12–14.
3 Samuel Huntington, *The Soldier and the State: The Theory and the Politics of Civil-Military Relations* (Cambridge, MA: Harvard University Press, 1957).
4 David Shambaugh, "The Soldier and the State in China: The Political Work System in the PLA," *The China Quarterly*, no. 127 (September 1991), pp. 527–68.
5 Ellis Joffe, "Party-Army Relations in China: Retrospect and Prospect," *The China Quarterly*, no. 146 (June 1996), pp. 299–314.
6 David Shambaugh, *Modernizing China's Military* (Berkeley: University of California Press, 2004), pp. 11–13.
7 Ellis Joffe, "Party-Army Relations in China: Retrospect and Prospect," *The China Quarterly*, no. 146 (June 1996), pp. 299–314.
8 Interviews with PLA veteran officers, 2007.
9 David Shambaugh, *China's Communist Party: Atrophy and Adaptation* (Berkeley: University of California Press, 2008), p. 1.
10 Zhang Xingxing, *Jundui zhengzhi gongguo de lishi fazhan* (Historical development of political work in the military), Beijing: Guofangdaxue chubanshe, 2005. Available at www.iccs.cn/detail_cg.aspx?sid=200.
11 Ibid.
12 Ibid.
13 Mao Zedong, "Renmin jiefangjun yongyuan shi yige zhaodoudui you shi yige gongzuodui" (The PLA is always both political work team and military fighting team), *Mao Zedong junshi wenji*, vol. 5. Available at www.mzdthought.com/html/mxzz/mzdjswj/5/6812.html
14 Jin Feng, "Lishi jiemi: 1958 nian Liu Bocheng zai Zhongnanhai gongkai jiantao qianhou" (Secrets exposed: Liu Bocheng's self-criticism at the Zhongnanhai in 1958), *Yanhuang chunqiu*, available at www.peacehall.com/forum/lishi/1169.shtml

15   Zhang Xingxing, *Jundui zhengzhi gongguo de lishi fazhan.*
16   Ibid.
17   *"Guanyu zhenli biaojun wenti de taolun"* (Debates on the criterion for truth), available at http://news.xinhuanet.com/ziliao/2003-01/20/content_698076.htm
18   Zhang Xingxing, *Jundui zhengzhi gongguo de lishi fazhan.*
19   Shao Huaze, "Zhongyang junwei guanyu xinshiqi zhengzhi gongzuo de jueding" (Resolution of the Central Military Commission of the Chinese Communist Party on Army Political Work in the New Period), http://140.137.101.73:8008/cpedia/Content.asp?ID=13638
20   Central Military Commission of the Chinese Communist Party, "Resolution of the Central Military Commission of the Chinese Communist Party on Army's Political Work in the New Period," Chinese version available at http://news.xinhuanet.com/ziliao/2005-02/05/content_2550929.htm
21   Interviews with PLA veterans, 2007.
22   Zhonggong Zhongyang zhuanfa zong zhengzhibu, "Guanyu xin xingshi xia jiaqiang he gaijin jundui zhengzhi gongzuo de ruogan wenti" (On several problems of reinforcement and improvement of army political work), available at http://news.xinhuanet.com/ziliao/2005-02/18/content_2592088.htm
23   Peng Xiaofeng, *Jiang Zemin guanyu guofang he jundui jianshe sixiang gangyao* (Jiang Zemin's thoughts on the construction of national defense and the military) (Beijing: Zhongyang wenxian yanjiu chubanshe, 2002), p. 7.
24   Ibid., pp. 7–10.
25   Ibid., pp. 10–14.
26   Ibid., pp. 10–14.
27   China's National Defense in 2004, available at http://english.gov.cn/official/2005-7/28/content_18078.htm
28   Huang Guozhu, Jia Yong and Cao Zhi, "Renmin jundui jianshe he fazhan de kexue zhinan" (Scientific guidance for the Development and Construction of a People's Army), *Xinhuashe*, August 19, 2003; www.pladaily.com.cn/item/studyjzm/gdwz/01.htm
29   Shambaugh, 1991.
30   Ibid.
31   For more information on the political commissar system see You Ji, "Unravelling the Myths about Political Commissars," in David M. Finkelstien and Kristen Gunness (eds.) *Civil-Military Relations in Today's China* (Lanham, MD: Rowman and Littlefield, 2007), pp. 146–70.
32   'The Political Work Regulations of the PLA, 2003," www.allzg.com/html/2006-8/1541.html
33   For more on this topic see Maryanne Kivlehan-Wise, "Demobilization and Resettlement: The Challenge of Downsizing the People's Liberation Army," in *Civil-Military Relations in Today's China*, pp. 255–69.
34   Shambaugh, 1991.
35   Ibid.
36   Ibid.
37   www.google.co.nz/search?hl=en& rlz = 1T4RNWN_enNZ223NZ224& q = %E5%85%9A%E5%A7%94%E4%B8%AD%E5%BF%83%E7%BB%84%E5%AD%A6%E4%B9%A0%E5%88%B6%E5%BA%A6& btnG = Search& meta = .
38   General Political Department, "Outline for the Ideological and Political Education of the PLA," July 1, 2007, http://news.xinhuanet.com/mil/2007-01/23/content_5640136.htm
39   Ibid.
40   Liu Dongxiao and Sun Zhenfeng, "Jundui dexue wenhua jiaoyu", (Science and Cultural Education in the Army), www.defence.org.cn/aspnet/article-2-19508.html

41   The Central Committee of Chinese Communist Party, "Political Work Regulations of the PLA 2003."

42   David Shambaugh, 2004.

43   Wu Cangjun and Jiang Jie, "Dangqian budui siixiang zhengzhi jiaoyu xin qingkuang xin wenti diaocha fenxi" (New situation with new problems in current education of ideological and political education in military campus), *Zhengzhi jiaoyu ziyuan wang* (Political Education Resources), November 27, 2005, www.allzg.com/html/2006-8/2199.html

44   Anonymous, "Zhengque duidai shenhua gaige zhong de liyi tiaozheng" (The right attitude toward interest change in further reform), *zhengzhi jiaoyu ziyuan wang* (Network of Political Education Resource), August 25, 2006, www.allzg.com/show.aspx?id=3442& cid = 101. See also Xiaoping Li, "The Impact of Social Changes on the PLA: A Chinese Military Perspective," in *Civil-Military Relations in Today's China*, pp. 26–47.

45   Anonymous, "Jiceng budui guanbing sixiang diaocha yu sikao" (The investigation and reflection of soldiers and officers thought at grass root level), *Zhengzhi jiaoyu ziyuan wang* (Network of Political Education Resource), December 9, 2005, www.allzg.com/html/2006-8/2202.html

46   Outline for Thought Politics Work of the PLA.

47   www.chinamil.com.cn/item/new16/txt300/323.htm

48   www.pladaily.com.cn/html/1999/12/a19991227_03.htm

49   www.chinamil.com.cn/pladaily/itnews/20000530/gb/20000630001027_qianyan.html.

50   http://www.chinamil.com.cn/pladaily/2001/01/08/20010108001237_army.html

51   www.chinamil.com.cn/item/new16/txt300/323.htm

52   *People's Daily*, October 23, 2005, p. 4.

53   www.edu.cn/20030826/3089813.shtml

54   Mao Zedong, "Forward to *Communist*" (*"Gongchandang ren" fakanci*). October 4, 1939. See www.wxseu.cn/llxx/mzd/mzd_xuanji/038.htm

55   Mao Zedong, speech on August 7, 1927. See www.people.com.cn/GB/shizheng/252/5303/5304/20010528/476230.html

56   Mao Zedong, speech at the CCP Seventh Congress Second Plenum. See www.sxgaoping.gov.cn/112/2006-12-25/1@4030.htm

57   *White Paper on National Defense* (2004), chapter 8.

58   www.godpp.gov.cn/llzh_/2006-12/29/content_8921398.htm

59   These are: Learn from Lei Feng Day (Mar. 5th), Arbor Day (Mar. 12th), World Water Day (Mar. 22nd), Safety Education for Primary and Middle School Pupils Day (Mar. 28th), World Health Day (April 7th), World Earth Day (April 22nd), Youth Day (May 4th), National Disabilities Day (3rd Sunday of May), World Environment Day (June 5th), National Land Day (June 25th), Anti-Japanese War Day (July 7th and August 15th), World Population Day (July 7th), International Anti-Illiteracy Day (September 8th), Teacher's Day (Sept. 10th), World Food Day (Oct. 16th), Fire Control Day (November 9th), World Children's Day (Nov. 20th), and World Disabled Day (Dec. 3rd).

60   National Defense Law, http://news.xinhuanet.com/legal/2003-01/22/content_701790.htm

61   See *Civil Network of National Education Online* at http://www.gf81.com.cn/.

62   See news about Celebration Activity on Military Training in Beijing at http://news.xinhuanet.com/politics/2005-10/16/content_3621802.htm

63   Chinese National Defense (2002), promulgated by PRC State Council News Express Office, December 2002. http://people.com.cn/GB/shizheng/20021209/884483.html

64   www.ycgfjy.com/Article_Show.asp?ArticleID=695

8 Prostitution and propaganda in the People's Republic of China

Elaine Jeffreys[1]

In 2006, a series of highly publicized events brought into question the history and nature of prostitution-related propaganda in the People's Republic of China (PRC). On 19 January, Zhou Ruijin – former deputy editor-in-chief of the *People's Daily* and *Jiefang Ribao* (Liberation Daily) – published an article on the *Dongfang* (Orient) website entitled 'Delegates at the National People's Congress (NPC) and the Chinese People's Political Consultative Congress Should Discuss Legalizing the Underground Sex Industry.'[2] In March, Chi Susheng, an NPC representative from Heilongjiang Province, similarly proposed that China should legalize prostitution.[3] Chinese academics have variously suggested that the PRC should overturn its historical ban on the prostitution industry in order to give womenin-prostitution legal protections, halt police and cadre corruption, and help the work of HIV/AIDS prevention.[4] However, Zhou and Chi's respective proposals that China's highest legislative body should make prostitution legal and open to a system of government management were heralded as extraordinary by China's media because of their standing as active members of the Chinese Communist Party (CCP), and due to the corollary claim that such actions would assist the PRC's current policy goal of 'developing a civilized and harmonious society'.[5]

Then, on 5 September, the PRC's Ministry of Health and the World Health Organization (WHO) issued regulations in Chongqing Municipality requiring 100 per cent provision of condoms in entertainment establishments that provide commercial sex and 100 per cent condom use by sellers and buyers of sex when engaging in the prostitution transaction.[6] On 11 October, the Centre for Disease Control and Prevention in Harbin City ran a training class for 50 'working girls' on how to use condoms and prevent the spread of HIV/AIDS and sexually transmissible infections (STIs).[7] These activities are part of the 100 Per Cent Condom Use Programme, which is being developed throughout China. As the programme expands, relevant government departments will not only sign health education protocols with owners and managers of recreational enterprises, but also provide them with publicity material and free condoms.[8]

Media coverage of these actions sparked public debate for signalling a potentially radical shift away from the CCP's historical opposition to the prostitution industry, and current policy of banning it, towards a response based on governmental toleration and regulation. In keeping with Marxist theory,[9] the early CCP viewed the institution of prostitution as an expression of the exploited and denigrated position of women under feudal-capitalist patriarchy, and therefore as incompatible with the desired goals of building socialism and establishing more equitable socio-sexual relations. Following its assumption of national political power in 1949, the CCP embarked upon a series of campaigns that purportedly eradicated the prostitution industry from mainland China by the late 1950s.[10] The extraordinary nature of this feat, irrespective of its actual validity, meant that the eradication of prostitution was (and is) vaunted as one of the major accomplishments of the new regime. Indeed, a PRC government white paper describes it as effecting an 'earth-shaking historic change in the social status and condition of women'.[11] However, along with China's post-1978 shift from a planned to a market-based economy, government authorities have acknowledged that prostitution has reappeared on the mainland and that it constitutes a growing social phenomenon. In terms of statistics, women-in-prostitution figures range from official estimates of 3 million women nationwide, to US State Department reports of 10 million, to 20 million sex workers, according to economist Yang Fan, who contends that they account for 'fully six percent of the country's gross domestic product'.[12]

But claims that the PRC is moving towards legalizing the prostitution industry were flatly contradicted on 29 November 2006 when police authorities in the booming city of Shenzhen held two consecutive public sentencing rallies to illustrate their success in apprehending more than 100 participants in the prostitution transaction, including 10 Hong Kong residents. At 3 p.m., a busy road intersection in the Futian District was cordoned off and a large banner was placed overhead which proclaimed the intention of the police to 'strike hard' at prostitution offences during a public meeting. By 4:30 p.m., a crowd of more than 1,000 people had gathered to watch as uniformed police escorted a group of people categorized as prostitution offenders from police vehicles to a designated area. The offenders, who were dressed either in yellow shirts and black pants or else in grey shirts and grey pants, and whose faces were covered by surgical masks, hung their heads as the deputy-director of the Futian police used a loudspeaker to read out in turn their name, date and place of birth, and the nature of their offence, and then sentenced each of them to 15 days administrative detention. News photographers took snapshots of the proceedings and the crowd applauded.[13]

These proceedings (hereafter 'the Futian Incident') elicited immediate controversy on China's Internet and in the print media on the grounds that the Chinese police had not only revived the heavy-handed denunciation tactics associated with the Maoist era (1949–76), but also violated the rights to reputation and privacy of those paraded as prostitution offenders.[14] The ensuing debate was quickly seized upon by foreign correspondents as indicative of an emerging concern for prostitute rights on the part of China's new professionals and the Chinese people in general, one that stands in stark contrast to the presumed traditional and repressive ethos of the Party–police–state. In the words of one foreign correspondent:

> What the authorities in Shenzhen, an industrial boomtown adjacent to Hong Kong seem not to have counted on was an angry nationwide backlash against their tactics, with many people around China joining in a common cause with the prostitutes over the violation of their human rights and expressing their outrage at the incident in one online forum after another.[15]

In the words of another: 'A parade of prostitutes and their clients aimed at naming and shaming sex workers in southern China has sparked a backlash by an unusual coalition of lawyers, academics and the All-China Women's Federation.'[16] These criticisms conform to existing English-language litera-ture on prostitution in China, the majority of which is highly critical of the PRC's response, claiming that it is premised on repressive modes of effecting social control and an out-dated ideological construction of 'socialist' morality.[17]

This chapter examines different approaches to the governance of prostitu-tion in present-day China and considers their implications for understanding the nature of contemporary propaganda and thought work (*xuanchuan yu sixiang gongzuo*). Propaganda – 'the attempt to transmit social and political values in the hope of affecting people's thinking, emotions, and thereby behaviour'[18] – was an integral component of Maoist-era efforts to build a new, socialist China and it is an integral, albeit transfigured, component of the current Party-state's efforts to create a 'new', new China.[19] The English-language term 'propaganda' has acquired negative connotations since World War I, being associated with the governmental provision of biased and mis-leading information to promote a problematic political agenda, for example, fascist totalitarianism in Hitler's Germany and communist totalitarianism in the former Soviet Union. However, the Chinese-language term *xuanchuan*, which is usually translated as propaganda, has no such negative connotations. It literally means to broadcast or spread information and to inform rather than indoctrinate. Thus, *fang ai xuanchuan jiaoyu* (propaganda and education on HIV/AIDS prevention) means promoting public awareness of how to prevent the spread of HIV/AIDS through public education.

A comparison of recent policing and HIV/AIDS prevention initiatives demonstrates that prostitution-related propaganda in the PRC is neither based on a unitary ideological position nor reflective of a policy-based divorce between rhetoric and reality. It is increasingly pragmatic and premised on the positioning of propaganda work along independent moral, security and public health concerns. It also plays a pivotal role in propagating public health awareness and repackaging the CCP as a modern and 'people-centred' government, as opposed to a traditionalist and revolutionary political party.

Contextualizing prostitution-related propaganda in China

Prostitution-related propaganda, in the form of the CCP's historic claim to have eradicated prostitution and venereal diseases from mainland China, is part of a foundational narrative that legitimized and defined the establishment of the PRC, under the leadership of the vanguard Party, as a new and modern nation. Following its assumption of national political power in 1949, the CCP demonstrated that it had the capacity not only to rescue China from foreign aggressors, but also to overturn its derogatory appellative as 'the Sick Man of Asia'. This appellative was sometimes ascribed to China by nineteenth-century Western political philosophers by virtue of its characteristic corruption, feudal-style servitude of peasants, and the debased position of women, and it was viewed by many Chinese intellectuals as a mark of national shame.[20] Despite facing a daunting set of problems – a ruined economy, a wary population, and ongoing civil war, the newly victorious CCP promptly set about eradicating the prostitution industry and simultaneously declared that syphilis and gonorrhoea were preventable social diseases stemming from the exploitation of man by man: their root causes being 'poverty, prostitution, ignorance, and the subordinate status of women'.[21] Through a combination of campaigns involving mass education, the virtual eradication of the prostitution industry, and the large-scale provision of costly penicillin, the CCP announced to the World Health Organization in 1964 that active venereal disease no longer existed in China. These achievements are lauded in Chinese-language documents for creating a 'New China' that was strong and disease-free, and for demonstrating the capacity of the CCP and Chinese Marxism to effect positive social change in areas that no other government in world history had managed to achieve.[22]

The resurgence of prostitution in 1980s China, coincident with the nation's adoption of a market-based economy and opening up to the rest of the world, undermined this foundational narrative and demanded a response in terms of the development of propaganda work. Government authorities initially attempted to explain away the resurgence of prostitution in the reform era by describing it as an 'ugly, feudal relic' that had made a temporary comeback due to the ideological 'uncertainty' that had accompanied the proclaimed disaster of the Cultural Revolution (1966–76) and the 'spiritually polluting' influence of foreign investment and Western ideas. This explanation was soon overlaid with the suggestion that prostitution was an inevitable, but unwelcome, side-effect of economic development and China's (re)location at the 'primary stage of socialism'.[23] Both explanations encouraged the targeting of prostitution activities as part of broader police-led crackdowns against China's new and escalating problem of crime.

Prostitution has been a periodic and explicit focus of police-led campaigns against crime and illegality since the late 1980s. The first and most notorious of China's reform-era policing campaigns was the 1983 'strike hard' (*yanda*) campaign against criminal activity, which was launched following a July meeting between Deng Xiaoping and leading members of the Ministry of Public Security. At this meeting, it was concluded that China's escalating crime problem could only be resolved by mobilizing 'the masses', but the nature of that mobilization had to be far more discrete than that which characterized the political movements of the Maoist era.[24] The campaign process, previously a Maoist tool of continuing class struggle, subsequently was resurrected as a pragmatic tool of policing, and prostitution-related propaganda was redirected towards the task of eliciting support for police-led crackdowns as part of a broader battle against crime in the context of rapid social change. Campaigns target different types of persons, places and behaviours according to local context and in keeping with China's post-1978 development of a legal system.[25] Prostitution was an explicit focus in 1989 of a campaign against the 'six evils' (*liuhai*) – prostitution, pornography, the sale of women and children, narcotics, gambling, and profiteering from superstition; and, as the Futian Incident shows, police-led campaigns against prostitution continue to this day.

Propaganda to prevent prostitution in the 2000s is coordinated by the propaganda department, police and other relevant departments and aims to elicit public support for police-led crackdowns in four broad ways. First, the media is used to educate the public that third-party involvement in the organization of prostitution is a criminal offence, punishable by a maximum of 10 years' imprisonment in cases of forced prostitution, with additional penalties for especially serious cases, according to Articles 358 and 359 of the PRC's 1997 *Criminal Law*.[26] First-party participation in the prostitution transaction is not criminalized, but rather is condemned as a social harm that disrupts public order, punishable by between 5 and 15 days' administrative detention, with the possible addition of a fine, according to Articles 66 and 67 of the PRC's 2005 *Public Security Administrative Punishment Law*, effective 1 March 2006.[27]

Second, the media is used to encourage the Chinese public to view prostitution as a social harm by publishing stories that highlight the links between prostitution, crime, and sexual exploitation. For example, from 1997 to the present day, China's media have covered the stories of more than 30 young women who have leapt from the windows of high-storey buildings, often resulting in crippling physical injuries and death, to escape from forced prostitution.[28] These women had moved to urban centres from poor agricultural provinces to accept offers of comparatively well-paid work as waitresses and receptionists in the hospitality industry, only to discover they were expected to engage in prostitution. Their recruiters had then used a variety of means to prevent them from leaving, such as threats, beatings, rape, and forcing them to sign promissory notes akin to debt-bondage to cover the costs of their travel and accommodation, i.e., debts that they could only pay off by engaging in prostitution.[29]

Third, the media is used to elicit public support for police-led crackdowns on prostitution by emphasizing the social and economic importance of efforts to regulate China's burgeoning hospitality and service industry. A standard argument is that the sex industry damages rather than promotes economic development. Hence, police efforts to curb prostitution in recreational enterprises by enforcing the PRC's *Regulations Concerning the Management of Public Places of Entertainment (yule changsuo guanli tiaoli)*, which were issued in 1999 and revised in 2006, are in the public interest.[30] These regulations forbid all forms of commercial sexual activities in recreational enterprises, including the provision of 'accompaniment' or 'hostess-style' services.[31]

Finally, the media is used to elicit public support for police-led crackdowns by publishing stories of policing successes, of which the Futian Incident constitutes a controversial example. During this campaign, 1,000 officers and 3,000 person-hours were used to investigate approximately 570 rental accommodations and recreational enterprises.[32] This led to the closure of 79 recreational enterprises and 78 rental accommodations for involvement in illegal activities or operating without a business license. It also resulted in the arrest of 17 people for criminal involvement in prostitution and a further 142 people for first-party involvement in the prostitution transaction and potential administrative punishment.

While rightly criticized, claims that the Futian Incident underscores the repressive, 'illegal' and unchanging nature of the Chinese Party-police-state and its prostitution controls are untenable. The PRC's 2005 *Public Security Administrative Punishment Law* gives the Chinese police, not the Chinese courts, the legal authority following appropriate investigation to determine who constitutes a minor prostitution offender and to detain them for between 5 and 15 days' administrative detention – not prison, in order to provide legal education and health checks for STIs-HIV/AIDS.[33] Although the practice of detaining first-party participants in the prostitution transaction may seem harsh, this law not only significantly reduces former penalties for minor prostitution offences, but also enables people who are sentenced to administrative detention to appeal that ruling. Previous regulations introduced in the mid-1980s allowed very little scope for appeal and empowered the Chinese police to detain minor prostitution offenders for legal and moral education for periods of up to six months and to detain repeat offenders for periods of up to two years.[34] Viewed from the perspective of Chinese law, the Futian Incident may have been designed as a public show of police might, but it also demonstrates the increasingly formalized and lenient nature of China's prostitution controls.

The Futian Incident highlights the increasingly formalized and lenient nature of China's prostitution controls in three additional ways. First, statistics released by the Futian police regarding the activities of 25–27 November 2006 suggest that the police had acted in keeping with Chinese law because the paraded offenders of 29 November were not people suspected of committing criminal offences, i.e. people who would need to go before the courts. They were people who had been apprehended by the police and then classified as minor prostitution offenders following routine investigation and questioning.[35] The two-day time-lapse between the end of the initial 'clean up' campaign and the 'parade' further suggests that the police had followed correct administrative procedures by establishing the identities of the said offenders, determining their degree of responsibility, and then notifying family members of their apprehension, anticipated punishment, and rights to appeal. Second, police officials ensured that the paraded offenders wore identical clothing and surgical masks to hide their identities, and did not read out their full names, referring to them more anonymously as Wang X and Zhou XX. Hence, rather than reviving the older practices of shaming and denouncing criminals in public (*youjieshizhong*), it could be argued that the Futian police were following the PRC's operative legal principle of making the law transparent and open to the public (*gongkai sifa*). Finally, and contrary to routine complaints of police corruption and inaction vis-à-vis places of prostitution, the number of police officers and targeted venues that were involved at the start of this campaign indicate that it was a carefully planned and coordinated affair.

A more compelling criticism of the PRC's policy of cracking down on prostitution, and one that has demanded the development of a different form of propaganda, is that it hinders the work of disease prevention. Although health-related propaganda was a feature of the Maoist period,[36] the resurgence of STIs in mid-1980s China demanded a new response, not least because the PRC's revolutionary history had ensured that no doctors under the age of 45–50 had even seen a case of active syphilis or gonorrhoea at that time.[37] Yet the incident rate of STIs has risen sharply over the last 20 years and STIs, such as non-gonococcal urethritis/cervicitis, gonorrhoea, syphilis, genital warts, and genital herpes, now rank among the PRC's most prevalent reportable infectious diseases. A total of 703,001 cases were registered in 2005, compared to 461,510 cases in 1997 and 5,838 cases in 1985.[38] Health officials further suggest that under-reporting makes these figures highly conservative, since STI patients frequently seek treatment from private – commercial, unlicensed and often illegal – clinics in order to avoid the social stigma associated with contracting an STI and having their details registered with government authorities.[39]

Domestic and international concerns over China's soaring rate of STIs, and HIV/AIDS, in particular, have demanded propaganda work focused on prostitution and disease prevention. Scholars usually divide the spread of HIV/AIDS in China into four stages.[40] Stage One (1985–88) began with the identification of China's first AIDS case in Beijing in 1985 and was followed by the identification of 22 more 'imported' cases. Stage Two (1989–93) relates to the identification of HIV-infected persons among intravenous drug users in southwest China (Yunnan Province and Guangxi Autonomous Region) and in the far western region of Xinjiang. Stage Three, starting in late 1994, is associated with commercial plasma donors or the practice of contaminated blood being circulated to original donors and the recipients of blood transfusions. Since 2001, the spread of HIV/AIDS in China has reached a Stage

Four pattern in that the rate of domestically generated HIV infections has increased and many new cases are linked to sexual transmission.[41]

Acknowledging the potential for an HIV epidemic, China's State Council issued a circular in 1998 stating that the unchecked spread of STIs–HIV/AIDS poses a serious public health problem, which could threaten national socio-economic development.[42] A 2001 UNAIDS report more dramatically described it as a 'titanic peril', claiming that the country is poised 'on the verge of a catastrophe that could result in unimaginable human suffering, economic loss and social devastation'.[43] Although China's HIV infection rate among adults is low by world standards (less than 0.1 per cent),[44] the threat of a widespread HIV epidemic stemming from sexual transmission has prompted domestic and international demands for immediate government action and encouraged a new focus on individual 'risk-taking' behaviours, including participation in the prostitution transaction.

Propaganda work on prostitution and HIV/AIDS prevention is viewed as essential for ensuring China's successful economic development and simultaneous construction of socialist spiritual civilization.[45] 'The notion of "socialist spiritual civilization" was first raised in 1979 by Ye Jianyang, then Minister of Defence and a Party conservative', as a means to criticize 'the Deng government's stress on "material construction" and economic development'.[46] Building socialist spiritual civilization was adopted as a fundamental policy objective in 1986, following Deng Xiaoping's corollary contention that the victory of Chinese socialism requires attention to both material and spiritual civilization because ignoring spiritual civilization will ultimately erode the economic domain.[47] Deng's successor, Jiang Zemin, reaffirmed this objective by claiming that the task of building socialism with Chinese characteristics requires attaching equal importance to material, economic development and spiritual civilization and therefore running the country 'by combining the rule of law with the rule of virtue'.[48] Although the question of what socialist spiritual civilization looks like remains unclear, there are guidelines about what kinds of beliefs and behaviours will help to promote it. Building a strong, prosperous and civilized China requires citizens who have good attitudes, morals and a scientific approach, based on the insights afforded by Marxism–Leninism, Mao Zedong Thought, Deng Xiaoping Thought, and Jiang Zeming's theory of the Three Represents. It also requires citizens who agree with and actively support China's combined battle against prostitution and HIV/AIDS.[49]

Propaganda on prostitution and HIV/AIDS prevention in present-day China is based on an eightfold strategy and aims to safeguard China's future generations by generating public support for a dual policy of cracking down on organized prostitution and providing STIs–HIV/AIDS education and training to first-party participants in the prostitution transaction.[50] First, the media are used to promote HIV/AIDS education. Second, information about STIs–HIV prevention is incorporated into the health education curriculum of schools, colleges and propaganda and education departments. Third, propaganda and education activities about HIV/AIDS prevention are conducted in recreational enterprises and urban places that cater to a large population of rural migrants. Fourth, propaganda materials provide information about hotlines, medical consultants, family and community education, psychological consultancy and peer-education organized by non-governmental organizations and community organizations. Fifth, good examples of successful HIV/AIDS propaganda activities are selectively reported in China's media to increase public awareness and participation. Sixth, training is provided to government officials in charge of propaganda and education on HIV prevention, as well as to HIV prevention and consultancy hotline personnel and the police. Seventh, the contents of such propaganda materials should be accurate, scientific and conform to existing policies. Finally, the media are discouraged from printing reports suggesting that the Chinese police use possession of condoms as evidence of involvement in prostitution.

The recent popularization of STIs–HIV/AIDS education for first-party participants in China's banned sex industry is a controversial aspect of this propaganda work. HIV-intervention propaganda teams based at state-affiliated disease control centres have begun to cooperate with international organizations, condom manufacturers, managers of recreational enterprises and the Chinese police, to provide sexual-health training, free boxes of condoms, and information about government-sponsored STI clinics and hotlines, to women who offer commercial sexual services in recreational enterprises.[51] They have also disseminated information in homosexual bars, and in urban-based rural migrant enclaves, that are designed to encourage men who buy sex, and men who have sex with men, to use condoms.[52] The popularization of training designed to encourage sellers and buyers of sex to govern their own sexual health is not only remarkable but also appears contradictory in the context of China's continued ban on the commercial sex industry. Indeed, it has required a minor propaganda campaign to stem criticisms that such actions undermine the PRC's historical opposition to the prostitution industry and the work of contemporary policing.

Popularizing propaganda on prostitution and STIs–HIV/AIDS prevention in China

Domestic and international concern over China's soaring rates of STIs and HIV/AIDS has resulted in propaganda work being explicitly targeted at participants in China's illegal sex industry. Based on the perceived success of Thailand's 100 Per Cent Condom Use Programme, which is credited with significant increases in consistent condom use and a declining incidence of STIs (at least in its initial stages), the PRC's Ministry of Health, in conjunction with WHO, implemented four pilot programmes in China during the early 2000s[53] These programmes aimed to prevent the spread of STIs–HIV/AIDS by encouraging a commitment to 100 per cent condom use in all commercial sex encounters on the part of women who sell sex, and by the owners, managers and employees of venues that facilitate the provision of commercial sex. Programme personnel offered participatory workshops on the nature of STIs–HIV/AIDS transmission and encouraged the managers of recreational enterprises to provide visible supplies of condoms and place programme-related posters in their establishments. 100 Per Cent Condom Use programmes are now being implemented throughout China with legal support. The PRC's 2006 'Regulations on HIV/AIDS Prevention and Control' state that condom use is an effective method of preventing sexually transmitted HIV infection and that condom use is to be promoted in order to prevent the spread of STIs–HIV/AIDS from key at-risk groups to the general population.[54]

Sexual-health training for female sex sellers began in pilot form as early as 2001 and is now being implemented throughout China as part of the nationwide rollout of a 100 Per Cent Condom Use programme. As part of this programme, HIV-intervention propaganda teams are running free STIs–HIV/AIDS education classes for women who provide commercial sexual services in recreational enterprises, providing them with free boxes of condoms and information about government-sponsored STI clinics and hotlines.[55] Propaganda teams and other official bodies have used a wide range of tactics to ensure attendance at such classes, primarily to limit the potential for low attendance flowing from the fact that the sex industry is banned in China and prostitutes experience social stigmatization. Such tactics include seeking support from managers of recreational enterprises, asking local police to halt anti-prostitution crackdowns temporarily, ensuring that local police do not arrest managers of recreational enterprises who support such initiatives, and attempting to gain the trust of women who sell sex by treating them with respect, taking them out for dinner and providing them with gifts.[56]

The PRC's Centre for Disease Control and Prevention, with the assistance of UNAIDS, has also published and disseminated a number of comic books that advise sellers and buyers of sex about the utility of condoms in preventing STIs–HIV/AIDS.[57] These low-literacy interventions aim to minimize the effects of limited attendance at formal sexual-health classes by encouraging those who engage in the prostitution transaction to share information about STIs–HIV/AIDS prevention among their peers. They not only stress the importance of safeguarding individual health by refusing to engage in unprotected sex, but also explain how STIs are transmitted, the long-term health implications of untreated STIs, how to use and dispose of condoms, and how to contact health authorities for further assistance. In doing so, they conform to the parameters outlined in the previously mentioned eightfold strategy for generating effective HIV/AIDS propaganda.

For example, a booklet that promotes sexual health and STIs–HIV/AIDS awareness for 'working girls' (*xiaojie*) begins by stating:

> Sisters, be careful! Pay attention to preventing HIV/AIDS. Having multiple sexual partners is the most dangerous; protecting yourself is the

most important. Always use a condom; it is very effective in preventing diseases. It also greatly reduces the risk of contracting STIs, HIV and Hepatitis B.[58]

The text uses catchphrases, often in the form of rhyming jingles, to aid memorization of the steps required to reduce the possibility of STIs–HIV infection. It reportedly was designed by propaganda and health teams who first spoke to female sex sellers working in recreational enterprises and then incorporated the language that they use to negotiate the prostitution transaction, such as referring to male consumers of commercial sexual services as *keren* (guests) who are after some 'fun' (*wan*).[59] The pictorial representations in the text also aim to match the sartorial and personal presentation style of the 'stereotypical prostitute' – young and wearing revealing clothes and lots of make-up.

Most importantly, the booklet has sections that tell 'working girls' how to encourage male buyers of sex to use condoms and how to say 'if it's not on, then, it's not on'.[60] Noting that many 'guests' will not want to use condoms, the text advises the prostitute-as-reader to say: 'Try it, its really fun', and to be prepared to cajole or trick a reluctant 'client' into using them. These tricks include having different types of novelty condoms available for use and explaining that condoms not only help to prevent STIs–HIV, but can also prolong the 'fun' time expended before ejaculation. If these tactics fail, the prostitute-as-reader is encouraged to act like a spoilt or sulky child to induce compliance, or to state that they do not take the contraceptive pill and are worried about getting pregnant. If these appeals to masculinity and responsibility also fail, then, the prostitute-as-reader is told to remember that their own health is of paramount importance and hence to say: 'no condom, no sex'.

Low-literacy interventions aimed at male buyers of commercial sexual services primarily target rural migrants working in the construction industry. Original plans to provide simultaneous training for sellers and buyers of sex in China's recreational enterprises were abandoned due to client mobility and the refusal of targeted men to admit that they actually engaged in the prostitution transaction.[61] Although there are little reliable data on the sexual consumption practices of male migrant workers, a government-sponsored project on 'HIV/AIDS Prevention Among Rural Migrant Workers' was launched in late 2005.[62] This project states that China has 120 million migrant workers from rural areas aged between 15 and 49 years, who may engage in unsafe sexual behaviours, or drug related needle sharing, due to limited knowledge of HIV/AIDS and sexual-health issues. The project therefore aims to popularize HIV/AIDS education among male migrant workers in order to increase their capacity to protect their own sexual health, and to reduce the potential spread of STIs–HIV/AIDS from this particular sub-population to the general population.

Propaganda materials in the form of comic booklets for male buyers of commercial sex highlight the importance of avoiding unprotected sex in order to protect individual health, the health of one's spouse, one's children, and ultimately the health of China's future generations. One text opens with the somewhat improbable image of a group of people who are smiling and holding hands to signify their unity in China's fight against STIs–HIV/AIDS.[63] As they say in unison: 'STIs and HIV/AIDS can be prevented. Having respect for yourself and looking after yourself means protecting yourself.' This group is 'improbable' because it is comprised of five people who probably would not be smiling in the following circumstances: (1) the head of a migrant worker construction gang; (2) the text's protagonist – a young man from the same village as the head of the construction gang who has joined him to work in the city; (3) the wife of the protagonist (presumably at home in her native village); (4) a migrant female prostitute from the rural countryside from whom the protagonist has contracted an STI; and (5) a female doctor from a government-run STI clinic who treats and cures the protagonist after his boss persuades him to go to the clinic, and who tells them about the nature of HIV/AIDS transmission, and the potential threat that the protagonist's engagement in unprotected sex poses to individual and national prosperity and security. The text concludes with an equally improbable image – the protagonist and his wife are smiling and standing with their arms around each other, saying: 'Learn how to protect yourself [be faithful or use a condom] and share what you know [about STIs–HIV/AIDS and condom use] with others'.

The popularization of such trainings, especially classes for 'working girls', generated immediate media controversy, with reporters capitalizing on the sex and novelty value of the story and suggesting that the provision of such training ran counter to the PRC's policy of opposing prostitution. A standard claim here is that state-affiliated HIV-intervention propaganda teams had undermined China's historical opposition to the prostitution industry by working with female prostitutes and managers of recreational enterprises that provide commercial sexual services.[64] A further claim is that state-affiliated HIV-intervention propaganda teams had compromised the work of policing by asking authorities to 'go soft' on prostitutes and managers of recreational enterprises that supported the 100 Per Cent Condom Use Programme in order to elicit support for the programme.[65]

This controversy led to a renewed propaganda response in the form of media reports asserting that the dual policies of attacking prostitution and popularizing sexual-health training for first-party participants in the prostitution transaction are complementary, not contradictory. In an online interview posted on the PRC government website on International AIDS Day, 1 December 2006, Qi Xiaoqiu and Wu Zunyou (director of the PRC's Centre for Disease Control and Prevention and director of the National Centre for AIDS/STD Control and Prevention respectively) stated that it is simply not possible to eliminate prostitution from China in the near future, i.e. the historical example of the 1950s cannot be repeated. Thus, the primary responsibility of the PRC government in the twenty-first century is to mobilize and teach all Chinese citizens how to protect themselves from STIs and HIV/

AIDS, especially since international experience has (scientifically) demonstrated the efficacy of condom use programmes in reaching at-risk sub-populations, such as participants in the prostitution transaction, whose unchecked 'risky behaviours' pose a potential threat to the health and wealth of the entire population.[66]

Other commentators similarly assert that the seemingly different responsibilities of the ministries of Public Security and Health – to attack prostitution and to carry out propaganda on HIV/AIDS prevention – are complementary and supported by Chinese law. As they argue, prostitution is identified as a potential major source of disease transmission and 'working girls', just like any other Chinese citizens, have the right to protect themselves from that threat and avail themselves of propaganda and education as provided by the PRC government. Moreover, health officials are not authorized to determine whether a person receiving sexual-health training is engaged in an illicit activity or not; and the Chinese police already assist with the primary goal of disease prevention by detaining minor prostitution offenders for medical checks.[67] Since the police are responsible for ensuring that managers of recreational enterprises comply with licensing and other regulations, policing and health authorities will presumably further cooperate on the implementation of the 100 Per Cent Condom Use Programme. Along with the programme's expansion, managers who fail to provide condom vending machines and HIV/AIDS prevention propaganda materials will be fined, and managers who demonstrate continued non-compliance will have their business suspended or their business license revoked.[68]

Propaganda surrounding the rollout of China's 100 per cent programme thus plays an important role in portraying the current CCP regime as a modern and 'people-centred' government, as opposed to a traditionalist, revolutionary party. It demonstrates that China's governmental authorities are prepared to prioritize different goals and mobilize different moral and legal arguments when faced with a major public health problem. It also demonstrates that China's governmental authorities are pragmatic and not bound to a fixed ideological position on prostitution and socialist morality, even though the construction of prostitution as a social harm remains intact and the policy of attacking prostitution as a social harm may well be given added impetus in the future by the focus on prostitution as a vector of disease in international discourses on STIs–HIV/AIDS prevention.

Conclusion

The recent provision of STIs–HIV/AIDS education by state-affiliated propaganda teams to members of China's banned commercial sex industry demonstrates that the PRC's old 'socialist art of government' is being overlaid with new calculations and strategies of government. Sexual-health awareness in China today is propagated through cooperation with international organizations, the involvement of diverse state and non-state organizations, such as municipal health authorities, managers of recreational enterprises and commercial condom manufacturers, and the cultivation by individuals themselves of the capacity to regulate their own health and behaviour. The devolving of responsibility for promoting and enacting STIs–HIV/AIDS prevention challenges the widespread view that power is concentrated in a monolithic Party-state, even though the Chinese police continue to govern the realm of commercial sexual relations. It suggests we need to further consider the meaning of propaganda and governance in the context of continued one-party rule.

Notes

1 The Australian Research Council supported this research.
2 Zhou Ruijin, '"Lianghui" daibiao bufang yiyi dixia "xingchanye"' (Delegates at the National People's Congress and the Chinese Political Consultative Conference should discuss legalizing the underground 'sex industry'), January 19, 2006, *People.com.cn*, http://opinion.people.com.cn/GB/35560/4042747.html
3 Zhou Jigang, 'Dalu dixia xingchanye "hefahua" fengbo' (Debating the 'legalization' of China's underground sex industry), *Boraid.com*, April 14, 2006, www.boraid.com/darticle3/list.asp?id=52261& page = 2& size =
4 Li Yinhe, 'Woguo yinggai ba maiyin dang daode wenti chuli' (China should handle prostitution as a moral [not legal] issue), *Nantong Daxue Zhifeng*, February 24, 2005, www.xici.net/main.asp?url=/u6489039/d25697757.htm; Pan Suiming, Huang Yingying and Liu Zhengying, *Qingjing yu ganyu: Xinan Zhongguo sange hongdengqu tansuo* (Situation and Inspiration: A Study of Three Red-Light Districts in Southwestern China) (Gaoxiong: Universal Press, 2005); Pan Suiming, Huang Yingying and Wang Jie, *Xiaojie: laodong de quanli – Zhongguo dongnan yan hai yu dongbei chengshi de duizhao kaocha* (Female Sex Workers and Labour Rights in Southeastern and Northeastern China) (Hong Kong: Dadao Press, 2005); Zhang Heqing, 'Female sex sellers and public policy in the People's Republic of China', in *Sex and Sexuality in the People's Republic of China*, edited by Elaine Jeffreys (Abingdon, Oxon; New York: Routledge, 2006), pp. 139–58.
5 Zhou Jigang, 'Dalu dixia xingchanye "hefahua" fengbo' (Debating the 'legalization' of China's underground sex industry), *Boraid.com*, April 14, 2006, www.boraid.com/darticle3/list.asp?id=52261& page = 2& size =
6 'Jiuyue wuri qi, Chongqing shi maiyinpiaochang hefa le?' (Is the selling and buying of sex legal in Chongqing City from September 2006?'), September 9, 2006, *Chongqing Chenbao*; Zhang Feng, 'Condom use promoted in fight against AIDS', September 7, 2006, *China Daily*; Raymond Zhou, 'Base rules on reality, not lofty ideals', September 16, 2006, *China Daily*.
7 'Haerbin shi "xiaojie" peixun ban yinfa de zhenglun' (The 'working girl' training class in Harbin City triggers debate), October 15, 2006, *Haerbin Ribao*, www.czcdc.com/Article2/ShowArticle.asp?ArticleID=2189; Li Fangchao, 'AIDS lecture sparks prostitution row', October 17, 2006, *China Daily*.
8 'Condoms mandatory for Lanzhou sex-workers', November 23, 2006, *China Daily*; 'Condom promotion at China's entertainment venues', January 3, 2007, *Xinhua News Agency*; 'Condom use promoted among sex workers in Guangdong', November 28, 2006, *Xinhua News Agency*.
9 Frederick Engels, *The Origins of the Family, Private Property and the State* (New York: International Publishers, [1884] 1972).
10 Elaine Jeffreys, *China, Sex and Prostitution* (London; New York: RoutledgeCurzon, 2004).

11   Information Office of the State Council of the People's Republic of China, 'Chapter 1: Historic liberation of Chinese women', in *The Situation of Chinese Women*, 1994, www.china.org.cn/e-white/chinesewoman/11-12.htm

12   Howard W. French, 'Letter from China: the sex industry is everywhere but nowhere', December 14, 2006, *New York Times*.

13   Jonathan Ansfield, 'Wrong to shame "chickens", won't scare monkeys – survey', 2 December, 2006, *China Digital Times*; Edward Cody, 'Public shaming of prostitutes misfires in China: traditional discipline draws angry outcry', December 9, 2006, *Washington Post*; Huang Xuemin, Gui Zeng, and Hao Yi, 'Shenzhen jingfang huiying cheng shehuang shizhong shijian yifa xingshi' (Shenzhen police say that public parading of prostitution offenders is lawful), December 6, 2006, *Sina.com*, http://news.sina.com.cn/c/l/2006-12-06/095611714666.shtml; Mark Magnier, 'Campaign of shame falls flat in China: public humiliation as punishment sets off debate over individual privacy and the limits of state intrusion', December 18, 2006, *Los Angeles Times*; Ran Xiang, 'Gongchu maiyinpiaochang, Shenzhen jingfang diulian' (Public handling of prostitution, Shenzhen police lose face), December 1, 2006, *Xingchen Zaixian*, http://xjpl.csonline.com.cn/2/200612/t20061201_542130.htm; Jonathan Watts, 'Backlash over humiliation of prostitutes', December 8, 2006, *Sydney Morning Herald*; Zhu Yongping 'Banghe shidai: Shenzhen jingfang gongshi maiyinnü piaoke ling falü mengxiu' (A timely rebuke: Shenzhen police shame the law by publicly parading prostitutes and prostitute clients), December 8, 2006, *Xinkuai Bao*, http://cul.book.sina.com.cn/t/2006-12-08/1200165337.html

14   Huang Xuemin, Gui Zeng, and Hao Yi, 'Shenzhen jingfang huiying cheng shehuang shizhong shijian yifa xingshi' (Shenzhen police say that public parading of prostitution offenders is lawful), December 6, 2006, *Sina.com*, http://news.sina.com.cn/c/l/2006-12-06/095611714666.shtml

15   Howard W. French, 'Shenzhen's public humiliation of sex workers provokes a backlash', December 8, 2006b, *International Herald Tribune*.

16   Jonathan Watts, 'Backlash over humiliation of prostitutes', December 8, 2006, *Sydney Morning Herald*.

17   Vincent E. Gil and Allen F. Anderson, 'State-sanctioned aggression and the control of prostitution in the People's Republic of China', *Aggression and Violent Behaviour*, vol. 3, 2 (1998), pp. 129–42.; Gail Hershatter, 'Chinese sex workers in the reform period', in *Remapping China: Fissures in Historical Terrain*, edited by Gail Hershatter, Emily Honig, Jonathan Lipman and Randall Stross (Stanford, CA: Stanford University Press, 1996), pp. 42–93; Zheng Tiantian, 'Cool masculinity: male clients' sex consumption and business alliance in urban China's sex industry', *Journal of Contemporary China*, vol. 15, 46 (2006), pp. 161–82.

18   Peter Kenez, *The Birth of the Propaganda State: Soviet Methods of Mass Mobilisation, 1917–1925* (Cambridge: Cambridge University Press, 1992), cited in Anne-Marie Brady, *Marketing Dictatorship: Propaganda and Thought Work in Contemporary China* (Buffalo, NY: Rowman and Littlefield, 2007), p. 3.

19   Anne-Marie Brady, *Marketing Dictatorship: Propaganda and Thought Work in Contemporary China* (Buffalo, NY: Rowman and Littlefield, 2007).

20   Elaine Jeffreys, 'Advanced producers or moral polluters? China's bureaucrat-entrepreneurs and sexual corruption', in *The New Rich in China: Future Rulers, Present Lives*, edited by David S. G. Goodman (Abingdon, Oxon; New York: Routledge, 2008), p. 234.

21   Herber K. Abrams, 'The resurgence of sexually transmitted disease in China', *Journal of Public Health Policy*, vol. 22, 4 (2001), pp. 429–40.

22   Information Office of the State Council of the People's Republic of China, 'Chapter 1: Historic liberation of Chinese women', in *The Situation of Chinese Women*, 1994, www.china.org.cn/e-white/chinesewoman/11-12.htm

23   Elaine Jeffreys, *China, Sex and Prostitution* (London; New York: Routledge-Curzon, 2004), pp. 96–122.

24   Deng Xiaoping, 'Crack down on crime', *Selected Works of Deng Xiaoping,* vol. 3 (Beijing: Foreign Languages Press, 2004), pp. 44–45.

25   Elaine Jeffreys, *China, Sex and Prostitution* (London; New York: Routledge-Curzon, 2004), pp. 150–82.

26   *Criminal Law of the People's Republic of China* (1997), adopted at the Second Session of the Fifth National People's Congress on July1, 1979, revised at the Fifth Session of the Eighth National People's Congress on March 14, 1997, www.cecc.gov/pages/newLaws/criminalLawENG.php

27   Quanguo renda changwu weiyuanhui (Standing committee of the National People's Congress), *Zhonghua Renmin Gongheguo zhian guanli chufa fa* (Public Security Administrative Punishment Law of the People's Republic of China), 2005, http://news.xinhuanet.com/newscenter/2005-8/28/content_3413618.htm

28   Elaine Jeffreys, 'Accidental celebrities: China's chastity heroines and charity', in *Celebrity in China*, edited by Louise P. Edwards and Elaine Jeffreys (Hong Kong: Hong Kong University Press, 2010), p. 67.

29   Elaine Jeffreys, '"Over my dead body!" Media constructions of forced prostitution in the People's Republic of China', *PORTAL Journal of Multidisciplinary International Studies*, vol. 3, 2 (2006), http://epress.lib.uts.edu.au/ojs/index.php/portal/article/view/126/342

30   'Chajin qudi maiyinpiaochang ying tupo liangda nandian' (Prohibiting the selling and buying of sex requires breakthroughs in two difficult areas), December 12, 2001, *Xinhua Wang*, http://news.xinhuanet.com/newscenter/2001-12/12/content_159370.htm

31   Zhonghua Renmin Gongheguo guowuyuan, di 458 hao (State Council of the PRC, Order Number 458), *Yule changsuo guanli tiaoli* (Regulations Concerning the Management of Public Places of Entertainment), passed on January 18, 2006 and coming into effect on March 1, 2006, http://news.sina.com.cn/c/2006-02-13/16299089243.shtml

32   Luo Shan, Huang Xuemin, Yu Yalian, Li Guohui, Ai Ke, Chen Jingjing, and Liang Zhiqiang, 'Shenzhen jingfang gongkai chuli maiyinnü shijian yinqi jilie zhengbian' (Shenzhen police public handling of 'female sex sellers incident' causes fierce controversy), December 7, 2006, *Xinkuai Bao*, http://news.xinhuanet.com/legal/2006-12/07/content_5447820.htm; 'Shenzhen jingfang qingcha "seqing" cun' (Shenzhen police investigate 'sex' village), November 27, 2006, *CCTV.com*, http://news.cctv.com/law/20061127/104418.shtml

33   Quanguo renda changwu weiyuanhui (Standing committee of the National People's Congress), *Zhonghua Renmin Gongheguo zhian guanli chufa fa* (Public Security Administrative Punishment Law of the People's Republic of China), 2005, http://news.xinhuanet.com/newscenter/2005-8/28/content_3413618.htm

34   Elaine Jeffreys, *China, Sex and Prostitution* (London; New York: Routledge-Curzon, 2004), pp.138–49.

35   'Shenzhen jingfang qingcha "seqing" cun' (Shenzhen police investigate 'sex' village), November 27, 2006, *CCTV.com*, http://news.cctv.com/law/20061127/104418.shtml

36   Marta Hanson, 'Maoist public-health campaigns, Chinese medicine, and SARS', *Lancet*, vol. 372, 9648 (2008), pp. 1457–58.

37   Herber K. Abrams, 'The resurgence of sexually transmitted disease in China', *Journal of Public Health Policy*, vol. 22, 4 (2001), pp. 429–40.

38   Elaine Jeffreys and Huang Yingying, 'Governing sexual health in the People's Republic of China', in *China's Governmentalities: Governing Change, Changing Government*, edited by Elaine Jeffreys (Abingdon, Oxon; New York: Routledge, 2009), pp. 152.

39   Ibid.
40   'HIV and AIDS in China', 2007, *Avert.org*, www.avert.org/aidschina.htm
41   Ibid.
42   State Council AIDS Working Committee Office and UN Theme Group on HIV/ AIDS in China, *A Joint Assessment of HIV/AIDS Prevention, Treatment and Care in China*, 2004, www.chinaaids.cn/worknet/download/2004/report2004en.pdf
43   UNAIDS, 'HIV/AIDS: China's titanic peril – 2001 update of the AIDS situation and needs assessment report', 2002, www.hivpolicy.org/Library/HPP000056.pdf
44   Zheng Tiantian, 'Cool masculinity: male clients' sex consumption and business alliance in urban China's sex industry', *Journal of Contemporary China*, vol. 15, 46 (2006), p. 39.
45   'Yufang aizibing xingbing xuanchuan jiaoyu yuanze' (The principles with regard to thought work and education on preventing HIV/AIDS and sexually transmissible infections), December 1, 2003, *Dayang Wang*, www.huaxia.com/zt/2003-60/ sh/00151548.html
46   Anne-Marie Brady, *Marketing Dictatorship: Propaganda and Thought Work in Contemporary China* (Buffalo, NY: Rowman and Littlefield, 2007), p. 25.
47   'Socialist Spiritual Civilization – China', *Encyclopedia of Modern Asia*, (USA: Macmillan Reference, 2001–6), www.bookrags.com/research/socialist-spiritual-civilizationchi-ema-05/
48   Jiang Zemin, 'Full text of Jiang Zemin's report at 16th Party Congress', November 12, 2002, *People's Daily*, http://english.people.com.cn/200211/18/ eng20021118_106985.shtml
49   'Yufang aizibing xingbing xuanchuan jiaoyu yuanze' (The principles with regard to thought work and education on preventing HIV/AIDS and sexually transmissible infections), December 1, 2003, *Dayang Wang*, www.huaxia.com/zt/2003-60/ sh/00151548.html
50   Ibid.
51   Elaine Jeffreys and Huang Yingying, 'Governing sexual health in the People's Republic of China', in *China's Governmentalities: Governing Change, Changing Government*, edited by Elaine Jeffreys, (Abingdon, Oxon; New York: Routledge, 2009), pp. 163–64.
52   Ibid.
53   World Health Organization Regional Office for the Western Pacific, *100% Condom Use Programme: Experience from China (2001–2004)*, World Health Organization Regional Office for the Western Pacific, Manila (2004).
54   Guowuyuan (State Council), *Aizibing fangzhi tiaoli* (Regulations on HIV/ AIDS Prevention), January 18, 2006, http://news.sina.com.cn/c/2006-02-12/ 12349079619.shtml
55   'Haerbin shi "xiaojie" peixun ban yinfa de zhenglun' (The 'working girl' training class in Harbin City triggers debate), October 15, 2006, *Haerbin Ribao*, www. czcdc.com/Article2/ShowArticle.asp?ArticleID=2189; Qiu Yulan and Wang Yequan 'Jiangsu jikong zhongxin jiaodao "xiaojie" youpian keren dai anquantao' (Jiangsu Centre for Disease Control and Prevention instructs 'working girls' on how to coax clients into using condoms), October, 18, 2006, *163.com*, http:// news.163.com/06/1018/10/2TN99MR50001124J.html
56   Ibid.
57   For example see Zhongguo jibing yufang kongzhi zhongxin (China Centre for Disease Control and Prevention), 'Yufang aizi: wo you yi "tao"' (Preventing HIV/ AIDS: I have a 'method' [a condom]), China Centre for Disease Control and Prevention and Qingdao/London Durex Company Ltd (n.d.) Also see Zhongguo xingbing aizibing fangzhi xiehui (Chinese Association of STD and AIDS Prevention), 'Huashuo "aizi"' (Talking about 'AIDS' with pictures), Beijing Xuanwu Qu, 27 Nanwei Road (n.d.).

58 Zhongguo jibing yufang kongzhi zhongxin (China Centre for Disease Control and Prevention), 'Yufang aizi: wo you yi "tao"' (Preventing HIV/AIDS: I have a 'method' [a condom]), China Centre for Disease Control and Prevention and Qingdao/London Durex Company Ltd (n.d.), p. 1, translated by Elaine Jeffreys.

59 Qiu Yulan and Wang Yequan 'Jiangsu jikong zhongxin jiaodao "xiaojie" youpian keren dai anquantao' (Jiangsu Centre for Disease Control and Prevention instructs 'working girls' on how to coax clients into using condoms), October, 18, 2006, *163.com*, http://news.163.com/06/1018/10/2TN99MR50001124J.html

60 Zhongguo jibing yufang kongzhi zhongxin (China Centre for Disease Control and Prevention), 'Yufang aizi: wo you yi "tao"' (Preventing HIV/AIDS: I have a 'method' [a condom]), China Centre for Disease Control and Prevention and Qingdao/London Durex Company Ltd (n.d.), pp. 10–13.

61 Qiu Yulan and Wang Yequan 'Jiangsu jikong zhongxin jiaodao "xiaojie" youpian keren dai anquantao' (Jiangsu Centre for Disease Control and Prevention instructs 'working girls' on how to coax clients into using condoms), October, 18, 2006, *163.com*, http://news.163.com/06/1018/10/2TN99MR50001124J.html

62 Guowuyuan fangzhi aizibing gongzuo weiyuanhui bangongshi (State Council AIDS Working Committee Office), 'Guanyu lianhe shishi quanguo nongmingong yufang aizibing xuanchuan de tongzhi' (Announcement on HIV/AIDS education project among migrant workers), 2005, *China.com.cn*, www.china.com.cn/chinese/PI-c/1045176.htm

63 Zhongguo xingbing aizibing fangzhi xiehui (Chinese Association of STD and AIDS Prevention), 'Huashuo "aizi"' (Talking about 'AIDS' with pictures), Beijing Xuanwu Qu, 27 Nanwei Road (n.d.).

64 Qiu Yulan and Wang Yequan 'Jiangsu jikong zhongxin jiaodao "xiaojie" youpian keren dai anquantao' (Jiangsu Centre for Disease Control and Prevention instructs 'working girls' on how to coax clients into using condoms), October, 18, 2006, *163.com*, http://news.163.com/06/1018/10/2TN99MR50001124J.html

65 Chen Jiu, 'Aizibingri de xingwenming sikao: xiaojie wenti shi jiaoyu haishi chengjie' (Thinking about sexual civilization on AIDS Day: is the 'working girl' question about education or punishment?), November 16, 2006, *022.net.com*, www.022net.com/2006/11-16/432559263265359.html; Qiu Yulan and Wang Yequan 'Jiangsu jikong zhongxin jiaodao "xiaojie" youpian keren dai anquantao' (Jiangsu Centre for Disease Control and Prevention instructs 'working girls' on how to coax clients into using condoms), October, 18, 2006, *163.com*, http://news.163.com/06/1018/10/2TN99MR50001124J.html

66 'Tuiguang anquantao fang aizibing yu daji maiyinpiaochang ying xiangfuxiangcheng' (The methods of popularizing the use of condoms to prevent HIV/AIDS and striking hard against prostitution are complimentary), December 2, 2006, *Xinjing Bao*, http://news.xinhuanet.com/politics/2006-12/02/content_5421519.htm

67 Dong Xue, ed., 'Fang ai xuanchuan jiaoyu yu guli maiyinpiaochang wushe' (Propaganda and education relating to the prevention of HIV/AIDS is not about encouraging the selling and buying of sex), October 16, 2006, *Nanfang Wang*, www.southcn.com/opinion/commentator/nanwuyan/200610160337.htm; Wu Mindong '"Xiaojie xuexiban": maiyin hefa' ('Working girl' training class: is selling and buying sex lawful?), October 18, 2006, *Nanfang Luntan*, www.southcn.com/nfsq/sqrdgz/200610180587.htm

68 Zhang Yiwei and Chen Yanli, 'Mingnian qi Xi'an gonggong changsuo bufang anquantao zuigao fa 5,000 yuan' (Starting next year, the maximum penalty for failure to provide condoms in public places of entertainment in Xi'an will be 5,000 yuan), October 27, 2006, *Sanqin Dushi Bao*, http://news.sohu.com/20061027/n246031654.shtml

9 'Hand-in-hand, heart-to-heart'

Thought management and the Overseas Chinese

James To

Introduction

Following the violent crackdown on students demonstrating in Tiananmen Square in June 1989, tens of thousands of sympathetic ethnic Chinese and People's Republic of China (PRC) nationals across the globe (hereafter described as the Overseas Chinese or OC[1]) were unified in protest against the Chinese Communist Party (CCP). While some were too afraid to speak out, others were much more critical and antagonistic in calling for democratic reform.[2] Fearing an escalation of anti-CCP sentiment amongst a diaspora crucial to its national interests, Beijing promptly intensified *huaqiao shiwu gongzuo*, or its shortened equivalent *qiaowu* (also referred to as OC work) to deal with the precarious situation. It employed a foreign legion of diplomats, agents and cadres to aggressively manage and control strategic OC communities under a comprehensive set of influential tools and persuasive techniques.[3] Over the next two decades, the CCP continually developed and improved *qiaowu* to the extent that it had become more successful in the current period than any other era. As such, the CCP has been able to influence the behaviour and direction of certain OC, particularly so with new migrants and PRC students. Such prowess became apparent in 2008, when large numbers of the OC again took to the streets in heated protest – this time not in defiance of the regime, but in strong support of China and its leaders.

How is *qiaowu* able to influence and manage the OC in this way? Why has the CPP become so confident in advancing OC work since the crisis of 1989? Why are *qiaowu* efforts working with such success? By examining a wide range of Chinese language references and primary source policy documents, this chapter explains the nature and development of *qiaowu*, details its specific work methods, and analyses the platforms employed to advance relations with the OC diaspora. It argues that despite decades of counter-efforts from rival political factions, gradual assimilation, changes in OC demographics, technology and the geo-political climate, *qiaowu* has been an accomplished part of the CCP's modernized propaganda and thought work system for influencing, managing and unifying a heterogeneous population of OC.

What is *Qiaowu*?

Since its formation, the CCP has attempted to use the OC for advancing its interests both at home and abroad. The OC are also vital to China's economic, scientific and technological development.[4] As such, the CCP has continuously raised *qiaowu* to the highest levels of national importance to achieve these goals. *Qiaowu* is also part of the broad spectrum of China's foreign affairs work (*waijiao shiwu* or *waishi*).[5] It shares many common aspects of *waishi* as a complimentary effort to China's other platforms for international relations (such as hard power, aid and financial assistance).

Qiaowu is a comprehensive effort that ostensibly seeks to maintain the rights and interests of the OC. Tasks include propagating OC policy, promoting OC affairs, research of OC needs, and resolution of their problems.[6] In practice however, *qiaowu* is not simply a platform for maintaining economic and cultural relations – rather, it encompasses all areas of the OC relationship, including people-to-people links, managing their perceptions, and influencing their behaviour for serving Beijing's interests. To achieve this, *qiaowu* has two aims: first to attract the OC back into the fold of the Chinese nation state, and second to convey and project to them the nation state agenda.[7] Central to both these goals is winning their loyalty and support in order to challenge and exterminate potential threats to China's integrity and sovereignty (such as the spiritual organization Falungong, and the Taiwanese, Tibetan and Xinjiang pro-independence movements), and thus preserve and enhance the CCP regime's legitimacy to power. These goals have remained consistent since 1949, with policies and programmes continually developed and modernized in accordance with changes in OC demographics and their social situation. In this context, elements of *qiaowu* (in particular references to Confucianism, Chineseness and ethnicity) fall into the CCP's wider external propaganda effort as a specialized field of 'thought management' directed towards the OC.[8]

The literal translation of *qiaowu* is 'OC affairs/matters'. One of its core responsibilities is 'service for the OC'[9] – essentially 'people-to-people work' that plays to human needs and desires. *Qiaowu* is a continuous long-term soft power effort employing social and psychological tools that seek to to influence the choices, direction and emotions of the OC by dispelling negative suspicions and misunderstandings concerning China, and replacing these with a positive understanding instead.[10] Handbooks outline to cadres the basic manner in which *qiaowu* is to be conducted: to contact and liaise with the OC; promote and give impetus to them and their interests; and ultimately, guide them under a continuous precondition of merging and unity.[11] This is qualified by a 'Three Do's and Don'ts' attitude (*san er bu*) that seeks to co-ordinate and assist OC activities from a distance without them being aware of it: 'support but don't depend upon' (retain sufficient independence from OC groups), 'penetrate but don't intervene' (understand their inner workings), 'to guide but don't lead' (simply influence them).[12] These principles make *qiaowu* an effective tool for intensive behavioural control and manipulation yet appearing benign, benevolent and helpful.

A brief history of *Qiaowu* and the CCP

Qiaowu programmes had existed since the 1950s to attract and manage the OC for China's domestic and external interests in an isolated Cold War environment. While the CCP quietly supported Southeast Asian OC who were engaged in revolutionary efforts, an overt political connection or inter- eference was carefully avoided in order to preserve friendly state-to-state relations. Although the 1955 Bandung Conference was meant to sever the political link with the OC, China maintained sentimental and emotional ties to ensure that they remained part of China's 'family'.[13] The OC were initially welcomed back to the mainland; however, this period also saw rising radical elements in the CCP disrupt domestic *qiaowu* policies and its institutions – with treatment of returning OC veering left and right over the next two dec- ades.[14] Those who went back to China found themselves the target of dis- crimination and oppression because of their foreign connections.[15] After suffering a decade of chaos during the Cultural Revolution, Beijing placed renewed importance on *qiaowu* in 1978.[16]

A 1983 meeting on *qiaowu* stated that OC work in the 1980s had the core goals of serving China's 'Four Modernizations', national reunification, and advancing CCP interests.[17] Attracting the limited numbers of *huaqiao* (PRC nationals living abroad) alone, however, was insufficient for the task. A wider target was required for China's massive development effort. The majority of OC were either *tongbao* (compatriots from Hong Kong, Macau or Taiwan) or *huaren* (ethnic Chinese of foreign nationality). This latter population was growing – comprising of the millions established in Southeast Asia over many centuries, those who had gone elsewhere and were emerging into their second and third generations, and other recent migrants who had changed their nationality. These OC had become an important and powerful pool of resources for China; many had status in society, participated in local politics, and therefore could be tapped as a trade network and export market for Chinese-made products.[18] However, OC associations, schools and media were becoming localized and less connected with China both culturally and ideo- logically. *Qiaowu* had to resolve this problem, with special policies addressing these concerns in the context of reconnection, cultural unity and rivalry with Taiwan's own *qiaowu* effort, which at the time was far superior and dominant in comparison (see below).

These policies continued steadily until the Tiananmen Incident of 4 June 1989, which sent shockwaves throughout the OC diaspora. Vehement and wipespread protests against the CCP erupted around the world – most (if not all) of which were led and dominated by OC groups. Beijing immediately went into damage control. Provincial governments mobilized those with OC family and business connections to make contact with them and explain the situation, supplemented with specially produced propaganda materials.[19] Delegations were dispatched worldwide to visit OC community groups in an urgent effort to win back their confidence and loyalty. Diplomats attempted to 'preserve the harmony' (*baohe*) between OC and Beijing by presenting the 'official' version of events.[20] This was a major turning point in OC affairs, with all ethnic Chinese becoming the targets of intensified efforts to unify them through mind and spirit.

One group deserved special attention. Although they were supposed to be agents of change for China in the context of its scientific and technological modernization, state-sponsored PRC students became a liability for Beijing. As a result of the Emergency Immigration Relief Act of 1989 for Chinese Nationals following the June 4 Incident, Washington accorded PRC students in the US special immigration conditions.[21] This precipitated the potential problem of thousands choosing to remain abroad and not return to participate in China's modernization, or worse yet, engage in anti-CCP activities. PRC students were the focus of a 'fierce political struggle over human talents'.[22]

Thus began a new phase in the development of OC work, whereby PRC students were the target of an aggressive form of *qiaowu* – comprising of group management, extra-territorial influence, counter-infiltration and counter-subversion. For example, the PRC consul in Vancouver had identified student leaders and demanded that they stop pro-democracy demonstrations. When they arrived to collect their scholarship cheques, he showed them the 'official videotape' of the crackdown and indirectly threatened their relatives by reminding them of their contractual obligations.[23] In March 1990, the PRC State Education Commission convened a meeting of education counsellors in Chinese embassies and consulates, instructing them to expand their influence over student organizations. In December 1990, senior foreign propaganda official Zhu Muzhi suggested rectifying any negative feelings by encouraging the most patriotic students to return to China, while strengthening the patriotism of those choosing to stay abroad.[24] To facilitate this, a 1992 order by the State Council Administrative Bureau provided amnesty for those who engaged in acts against the PRC or its interests when returning to China.[25] The remainder staying abroad would be categorized dependant on their loyalty to Beijing, and each group addressed with specific measures. Relationships with pro-CCP students would be maintained and strengthened; for the less-patriotic, propaganda methods would be used to win them over; finally, those elements deemed dangerous to PRC national interests would be exposed and attacked. These measures would ensure that PRC students would remain a controllable asset for the CCP.[26]

The CCP has continued its effort to co-ordinate pro-Beijing activity among these groups. Although students initially formed ther own organizations, branches of the Chinese Students and Scholars Association (CSSA) were established on various campuses around the world after 1989 to manage various groups under one umbrella.[27] Furthermore, *qiaowu* efforts sought to network such PRC student groups with other local OC organizations and business associations for increased influence and exchange.[28] These groups are eager to enhance their political connections for prestige and status and readily demonstrate their support for the regime with red flags and banners.[29] For example, pro-China sentiment amongst the OC reached unprecented levels in 2008 following what was perceived by many to be an anti-Chinese conspiracy. These OC reacted negatively to the way the Tibetan riots of March 2008 riots were covered by the Western media (especially by CNN, the BBC and Deutsche Welle). Worldwide protests against the Olympic Torch relay (in light of recent events in Tibet and Darfur[30]) and racist comments aired on CNN also sparked outrage. Consequently, OC in major cities all around the world (mostly PRC students and 'new' migrants) turned out in huge numbers to support the Beijing games, oppose Tibetan independence and protest against distorted Western reporting. They wore red T-shirts emblazoned with the slogan 'One China, One Family', sang patriotic songs and chanted 'Go Beijing!' This was a complete reversal of the anti-CCP sentiment of 1989. How was this apparent level of widespread support for China and its leaders achieved amongst the OC?

The OC are mobilized to contribute to China's development and to support its regime through techniques and methodologies that appeal to ethnographic sensitivities and national pride. While much of the work is aimed at attracting remittances, foreign investment, skills and expertise, it can sometimes include encouraging subversive activity.[31] The 1999 Cox Report alleged that the PRC actively identified OC scientists, business connections and exchanges in the US with access to sensitive information and actively enlisted their cooperation.[32] Many respond positively and voluntarily, while others may require more persuasion, incentive or corrective tools to ensure obedience.

However, most efforts to cement relations between China and the OC are implemented through less covert methods. Diplomats host meetings and dinners, stoke OC patriotism and enthusiasm for the motherland.[33] For example, they remind students of how this relationship should be strengthened in combination with diligent study to make their parents' hopes and dreams a reality, and to make the Chinese nation proud of their success. Consequently, many feel a responsibility to do well in representing their country and are ready and willing to support China's leaders.[34]

This was clearly evident during the 2008 Olympic Torch rallies. Australia and Japan were labelled as 'relatively dangerous' destinations for the torch relay due to the anticipated presence of pro-Tibetan independence and Falungong protestors. As 'the last sentry', OC in these areas were organized well in advance to prevent a repeat of the embarrassment in London and Paris days earlier.[35] A patriotic call rallied descendants of the Yellow Emperor, no matter what their nationality or origin.[36] OC were encouraged to stand up against anti-China forces and be heard as part of mainstream society.[37] The embassies actively co-ordinated the thousands of supporters to challenge any potential threats to a successful Olympic Torch relay. Pro-Beijing student groups in Australia were ferried to rallies by chartered bus and provided with accommodation.[38] In Japan, the embassy advised the local police to ensure safety and security of students.[39] Protest paraphernalia (such as thousands of Chinese flags and red T-shirts) was sent to organizers in the form of 'donations' from China. Olympic souvenir items and certificates were given to those attending.

Reports concerning overt PRC involvement soon surfaced in the international media. Accusations of the PRC employing 'rent-a-crowds' to denounce pro-Tibetan protestors could not be allowed to persist. Beijing was obliged to make a public about-face on openly mobilizing OC to attend the rallies. Consequently, *Xinhua* reports emphasized that students had organized the rallies at their own will. PRC officials denied any involvement in stirring up OC nationalism by suggesting such groups took their own initiative.[40] Student groups were instructed to deny any links between the rallies and the embassy. Despite this cover-up, relations between the embassy and consulates and PRC student groups continued as before. After the London relay, representatives of the All England Chinese Students and Scholars Federation were among guests invited to an official function at the PRC embassy.[41] Following the Canberra demonstrations, an embassy statement thanked PRC students for successfully supporting the Olympic spirit and maintaining Chinese/Australian relations – their 'exceptional management and organization efforts' were singled out as a point of high praise.[42]

Cementing the relationship between the PRC and OC: root-seeking

Successfully raising nationalism amongst certain OC can be partly attributed to years of *qiaowu* efforts in the context of several major changes to the geopolitical environment and OC demographic landscape since 1989. First, appealing to their sense of connectedness to China through ethnicity and Chineseness has been a key to gaining a broad spectrum of support. The CCP has recognized that the OC are attracted by the rituals and language of traditional Chinese culture. Anne-Marie Brady points out in Chapter 3 that this work is part of its external (*duiwai*) propaganda – by supporting activities which promote traditional Chinese culture, the CCP is able to frame the public discourse in directions friendly to CCP interests, build bridges with potentially hostile groups, stoke up patriotism for China, and stir up antagonism against foreign aggression.

In reaching out to the OC (in particular youth and *huaren*), *qiaowu* has placed significant emphasis on the notion of *luoye guigen* (literally 'falling leaves return to their roots'). As Brady notes, after China opened up its borders to foreign tourists and foreign investment in 1978, increasing numbers of ethnic Chinese also travelled to China in search of their roots (*xun gen*). Encouraging reconnection has been an extremely successful method of building patriotism and sentiment – particularly in light of China's re-emergence. The themes have remained much the same – promoting cultural and economic opportunities, ethnographic connections, and challenging threats to the

CCP and China's national integrity. Moreover, efforts have gone from strength to strength, targeting a wider range of OC (*huaren, xinqiao*, as well as non-Han minorities) and offering them specially tailored activities in order to rouse pro-China sentiment.[43]

In exceeding the context of conventional tourism, root-seeking serves to complete one's identity by providing an authentic and fulfilling experience.[44] Tours began in the early 1970s with visits carefully managed to impress upon visitors the socialist advances that China had achieved.[45] Tours are historically and personally significant for participants in that they actually visit their ancestral *qiaoxiang* villages and houses. There they take part in activities such as rebuilding ancestral halls, restoring graves, and re-establishing special bonds between themselves and the local authorities (who may bestow their OC visitors with honorary titles).[46] The goal is that they will reignite their sense of Chineseness and willingness to contribute back to their homeland after years of integration and assimilation abroad.

In recent years, provincial authorities have taken a more pro-active approach to organizing reconnection tours with specific goals in mind.[47] For example, in 2007 hundreds of well-known artists and experts attended a special 'Artists Forum' that ostensibly sought to raise cultural standards amongst OC and propagate the 'culture of the motherland'.[48] It was a United Front effort to find common ground with OC artists known for producing dissident art. Another development is the targeting of non-Han minority OC. Representatives from these groups are regularly invited to showcase their unique regional music, song, dance and art through international arts festivals celebrating the diversity within Chinese culture. Alternatively, special delegations from the PRC are encouraged to 'go out' as performance troupes or hold exhibitions to show OC minorities that China is accommodating and supportive of all its peoples. Second and third generation youth of ethnic minorities are key targets for this kind of inclusionist effort.[49]

Another major theme of *qiaowu* is how the OC can contribute and benefit from a reinterpretation of OC modernity. OC (in particular *xinqiao*) are encouraged to feel as if they have moved beyond being a labouring class, and even beyond being professionals, to become an important force of global technological and scientific development.[50] This in turn has allowed China to become confident in satisfying their cultural and organizational needs. Thus another important development of reconnection work has been the targeting of elite (*jingying*) OC for fully subsidized organizational capacity building, and linking them to a dynamic new China full of career opportunities. Top academic, youth, community and business leaders of high calibre, suitable age and experience are invited to attend conferences, workshops, and training courses that promote networking, management and and team-building under PRC methods. These programmes directly influence the development of OC communities – educating their future leaders on how to manage their associations and build capacity in the context of the *qiaowu* infrastructure and philosophy.[51]

Raising OC nationalism

Other developments in the geo-political environment and OC demographic landscape have also raised OC nationalism. Since immigration from China was relaxed after 1985, 'new' *xinqiao* migrants have gradually exerted their dominance over 'old' migrants, both in numbers and organizational capacity. While 'old' established *laoqiao* OC have integrated and identified with their host countries, 'new' OC relate more to the modern Chinese state both politically and emotionally.[52] There is less antagonism towards the CCP than in the past, and consequently overall identification with China and Chineseness has become more pronounced. Second, the OC no longer feel ashamed of China as the poor and sick man of Asia. China's re-emergence as an economic and political power since 1989 has become a great source of pride, respect, self-confidence and strength for all OC, regardless of the regime.

In this context, the Olympic movement was recognized as a potent source of national pride for the OC, and thus heavily exploited by Beijing. The successful bid for the 2008 Games was described by PRC officials as a result of 'joint efforts made by the overseas Chinese throughout the world'.[53] Giving them input into China's affairs and development through the Olympic movement was another way of getting the OC to identify with China. They were extremely positive in their response.[54] For example, 330,000 OC from around the world gave more than 900 million yuan towards the effort. Proposals for the construction of venues were welcomed, with the 'Watercube' complex representing the foremost symbol of OC contribution.[55] Overseas Chinese of foreign citizenship were invited to participate as volunteers, with a special programme to recruit from abroad. Many OC viewed this as an opportunity that they, as Chinese descendants 'should not miss'.[56] With such a feeling of 'ownership', anything negative about the Olympics was considered a direct affront not only to China, but also to many of those who identified themselves as Chinese.

Such feelings of nationalism and pride for China are encouraged amongst the OC as part of propaganda efforts overseen by the Office of Foreign Propaganda and implemented by provincial level offices. The media environment in which these offices operate has undergone significant changes since 1989.[57] While Taiwanese and Hong Kong newspapers (such as the *Independent Daily* and *Sing Tao*) were once the mainstream sources of Chinese news up to the late 1990s and early 2000s, they have since been eliminated by free advertorial newspapers distributed by PRC-friendly media companies that mushroomed in the wake of increased *xinqiao* migration. The only non-PRC OC media sources able to communicate with OC on a global scale are the *Epoch Times*, New Tang Dynasty Television (both backed by the Falungong) and Taiwan's Macroview Television. However, the first two lack credibility amongst foreign audiences, and all three reach only limited sections of the OC diaspora. Independent OC media simply cannot compete with the wider distribution channels that PRC-influenced media enjoys.

Beijing's overwhelming dominance over this industry has occurred as a direct result of collaborating with the media companies themselves. Following a meeting of propaganda officials in 1992, PRC media companies were encouraged by provincial authorities to establish partnerships abroad.[58] Chinese sources call this 'borrowing ships to go to sea', whereby foreign companies carry content approved by centralized China-based bodies (such as the World Chinese Language Press Institute, World Chinese Media Forum, and World Chinese Newspaper Association).[59] Through these channels, articles, layouts, editing and typesetting are arranged before forwarding for publication abroad. Moreover, PRC embassies work closely with the OC media in order to manage their operations – or euphemistically speaking, 'guide them by service'.[60] For example, representatives of Chinese language media in important markets are brought together regularly for discussions with embassy staff. Diplomats visit OC newspapers, meet their editors, pose for photos and praise them for their cooperation. They advise them to strengthen their relationship with the embassy.[61] By aligning themselves with the PRC, media companies expect in return economic benefit, funding and prestige.[62]

The OC media are the key to improving China's image by connecting with and influencing the mainstream media and in turn, dispelling Western society's 'demonized' view of China.[63] As part of *qiaowu*, media work involves managing and influencing OC reporters when visiting China. OC journalists are charged with unifying and harmonizing OC society by propagating a modern perspective of China, its friendly intentions, and its leaders.[64] Special media tours are tailored for the different political and environmental expectations and interests of journalists.[65] They are invited to attend special forums and conferences with the aim of promoting 'objective' reporting on China, and encouraged to gather 'independent' news with a 'different' perspective. These are all techniques that have changed little in the contemporary period. For example, OC 'independent reporters' were invited to cover preparations for the 2008 Olympics in an effort to portray China as 'clean' and 'civilized' – especially after the 2003 SARS outbreak.[66]

Qiaowu has also evolved since 1989 as a result of the advance in telecommunications technology. New multi-media and electronic platforms have advantages of broader and more effective delivery, attractiveness, and dissemination than traditional platforms – particularly for ethnic Chinese and second or third generation OC.[67] To reach as many OC as possible, Beijing has produced a 'multi-faceted cultural product'.[68] The goal is to develop OC media into a 'New Chinatown' – a comprehensive 'supermarket' of Chineseness and OC work, which is then used to the full extent (including advertisements and articles) in conducting and promoting *qiaowu*.[69] As a result, audio-visual propaganda has been particularly effective in directly penetrating OC homes. PRC-directed portals and Chinese-language websites have become the leading sources of mainland and OC news and information amongst OC.[70]

Some OC websites are linked directly to Chinese government mouthpieces, which disseminate PRC government initiatives, policy and news. Other OC websites function to share and promote topics important to managing OC behaviour and participation. In this manner, China-based Chinese language websites, blogs and chatrooms provided detailed instructions to rally participants for the 2008 rallies. For example, students were told when and where to meet, how to dress, what to bring, and what to do so as to present the Chinese protestors as civil, friendly and peaceful in front of Western media.[71] For example, a statement was issued on the PRC embassy website the day before the Canberra protests stressing the importance to promote bilateral friendship, trust and goodwill.[72] In New Zealand, supporters were instructed to display only Chinese and local flags and banners, and not to engage in confrontation with opponents. In Japan, they were ordered to arrive and leave together and not participate in independent activities.

China's goal with *qiaowu* on the internet is to create a 'Global Chinese Village' in the hope of unifying the OC as a single virtual entity.[73] The 'red heart' campaign demonstrated how this could be achieved. Millions of OC added red hearts to their online avatars as part of an international 'Love China' campaign.[74] This concept was apparently initiated by users themselves and later adopted as a branding strategy for MSN China.[75] *Xinhua* was fully supportive of the effort, calling for netizens to maintain an 'open mind against anti-China propaganda while keeping patriotic'.[76] Many OC responded by adding pro-China and anti-Western media comments alongside their 'heart', and shared videos or songs criticizing CNN and the BBC. The most extreme form of online OC nationalism was the rise of 'human flesh search engines' – virtual witch-hunts that tracked down and attacked 'traitors' who supported pro-Tibetan or anti-China efforts.[77] Beijing's goal of inspiring nationalist activity and unity amongst pro-Beijing *xinqiao* and PRC students was a global success.

The Taiwan factor

Part of Beijing's successful effort to reclaim the OC can also be attributed to 'Taiwanization'. As an anti-communist alternative to Beijing after 1949, for decades Taipei had maintained dominance over strategic powerbases of the Chinese diaspora by ensuring local leaders were loyal to the Kuomintang (KMT) under its own version of *qiaowu*. As the government of the Republic of China (ROC), the KMT based its legitimacy on being the guardian of Chinese high culture and providing education and cultural resources to OC communities and schools. This formula continued up until the 1990s, after which a distinctive pro-Taiwanese identity began to emerge at the expense of Chineseness. Consequently, Taipei's OC policy tended to favour *Taiqiao* (OC of Taiwanese origin) and pro-Taiwan groups, but alienated and angered many *laoqiao* (old OC) groups and pro-reunification (mostly old KMT) supporters. Taiwanization reached its apex when the Democratic Progressive Party (DPP) regime was in power between 2000 and 2008. As such, preventing the threat of Taiwan achieving independence became China's leading foreign policy objective. Recognizing that the OC had a major role to play in this matter, China engaged with them using methods similar to those of 1989. It pursued an aggressive and widespread strategy under the co-ordination of PRC embassies and consulates around the world that sought to rally pro-Beijing supporters while opposing anti-China forces.[78]

Confident that a trend for *laoqiao* and anti-independence OC to turn away from Taipei would only increase, Beijing seized on this opportunity by focusing much of its *qiaowu* work around persuading the OC to embrace the *People's* Republic of China (emphasis added). Termed as transformation work (*zhuanbian*),[79] this form of *qiaowu* attempts to extricate the OC from years of Taiwanese dominance and influence – by propagating the 'One China' policy, persuading OC to 'advance the PRC/CCP stance, and reducing mutual misunderstanding'.[80] This work was especially important in OC schools where ROC textbooks and teaching methods were still being used, or in areas where staunch pro-Taiwan feelings remain (such as amongst members of the Fijian *laoqiao* community who hold strong historical KMT links).[81] To achieve 'transformation', cadres worked with backbone members of the Taiwan-friendly community and attempted to reduce their sense of distance with China. One theme was to propagate ethnic Chinese culture, friendship, sentimentality, common blood, ancestry and village connections in the face of Taiwanization. For example, organizations such as the China Mazu Cultural Exchange Association work to improve relations between *Taiqiao* and China as part of religious exchange and building links with the 'homeland'. Under such methods, Beijing hopes that the world's OC can come together 'hand-in-hand, heart-to-heart'.[82]

These efforts to embrace the wider OC diaspora gained additional traction after the KMT's re-ascension to power in 2008. Under the new regime, Taiwanese diplomats moved away from the previously politically motivated relationship of the DPP years, preferring to return to the KMT style of supporting their long term prosperity and encouraging more pragmatic relations with them. Although this change may have signalled some improvements with *laoqiao*, it is clear that Taiwan can never return to the level of relations that it enjoyed with the OC in times past. Despite its promises to reinstate KMT OC policy, it appeared that its own particular *qiaowu* effort was still very much influenced by Taiwan's domestic political situation. Reports that Ma Ying-jeou's administration intended to scrap the Overseas Chinese Affairs Commission (OCAC) soon surfaced after his successful election. Not long after, Ma announced that the OCAC would merge with Taiwan's Ministry of Foreign Affairs in order to provide 'better services to overseas Chinese'.[83] *Laoqiao* groups around the world with long historical links to the OCAC sent petitions of protest and threatened to boycott Taiwanese exchanges and visits in the face of this move. Finally in April 2009, given these concerns, Ma made a last-minute change to the proposal, and the OCAC was able to continue with its functions fully intact.[84]

However, whether the KMT is able to count on support from both *Taiqiao* and *laoqiao* remains to be seen. There have been significant changes to Taipei's relationship with certain OC groups. For example, while it has attempted to strengthen its links with *laoqiao*, its relationship with the Falungong and pro-Tibet movement has faltered – since the change of government, Taipei has refrained from further supporting such groups despite repeated requests for assistance, or refused to meet with pro-democracy activists.[85] These actions reflect the KMT's conciliatory approach towards dealing with Beijing. As such, the threat of Taiwan's quest for independence has been significantly muted. This apparent détente between the two Chinas has resulted in more engagements between rival OC groups. Diplomats from both sides are taking a leading role by considering organizing joint celebrations for traditional festivals.[86]

Ultimately, the 'truce' between the two Chinas is conditional upon Taiwan's eventual reunification on terms acceptable to Beijing. While Ma has demonstrated he is willing to work with mainland officials by improving economic and cultural links with China, he is careful in dealing with the political aspects of the warming relationship. Sooner or later, Taiwan will have to address the issue of reunification. As mentioned earlier, pressure from Taiwan's domestic constituency and the OC are key factors influencing when this might happen. However, in the contemporary period, Taiwan simply does not have the resources nor the political support to deal with such a large and diverse community; nor does it possess a sufficiently robust or attractive enough platform that ethnic Chinese can readily identify with. In contrast, Beijing's rival *qiaowu* efforts to reconnect with the OC have been very successful in addressing Taipei's weaknesses. For example, Beijing immediately capitalized on the sentiments of disaffected *laoqiao* OC frustrated at Ma's original plans for scrapping the OCAC – top PRC *qiaowu* official Li Haifeng appealed to these groups by telling them that the mainland would accept them if they were ever abandoned.[87]

Conclusion

Qiaowu has evolved and strengthened over the last twenty years to the extent that it has become a significant influence in determining the future direction of the OC diaspora. A comprehensive set of programmes and policies ensures that anyone of ethnic Chinese descent has unprecedented access to cultural, economic and political development in a PRC-friendly context. By embracing common themes of Chinese unity and modernity, and implemented through articulate persuasion and systematic management, *qiaowu* has enjoyed considerable success with certain groups of the OC. While it is pro-Beijing *xinqiao* and *huaqiao* who are most likely to react positively to *qiaowu* by making a conscious decision to reconnect or network with China, other OC may only be affected subconsciously. At the least, Beijing seeks to expose all OC to a 'fresh' perception of China in the hope they might look to China with renewed interest.

In contrast, rival factions vying for OC support have been rendered largely impotent in challenging China's better-resourced, more attractive and well subsidized *qiaowu* efforts. As the only serious threat to China's relationship with the OC in recent years, Taiwan (particularly during the DPP years) has largely focused only on the pro-Taiwan cohort, while *laoqiao* and pro-unification OC lean ever closer to Beijing. As another contender, Falungong has been isolated, weakened and discredited as a cult by the CCP, while the Tibetan and Xinjiang separatist movements have either been subdued or shouted down. In short, China's *qiaowu* effort simply has no effective competitor. Even Western liberalist ideology has failed to diminish the OC's nationalistic support for China's leaders. Domestically, the CCP authoritarian regime has tightened its grip on power by ensuring that the return of Western-educated PRC students serves only to further its economic policy, and not its political reform.[88] Externally, *qiaowu* has been successful in grounding 'grand-unification' nationalism amongst OC communities – the majority of pro-Beijing OC refuse to accept Taiwan's right to self-determination, and embrace the CCP discourse that sovereignty and economic development take priority over democratization.[89]

Although Beijing actively encourages the OC to support the CCP, boost Chinese pride, and to challenge threats to its national integrity, some have also been quietly mobilized for fifth-column activity (such as spying or espionage). However, the main task of OC is to promote China's national interests by projecting a positive image to the world while raising their own social, political and economic profile as the new Chinese modernity. *Qiaowu* has captured the hearts and minds of OC in a pre-emptive effort to challenge any other groups who may seek their loyalty. By taking advantage of its growing economy, geo-political might and long history, a confident PRC has prompted the OC to acknowledge the importance of being Chinese, and are encouraged to advance China's development as part of its 'family'. *Qiaowu*, as a pragmatic and attractive means of 'service to the OC' has been, and will continue to be developed as a significant frontline strategy in advancing China's relationship not only with its diaspora, but also the rest of the world.

Notes

1   This paper uses the term OC in a generic manner to include ethnic Chinese living outside of China (including the Special Administrative Regions of Hong Kong and Macau) or Taiwan, irrespective of citizenship. Where specific types of OC are referred to, the term will be qualified.
2   Franka Cordua-von Specht, 'Discourse on the China Crisis: Three Perspectives', *The Ubyssey*, vol. 8, no. 1, 5 July 1989, 5, www.library.ubc.ca/archives/pdfs/ubyssey/UBYSSEY_1989_07_05.pdf
3   Anne-Marie Brady, *Marketing Dictatorship: Propaganda and Thought Work in Contemporary China* (Lanham MD: Rowman & Littlefield, 2008): 163–64.
4   Gregor Benton, *Chinese Migrants and Internationalism: Forgotten Histories, 1917–1945* (London: Routledge, 2007): 118–20; Wu Zhiling, '*Zuohao xinshiqi qiaowu gongzuo*' (Succeeding with New Age OC Work) 12 February 2003,

www.gqb.gov.cn/news/2003/0212/1/311.shtml; Wang Jingzhi, ed., *Qiaowu zhishi shouce* (Handbook of Overseas Chinese Affairs Knowledge) (Beijing: Zhongguo huaqiao chuban gongsi, 1989): 69–70; *Qiaowu gongzuo gailun* (Outline of Overseas Chinese Work) (Beijing: Guowuyuan qiaoban qiaowu ganbu xuexiao, October 1993): 1, 13.

5　Anne-Marie Brady, *Making the Foreign Serve China: Managing Foreigners in the People's Republic* (Lanham MD: Rowman & Littlefield, 2003): xi; '*Qiaowu gongzuo "shehuihua" de zhiyi*' (Query into OC Work and Socialization) in Wang Tang, ed., *Qiaowu chunqiu* (The Era of Overseas Chinese Affairs) (Beijing: Zhongguo guojiguangbo chubanshe, 1997): 73–74; '*Zhuanjia xixun weiyuanhui wei qiaowu gongzuo xianji xiance*' (Specialist Advisory Committee Offer Suggestions for OC Work) *Qiaoqing*, no. 8, 15 March 2005, 9–10.

6　Wu Ruicheng, '*Zhangwo xinfangfa, katuo Guangdong qiaowu xinjumian*' (Master New Techniques, Open Up New Phase of Guangdong OC Work) 30 August 2007, www.gqb.gov.cn/news/2007/0830/1/6401.shtml

7　Hong Liu, 'New Migrants and the Revival of Overseas Chinese Nationalism', *Journal of Contemporary China*, vol. 14, no. 43, May 2005, 302–3.

8　Brady, *Marketing Dictatorship*, 73.

9　*Qiaowu gongzuo gailun*, 9.

10　'*Guanyu qiaowu gongzuo xingzhi wenti de tantao*' (Enquiry Into Quality of OC Work) 1986 in *Qiaowu chunqiu*, 63–64.

11　*Qiaowu gongzuo gailun* (Outline of Overseas Chinese Work) (Beijing: Guowuyuan qiaoban qiaowu ganbu xuexiao, October 1993): 2, 4–5, 10–17, 29–31.

12　'*Fu Xinxilan diaoyanhou de xinsikao*' (New Thoughts Following Research in New Zealand) *Qiaoqing*, no. 11, 1 March 2004, 2, 6.

13　'*Zhou Enlai zhongli dui Miandian huaqiao de jianghua*' (Premier Zhou Enlai Speaks to Myanmar OC) 18 December 1956, in *Qiaowu zhengce wenji* (Collection of OC Policy) (Beijing: Renmin chubanshe, 1957): 1–10.

14　Stephen Fitzgerald, *China and the Overseas Chinese: A Study of Beijing's Changing Policy, 1949–1970* (Cambridge: Cambridge University Press, 1972).

15　Anne-Marie Brady, 'The War That Never Was, or, New Zealand-China Relations in the Cold War Era', in *Lenin's Legacy Down Under: New Zealand and the New Cold War History*, eds. Aaron Fox and Alex Trapeznik (Dunedin: University of Otago Press, 2003): 12; Michael R. Godley, 'The Sojourners: Returned Overseas Chinese in the People's Republic of China', *Pacific Affairs*, vol. 62, no. 3, Autumn 1989, 330–52.

16　Wang Gungwu, 'South China Perspectives on Overseas Chinese', *The Australian Journal of Chinese Affairs*, no. 3, January 1985, 69–84.

17　The Four Modernizations were a reversal of Mao's policy of economic self-reliance that comprised of accelerating export-led economic growth, foreign trade and investment to make advances in agriculture, industry, science and technology and the military. '*Zai yici yewu zuotanhui shang de fayan*' (Statement from a Vocational Forum) 1983 in *Qiaowu chunqiu*, 118.

18　'*Huaqiao, waiji huaren shehui jiegou de bianhua*' (Changes in the Structure of OC Society) 1982 in *Qiaowu chunqiu*, 84–89.

19　Chen Xitong, *Report and Checking the Turmoil and Quelling the Counter-Revolutionary Rebellion* (Beijing: New Star Publishers, 1989); Brady, *Marketing Dictatorship*, 163.

20　Pal Nyiri, 'The New Migrant: State and Market Constructions of Modernity and Patriotism', http://cio.ceu.hu/courses/CIO/modules/Modul01Nyiri/print.html.

21　Canada, Australia and New Zealand passed similar legislation allowing students to remain as refugees, and later as permanent residents.

22　Eighty per cent of the 50000 PRC students were thought to remain in North America and 10 per cent were actively anti-CCP. See Appendix I ('Summary of the Meeting of Educational Counselors (Consuls) in Chinese Embassies and Consulates') and II ('Directive on Policy Toward Chinese Students and Scholars in the United States and Canada, March 1990') in Nicholas Eftimiades, *Chinese Intelligence Operations* (Annapolis MD: Naval Institute Press, 1994): 117–39.

23 Franka Cordua-von Specht, 'Chinese Students Fear Spies', *The Ubyssey*, vol. 8, no. 1, 5 July 1989.

24 Zhu Muzhi, '*Jiaqiang dui liuxue renyuan de xuanchuan gongzuo*' (Strengthen Propaganda Work Towards Foreign Students), 15 December 1990 in *Zhu Muzhi Lun Duiwai xuanchuan* (Zhu Muzhi Discusses Foreign Propaganda) (Beijing: Wuzhou chuanbo chubanshe, 1995): 292–93.

25 Order no. 44. as noted by Qian Ning, *Liuxue Meiguo* (Studying in America) (Nanjing: Jiangsu wenyi chubanshe, 1996): 285.

26 Eftimiades, *Chinese Intelligence Operations*, 117–39.

27 Branches have direct links with the PRC embassy. See http://umdcssa.org/

28 '*Beimei qiaoqing xin bianhua*' (New Changes in North American OC Affairs) *Qiaoqing*, no. 56, 20 December 2003, 8; Wu Zhiling, '*Jiada lidu pushe yinjin haiwai rencai de "luse tongdao"*', (Increase Strength for Laying the 'Green Passage' in Attracting Overseas Talent) 6 March 2003, www.gqb.gov.cn/news/2003/0306/1/321.shtml

29 'Chinese Naval Fleet Calls on New Zealand', *Xinhua*, 11 October 2001; 'Hu Winds Up US Visit Amid Protests', *Stuff.co.nz*, 22 April 2006, www.stuff.co.nz/stuff/0,2106,3645313a12,00.html.

30 Beijing was criticized for its involvement in Darfur and refusing to put pressure on the Sudan government to end the humanitarian crisis. Jane Macartney, 'China Lashes Out Against Darfur Critics in Olympic Row', *Times Online*, 14 February 2008, www.timesonline.co.uk/tol/news/world/asia/article3367440.ece

31 John Diamond, 'China Broadens Espionage Operations', *USA Today*, 18 May 2006.

32 House Report 105-851, 'Report of the Select Committee on US National Security and Military/Commercial Concerns with the People's Republic of China, submitted by Mr. Cox of California, Chairman', www.access.gpo.gov/congress/house/hr105851/

33 '*Aozhou guoli daxue juban "qingqian aoyun xinxi Zhongguo"*' (ANU Organizes 'Love Leads the Olympics, Hearts Tied to China'), 31 August 2007, www.eduwo.com/eduwo/news/10/hotnews/ProviderNews/files/1719.shtml; Xia Wenhui, '*Xinxilan Zhongguo liuxuesheng juxing guoqing lianhuanhui*' (New Zealand Chinese Foreign Students Organise National Day Celebrations), *The Sun*, 6 October 2005, 5.

34 Embassy of the People's Republic of China, '*Liuxuesheng qieji: jiazhangmen wei ni qianchang guadu!*' (Foreign Students Remember: Parents Are Concerned About You!), *New Zealand Messenger*, 17 November 2004; 'Cheers and Jeers Greet Chinese President', *The Press*, 10 November 2005.

35 Paul Walker and David Batty, 'Olympic Torch Relay Cut Short Amidst Paris Protests', *Guardian*, 7 April 2008, www.guardian.co.uk/world/2008/apr/07/france.olympicgames2008

36 '*Aodaliya huaren shouhao shenghuo "zuihou yiban gang"*; *Yun huoju weidao Aozhou, huaren shetuan yishi xiaoyan miman*' (Before the Torch Reaches Australia, Smoke of OC Group's Gunpowder Already Fills the Air), 15 April 2008, http://cn-view.blogspot.com/2008/04/g2g_6775.html

37 '*Huang yiyuan, Huolushi, Wang Xiansheng: qing chuxi 4.27 jihui!*' (Pansy Wong, Lawyer Huo, Mr Wang: Please Attend the April 27 Rally!) www.nzchinese.net.nz/news.asp?p=561933.

38 '*Mianfei daba Kanpeila Beijing aoyun shenghuo chuandi zi lu*' (Free Coach for Canberra Beijing Olympic Torch Relay Trip), from Sydney Eat, Drink Fun Club website, www.ozchinese.com/bbs/archiver/tid-150584.html

39   Jesse McKinley, 'Olympic Torch Route Changed in San Francisco', *New York Times*, 10 April 2008, www.nytimes.com/2008/04/10/us/10torch.html?_r=1&scp=5& sq=torch+protest&st=nyt&oref=slogin; John Garnaut, 'Students Plan Mass Torch "Defense"', *The Age*, 16 April 2008, www.theage.com.au/articles/2008/04/ 15/1208025189581.html

40   '*Aodaliya bufen meiti feinan huaren canyu aoyun huoju chuandi*' (Some Australian Media's Reproach of Chinese Participation in Olympic Torch Relay) *Xinhua*, 25 April 2008, http://news.xinhuanet.com/overseas/2008-04/25/content_8049791.htm; 'Foreign Ministry Spokesperson Jiang Yu's Regular Press Conference on April 8, 2008', *PRC Embassy Website*, 9 April 2008, www.china-embassy.ch/eng/fyrth/ t423126.htm

41   '*Zhongguo zhu Ying shiguan juxing qing aoyun huoju chuandi zhaodaihui*' (PRC Embassy in England Hosts Olympic Torch Relay Ceremony) www.ukchinese. com/www/18/2008–04/590.html

42   Zhang Junsai, '*Zhi zaiAo huaren huaqiao he liuxueheng pengyou de yifeng xin*' (A Letter to Australian Chinese, OC, Foreign Students and Friends), 24 April 2008, http://au.china-embassy.org/chn/sgjs/sghd/t428847.htm

43   *Qiaowu gongzuo gailun*, 101; Wu, '*Jiada lidu pushe yinjin haiwai rencai de "luse tongdao"*'.

44   Andrea Louie, 'When You Are Related to the 'Other': (Re)locating the Chinese Homeland in Asian American Politics Through Cultural Tourism', *Positions*, vol. 11, no. 3, Winter 2003, 735–63.

45   Jan Wong, *Red China Blues* (New York: Anchor Books, 1996).

46   Flemming Christiansen, 'Beyond Chinese Statehood? Authoritative Representations of Nation and Ethnicity in the Late 1990s and Early 2000s', Department of East Asian Studies, University of Leeds, www.personal.leeds.ac.uk/~chifc/nation.pdf, 7

47   '*Liebian, chongzu, xinsheng, ronghe*' (Split, Reconstitute, New Born, Fusion) *Qiaoqing*, no. 11, 1 March 2004, 9, 12–15; '*Shenri shehui, tanjiu qiaoqing*' (Penetrate Chinese Society, Investigate Overseas Chinese Affairs) *Qiao qing*, no. 27, 5 August 2005, 1–12; Wu Ruicheng, '*Qiaowu gongzuoju zhanluexing qianzhanxing*' (Strategic and Forward Looking Nature of OC Work Tools), 15 February 2007, www.gqb.gov.cn/news/2007/0215/1/3993.shtml

48   '*Wenhua Zhongguo, Mingjia jiantan: tuijie Zhonghua wenhua de xinpinpai*' (Cultural China Artists Forum: Promoting New Brands of Chinese Culture), *Qiao qing* no. 23, 23 August 2007, 6–8.

49   '*Jiaqiang qiaowu wenhua gongzuo, xuanchuan hongyang Zhonghua wenhua*' (Intensify Overseas Chinese Cultural Work, Propagate and Enhance Chinese Culture) *Qiaoqing*, no. 16, 24 May 2005, 1–5; '*Dui jiaqiang xinxingshi xia Xinjiangji huaqiao huaren gongzuo de sikao*' (Thoughts on Strengthening Xinjiang OC Work In Light of a New Situation), *Qiaoqing*, no. 14, 6 June 2007, 1–6.

50   Nie Chuanqing, '*Chaoyue chuantong "san ba dao" haiwai xinhuaqiao huaren zhuangong zhuliu hangye*' (Transcending the Traditional 'Three Knives': Overseas Chinese and Ethnic Chinese Change into Mainstream Industries), *People's Daily* (Overseas Edition), 11 September 2007, http://big5.cri.cn/gate/big5/gb.cri.cn/1321/ 2007/09/11/1766@1757543,htm

51   Lu Weixiong (director of the Guangdong Overseas Chinese Affairs Office), letter to OC leaders, 26 June 2008. '*Shenri shehui, tanjiu qiaoqing*', 11; '*Shenri qiaoshe, tuozhan Feizhou diqu qiaowu gongzuo*' (Penetration of Overseas Chinese Society, Develop African Overseas Chinese Work), *Qiaoqing*, no. 24, 15 July 2005, 3–4.

52   Bertil Lintner, 'The Third Wave', *Far Eastern Economic Review*, 24 June 1999, 28; Liu, 'New Migrants and the Revival of Overseas Chinese Nationalism', 300.

53   Zhao Xiangling (Auckland Consul General) as quoted in 'Celebrations on Beijing's Succesful Bid for Hosting the 2008 Olympic Games', *Auckland PRC Consulate Website*, 14 July 2001, www.chinaconsulate.org.nz/eng/xwdt/t44155.htm

54   'Jia Qinglin Meets Fuzhou-Originated Overseas Chinese', *Xinhua*, 11 October 2001.
55   '*Guojia youyong zhongxin "Suilifang" huo gangaotaiqiao juanzhi jiangchao jiuy,i*' (National Aquatic Centre 'Watercube' Captures Almost Over 900 Million Yuan from OC Donations) *Xinjingbao*, 7 November 2007; Jia Qinglin (Secretary of the Beijing Municipal Committee of the CCP).
56   Statement by the Preparatory Group of the Volunteer Department from the official website of the Beijing 2008 Olympic Games, as noted in www.sportingfemale. com/www_en/NewsInfo.asp?NewsId=180; Liu Xing, 'Everyone Can Lend a Hand to Olympic Programmes', *China Daily*, 9 April 2006, www.cctv.com/ program/worldinsight/20060904/102625.shtml
57   Brady, *Marketing Dictatorship*, 156–70.
58   Ibid., 12, 157, 162. There are similar strategies for the contemporary period. '*Tigao waisuan youxiaoxing de wudian kianyi*' (Five Suggestions for Raising Effective Foreign Propaganda) as found in *China Reporter*, vol. 2, 2004, http:// 203.192.6.68/2004/2/2-23.htm; 'Guangdong Encourages Media to Operate Overseas', *China Daily*, 1 October 2003, www.chinadaily.com.cn/en/doc/2003-10/01/ content_269049.htm
59   Elena Barabantseva, 'The Party-State's Transnational Outreach Overseas Chinese Policies of the PRC's Central Government', Greater China Occasional Papers no. 2, Institute of Chinese and Korean Studies, University of Tübingen, August 2005, www.uni-tuebingen.de/sinologie/sino/gcs/papers/paper2.pdf, 23.
60   *Qiaowu gongzuo gailun*, 83, 88–89; Lu Weixiong, '*"San ge jianchi" quanmian tuozhan qiaowu gongzuo*' (Three Perseverances for Comprehensive Development of OC Work), 22 February 2006, www.gqb.gov.cn/news/2006/0222/1/1925.shtml
61   Wei Ran, '*Zhang dashi canguan benbao qiwang Zhongwen meiti chuancheng Zhonghua wenhua goujian yulun pingtai*' (Ambassador Zhang Visits Newspaper, Hopes Chinese Language Media Can Disseminate Chinese Culture and Construct a Platform for Public Dialogue), *New Zealand Chinese Herald*, 6 May 2006, B3.
62   *Qiaoqing*, no. 13, 15 March 2004, 9; Xu Mingyang, 'Thai Chinese Journalists Enhanced Cooperation', *Guangdong OCAO Website*, 11 June 2004, http://gocn. southcn.com/english/whatson/200406110013.htm
63   '*Guanyu Fa, He, Ying sanguo huaqiao huaren rongre zhuliu shehui qingkuang de diaoyan baogao*' (Investigative Report of the Situation Concerning Integration of French, Dutch and English OC in Mainstream Society), *Qiaoqing*, no. 24, 5 September 2007, 14–15; '*Yaoqing haiwai huawen meiti xuanchuan Beijing aoyun*' (Invite OC Media to Propagate Beijing Olympics), *Qiaoqing*, no. 23, 23 August 2007, 2–3.
64   Wu, '*Zhangwo xinfangfa, katuo Guangdong qiaowu xinjumian*'; '*Haiwai huaqiao huaren he huawen meiti gaodu pingjia Zhonggong shiqi da zhaokai*' (OC and Chinese Media Make a High-level Appraisal of 17th CCP Conference), *Xinhuanet*, 18 October 2007.
65   '*Chuangxin waixuan celue, chuanbo guojia xingxiang*' (Bring Forth New Overseas Propaganda Tactics, Disseminate the National Image), *Qiaoqing*, no. 22, 14 August 2007, 10–11, 14–15.
66   '*Yaoqing haiwai huawen meiti xuanchuan Beijing aoyun*', 1.
67   '*Chuangxin waixuan celue, chuanbo guojia xingxiang*', 15; Wu, '*Zuohao xinshiqi qiaowu gongzuo*'.
68   '*Lian Song fangwen Dalu dui haiwai qiaoshe de yinxiang ji wo gongzuo duice*' (Effects on Overseas Chinese from the Lian Song Visits to China and Our Countermeasures), *Qiao qing*, no. 19, 27 June 2005, 9–10.
69   '*Fu Xinxilan diaoyanhou de xinsikao*', 6.
70   *Qiaowu gongzuo gailun*, 87–89; Lu, '*"San ge jianchi" quanmian tuozhan qiaowu gongzuo*'; '*Dui wai xuanchuan baodao youxiaoxing de jiben pingjie*' (Report on Effectiveness of Overseas Propaganda), http://203.192.6.68/2004/2/2-18.htm.

71 '*4.27 jihui xuzhi! Qing wubi zixi yuedu! Yange zunshou!*' (Important Notice for April 27 Rally! Please Be Sure to Read Carefully! Observe Strictly!), notice posted by New Zealand Chinese Students in Support of Olympics, http://hi.baidu.com/%CD% B5%B5%C3%B0%EB%C8%D5%CF%D0/blog/item/a27910bf2da8a40f19d81f34. html; '*Gedi liuxuesheng huwei aoyun shenghuo: women de xin yu zuguo xiangyi*' (Foreign Students All Over Protect the Olympic Flame: Our Hearts and the Motherland are Interdependent), 24 April 2008, http://2008.sohu.com/20080424/ n256483814.shtml; '*Zai Ri huaren liuxuesheng aoyun shenghuo shengyuan huodong lakai weimu*' (In Japan, Chinese Foreign Students' Support of Olympic Flame Lift Open Curtain), 17 April 2008, www.peacehall.com/news/gb/intl/ 2008/04/200804170715.shtml; '*Aodaliya huaren shouhao shenghuo "zuihou yiban gang"*' (Australian Chinese Guarding the Olympic Flame the 'Last Sentry'), *Guoji Xianqu Daobao*, 25 April 2008, http://bak.zxtv.com.cn/News/Print.asp? ArticleID=10760.

72 '*Zhang Junsai: wo qidai aoyun huoju zai Kanpeila chuandi chenggong*' (Zhang Junsai: I Hope the Olympic Torch Relay in Canberra is Successful), 23 April 2008, http://au.china-embassy.org/chn/sgfyrth/t428056.htm

73 '*Minjindang zhizheng houtai 'qiaoweihui' de zhuyao gongzuo ji fazhan fangxiang*' (Essential Development and Direction Behind the Scenes of Overseas Chinese Affairs Commission Following DDP Ascent to Power), *Qiaoqing*, no., 29, 15 August 2000, 6–7, 10.

74 'Chinese Holding Rallies to Back Beijing Games', *China Daily*, 20 April 2008. www.chinadaily.com.cn/china/2008-04/20/content_6630183.htm; 'Overseas Chinese Rally in Support of Beijing Olympics, Against Western Media's Biased Coverage', *Xinhua*, 21 April 2008, http://english.people.com.cn/90001/90776/ 90883/6395679.html; Paul Dixon, 'Patriotic Web Users Defend China', *Guardian*, 18 April 2008, www.guardian.co.uk/media/2008/apr/18/digitalmedia.china? gusrc=rss& feed = technology.

75 '"Red Heart China" Appears in Netizens' MSN Signatures', *Xinhua*, 18 April 2008, http://english.people.com.cn/90001/90776/90882/6395205.html

76 Zhang Yuke, '*"Hongxin China" xijuan MSN women gai zenyang biaoda aiguo reqing*' ('Red Heart China' Sweeps Across MSN, How Should We Express our Patriotic Zeal?), *Xinhua*, 17 April 2008, http://news.xinhuanet.com/world/2008-04/ 17/content_7997010.htm

77 'China Online: Tibet and Torch Reaction', *BBC News*, 17 April 2008, http://news. bbc.co.uk/2/hi/asia-pacific/7347821.stm; Cara Anna, 'China's Olympic Torch Defender Speaks Out', *San Francisco Chronicle*, 17 April 2008, www.sfgate.com/ cgi-bin/article.cgi?f=/n/a/2008/04/17/international/il23226D67.DTL&w=chinese+ students&sn=001&sc=1000

78 '*Jinnian lai qiaowu dui Tai gongzuo qingkuang*' (The Situation of OC Work Towards Taiwan in Recent Years), *Qiaoqing*, no. 31, 23 October 2007, 5, 13; '*Haiwai huaqiao huaren yongyue weifan "du" cutong jianyan xiance*' (OC Enthusiastically Oppose Independence, Promote Unification, Offer Advice), *Qiaoqing*, no. 17, 2 June 2005, 8–9.

79 '*Taiwan dasuan dui wo qiaowu dui Tai gongzuo de yingxiang*' (Effect of Taiwanese Elections on Our Overseas Chinese and Taiwan Work), *Qiao qing*, no. 28, 23 June 2004, 2–9; '*Beimei qiaoqing xin bianhua*', 1.

80 '*Lian Song fangwen Dalu dui haiwai qiaoshe de yinxiang ji wo gongzuo duice*', 9.

81 '*Xinlao qiaotuan lianghao hezuo, huawen jiaoyu zaixian shengji*' (Good Cooperation Between New and Old OC Groups, Produce New Opportunities for Chinese Education), *Qiaoqing*, no. 34, 2 August 2004, 7.

82 As goddess of the sea, Mazu is widely and commonly worshipped throughout southeastern coastal regions of China, Taiwan and amongst OC communities. 'Cross-Strait Relations Irresistable', *People's Daily*, 13 January 2005,

http://english.people.com.cn/200501/13/eng20050113_170564.html;   '*Meizhou mazu haixia luntan: chuancheng mazu wenhua hongyang mazu jingshen*' (Meizhou Motherland Taiwan Straits Forum: Propogating Motherland Culture for Enhancing Motherland Spirit), *Xinhuanet*, 31 October 2007.

83   http://english.csie.ncnu.edu.tw/modules/iWSML/Ben/html/200903250950.html

84   Shih Hsiu-chuan, 'OCAC Escapes Inclusion in Foreign Ministry', *Taipei Times*, 19 April 2009, www.taipeitimes.com/News/taiwan/archives/2009/04/19/2003441459

85   'Taiwan DPP to Propose Tiananmen Motion as Dissident Wang Dan Fails to Meet President', *Taiwan News*, 24 May 2009, www.taiwannews.com.tw/etn/news_content.php?id=957998& lang = eng_news

86   'Taiwan, China Expatriates May Hold Joint Celebrations', *Central News Agency*, 24 July 2009, www.taiwannews.com.tw/etn/news_content.php?id=1011924& lang = eng_ne

87   'Merger of Overseas Compatriot Affairs Commission Opposed', KMT website, 11 March 2009, www.kmt.org.tw/english/page.aspx?type=article& mnum = 112& anum = 5891

88   '*Woguo Dalu renkou guoji qianyi de xianzhuang, qushi ji xiangguan duice jianyi*' (Current Situation of China's Global Migrant Population, Countermeasures and Recommendations for Trends and Implications), *Qiaoqing*, no. 24, 5 September 2007, 18; He Li, 'Returned Students and Political Change in China', *Asian Perspective*, vol. 30, no. 2, 2006, 5–29.

89   Chiou Chwei-liang, 'Old China Versus Modern Taiwan', *Taipei Times*, 24 September 2003, 8, www.taipeitimes.com/Newz/editorials/archives/2003/09/24/2003069059

10 Conclusion: the velvet fist in the velvet glove

Political and social control in contemporary China

Anne-Marie Brady

> People in the West are often inclined to consider the lot of converted countries in terms of might and coercion. That is wrong. There is an internal longing for harmony and happiness that lies deeper than ordinary fear or the desire to escape misery or physical destruction.[1]

Czeslaw Milosz was writing of the Eastern Bloc in the early 1950s, but his words seem equally apt for contemporary China. Many outside commentators still assume China's current one-party political system relies on force to stay in power.[2] Yet Milosz's words show how rather than fear, a craving for harmony and happiness can compel individuals to accept the political status quo in societies which, to outsiders, may appear oppressive. Raven and French have identified five bases for social and political control: reward power, coercive power, legitimate power, referent power, and expert power.[3] All of these approaches can be observed in contemporary China. In recent years, the CCP leadership has clearly understood that in order to stay in power it needs to emphasize policies that satisfy the human craving for stability and 'harmony' and be selective about when to display coercive might. It is surely not by chance that the Chinese government currently stresses 'harmonious society' (*hexie shehui*) or that the 2006–8 Olympic slogan targeted at Chinese citizens urged them to 'Participate, contribute and be happy' (*wo canyu, wo fengxian, wo kuaile*).

This chapter concludes the discussions in the book by exploring the question of how, in this globalized world, when liberal democracy is the dominant paradigm in the international system, the CCP government has managed to persuade the Chinese people to continue to accept the one-party state. The CCP appears to have succeeded in 'marketing dictatorship'[4] not only to the older generation, but even to its large population of globalized, urbanized, ICT-savvy youth – the same group who forged colour revolutions in the former Eastern Bloc in the 2000s, and political upheavals in North Africa and the Middle East in 2011. In this concluding chapter of *China's Thought Management* I argue that political stability has been strengthened in recent years, because the Chinese Party-state has increasingly preferred softer means of political and social control over coercive tactics – this is what I call a velvet fist in a velvet glove. As Milosz predicts, utilizing softer means has a better long term success rate for political stability than relying on coercion – though force is always a back-up if softer means fail. Political control and legitimacy are the foundations of state security; and a secure state is a tolerant state. All insecure states – regardless of ideology – will adopt more draconian measures when required.

Twenty-two years after the watershed of 1989, the PRC is a strong, united, economic powerhouse and the CCP government has regained the approval of the majority of its citizens, especially crucial interest groups such as intellectuals and business people. As a result of the influence of the 'collapse thesis'[5] in contemporary studies of Chinese politics, many scholars have focused their research on forms of resistance in Chinese society. Yet as Foucault reminds us, where there is resistance, there must also be control. Studying some of the new forms of control provides a key to defining the political order in China today. The chapter is based on primary and secondary source research in Chinese, secondary sources in English, and extensive interviews with Chinese bureaucrats and scholars while on fieldwork trips to China in 1998, 1999, 2000, 2001, 2002, 2004, 2005–6, 2007, 2009, and 2010.

Mao-era methods of social and political control

> A revolution is not a dinner party, or writing an essay, or painting a picture, or doing embroidery. A revolution is an insurrection, an act of violence by which one class overthrows another.[6]

From 1949 to 1976 the revolution in Chinese society was the ongoing legitimating project of the Party-state.[7] This period was typified by a radical, and frequently violent, transformation of the economic, social, and political structures of Chinese society into a whole new order. The revolution in Chinese society occurred in several stages, with different sections of society targeted for attack and transformation. In its first few years in power, one of the earliest acts of the regime was to take over the leadership of all economic and social units, however big or small. Although nominally there was always a separation between Party and state, in most work units the Party secretary always had more authority than the formal head of any organization.

For Mao and many other CCP leaders, the successful completion of the Chinese Revolution meant more than just seizing control of the infrastructure; it necessitated a revolution in the thinking of everyone in this new society. During the series of mass movements the CCP launched from 1949 to 1976, political undesirables and their descendants were subjected to mass vilification and discrimination. The violence was justified in quotes such as the one above from Mao. As an inevitable outcome of 'class struggle', violence was regarded as a necessary tactic in the goal of creating a more equitable society. Mao's assertion that a 'revolution is not a dinner party' was first made in 1927, and repeatedly cited after that; most notably in *Quotations from Mao Tse-tung*, the infamous Little Red Book of the Cultural Revolution (1966–69). Mob violence ruled throughout the Cultural Revolution years.

From 1949 to 1976 the whole of Chinese society was involved in mass ideological indoctrination which was conducted through political study sessions in every work unit, classroom, and mass organization in the country. The CCP utilized every tool of mass communication available at the time for this indoctrination project and the media, culture, and education systems were tightly controlled. Only when factional struggles within the CCP leadership played out would there be brief periods of free speech. From 1949 to 1979 China was a closed society with any political problems micro-controlled.

In the Mao years (and indeed up until the late 1990s) the work unit (*danwei*) was the foundation of the CCP system of political and social control.[8] Most (but not all) adult urban Chinese citizens belonged to a *danwei*. In 1957 only 3 per cent of urban workers did not belong to either a state or local *danwei*.[9] Rural workers were organized into collectives, which evolved into the 'people's communes' (*renmin gongshe*). Mass organizations such as the All-China Women's Federation were used to link non-workers into the Party-state system. All the essential concerns of most Chinese people's lives – income, housing, health, permission to get married, birth control, education for their children, access to welfare benefits, Party membership, permission to apply for a passport, and so on – were determined by the work unit, the village collective or the neighbourhood committee. Personnel matters and national policies were frequently decided on a highly political basis. The Mao-era Party-state system was the very opposite of Max Weber's 'rational bureaucracy'.[10] Eddie U has described it as a 'counter-bureaucracy', which ultimately sowed the seeds of its own destruction. It is worth noting that in the last ten years Chinese scholars of public administration have now embraced Weber's theories on 'rational bureaucracy' and are making it their own.[11]

Post-Mao era challenges to political and social control

By the end of the Mao era there was a strong awareness within the CCP and within Chinese society of the need for change, but it took some time for the Party leadership to devise a new approach to political and social control that would both maintain their dominance in the political system, at the same time as revitalizing China. The 1980s was a time marked by experimentation and increasing political openness, contrasted with the conservative reaction against such change. Many of the systems of political and social control we now see in place in contemporary China were first proposed in these years, such as the creation of a modern, highly qualified bureaucracy, the radical restructuring of the state-owned enterprise (SOE) sector, and a modernized approach to propaganda and thought work which would match the changes in China's economic sphere.

1989 is significant as the date when inner-Party and intra-societal conflicts regarding the potential paths for China's future development came to a head.

Conservative factions won the power struggle, but in the long run they ended up co-opting many of the policies of their liberal rivals. The crackdown in 1989 only briefly slowed China's economic reform, and from 1992 the pace of economic change was reset to rapid. Political reform also continued, albeit at a considerably slower and even more cautious pace. Nonetheless, the bottom line continued to be the maintenance of the Chinese Communist Party's pre-eminent place in Chinese politics, and this is still the ultimate proviso of any economic and political change.

As noted in earlier chapters, in the years since the crisis of 1989 the CCP rebranded itself as a political 'party in power' and dumped its previous Leninist rhetoric of being a revolutionary party holding power by right of ideology. The CCP's rebranding is highly significant; reflecting an under-standing that the government needs to take a significantly altered approach to governance and social and political control in order to maintain its long term political stability. Since the crisis of 1989 the Chinese Party-state has progressively reinvented itself on more democratic lines (anti-corruption campaigns, lower-level elections, e-government, improved transparency, inner-party democracy, and talk of social justice) while maintaining the political status quo of one-party rule. China has also adopted many of the means of persuasion more commonly seen in Western democratic societies such as spin doctors, political PR, and careful monitoring of public opinion.[12] The inspiration for China's new policies has become increasingly eclectic over the years since 1989; the US, Japan, Mexico, Singapore, France, Germany, Sweden, and North Korea have all been models in different aspects of society, while the Soviet Union under Gorbachev and post-communism in Serbia, Georgia, Ukraine, and Kyrgyzstan have served as anti-models.

Reformers in the mid-1980s critiqued the *danwei* system, saying it under-mined effective production and muddied the relationship between employer and employee.[13] The SOE sector was formerly the bulwark of the *danwei* system. Of all the changes in China's economic and political system since 1979, reforming the SOEs has been the hardest and most fraught task for the government, as it affected so many people and unravelling it would shake the foundations of the CCP's post-1949 system of political and social control. The government delayed major reforms in the SOEs until the mid-1990s, after fifteen years of economic reform policies when there was already a large (and growing) export sector that could soak up some of the jobless. From the mid-1990s large numbers of SOE employees lost their jobs and either found new positions in the non-state sector (*fei gongyouzhi*) – which provided none of the benefits or the constraints of the *danwei* system – or remained unemployed. With the exception of the wealthiest sectors in the Chinese bureaucracy – such as banks, railways, and the taxation department – those who are still employed by the state sector receive considerably less benefits than in the past. In 1979, 79 per cent of the urban workforce worked in the state sector.[14] But by 2010 more than 70 per cent of Chinese workers were employed in the private sector.[15]

There have also been radical reforms in the rural sector since the end of the Mao era, and this has had a significant impact on the need for new forms of political and social control. From the late 1970s on, the rural population was increasingly released from the administrative constraints of the Mao years. First, farmers were allowed to sell off surplus produce under the 'responsibility system'. Then, from 1982 to 1985 the commune system was disbanded, and rural residents were permitted to move to the cities on temporary resident permits to look for work. In the early 2000s adjustments to residency requirements allowed rural residents to settle more permanently in the cities and obtain access to education for their children. In the Mao years close to 75 per cent of the Chinese population lived in rural areas; yet in 2010 only 50 per cent have rural residency.[16] However, this figure does not accurately reveal the true picture of China's massive change in social structure as it incorporates the 211 million migrant workers who live and work in the cities.[17] This means that China has already reached the 60 per cent threshold when a country is considered to be urbanized,[18] and it has done so at a much more rapid rate than any other nation in history. These rural migrants don't fit easily into traditional systems of political and social control. Zhai Zhenkou, a population specialist at Renmin University, calls the floating population a 'third sector' after China's urban and rural sectors. In 2008 the powerful National Development and Reform Commission set up the Floating Population Service and Management Department to better manage this 'third sector'.[19] Some rural communities in suburbs of Beijing are taking matters into their own hands, setting up 'sealed villages' (*fengcun*). These lock in resident migrant workers and keep out undesirables.[20]

The reform of the SOE system and the break-up of rural collectives has led to fragmentation of the work force, causing what propaganda specialists call propaganda 'blind spots'.[21] In a short space of time, especially since the period of radical SOE restructuring in the late 1990s, the Party's previous close connection to most of the adult population has been completely severed. There are now large gaps in Chinese society where the government's previous means of political and social controls do not function. Moreover, large numbers of Party members have been separated from their traditional networks; and since many people experienced job loss or re-assignment, the Party organization structure has had to adjust to the needs of a more mobile population. Greater flexibility in the system for managing Chinese people's internal residency status (*hukou*) has also affected political and social control;[22] large numbers of Chinese people are now on the move, both within China and globally. Globalization and increased contact with the outside world also pose a threat to China's traditional methods of social and political control.[23]

The uneven pace of economic growth after 1979 brought many new challenges for the previous system of social and political control. Whereas the economic policies of the Mao years succeeded in raising basic living standards for many in China (while creating new elites), by the late 1990s the post-Mao economic reform process led to a yawning gap between the 'haves' and 'have nots'. China's social welfare system has been slow to develop. Welfare assistance for urban workers had always been linked to the *danwei*, while agricultural workers were expected to rely on family. A further challenge came from the commercialization and expansion of the public sphere from the mid-1990s on; this brought benefits in terms of reducing the heavy burden of state subsidies, but created disadvantages for traditional Party propaganda work. Unlike some other modern authoritarian societies such as Saudi Arabia, North Korea and Cuba, China embraced the potential of information communication technology (ICT) such as the Internet and mobile phone, while attempting to manage its damaging aspects. ICT helped to open up China's previously closed information borders and Chinese citizens can now easily tune in to the global marketplace of ideas.

Party theorists coined a new phrase to acknowledge the consequences of all these shifts in Chinese society: 'the "work unit member" became a "member of society"' (*danwei ren biancheng shehuiren*).[24] This means Chinese people no longer have their lives ruled by the *danwei* or the collective. Like citizens in other modern industrialized nations, they have become atomized units within society. As a consequence of these changes, Chinese citizens now have more freedom than they ever had in the past. Yet, as Michel Foucault's work has shown us, the paradox of less forceful means of political control being used in modern societies is that even more invasive forms of state power then enter everyday life.[25] Foucault's analysis echoes the views of the US political scientist and propaganda guru Harold Lasswell who as early as 1927 noted that 'if the mass will be free of chains of iron, it must expect chains of silver. If it will not love, honor, and obey, it must not expect to escape seduction.'[26] Lasswell's writings have been extremely influential on a new generation of CCP policy makers tasked with investigating forms of political and social control more suitable for China's modern economy and increasingly open society.[27]

China's chains of silver

> Government by force cannot guarantee social stability.[28]

By the early 2000s, as the quote above demonstrates, the awareness that the CCP government must adjust its means of social and political control was widespread. In 2007, an internal publication by Professor Ding Yuanzhu of the Central Party School articulated the reasons behind the change in approach and some potential policies China might follow for an updated system of 'social management' (*shehui guanli*). Professor Ding's suggestions included: (1) create a public service with national standards of service to the public, in order to improve social justice – an indirect reference to the problems of the Party-state model of bureaucracy; (2) control, but don't ban, NGOs; and (3) encourage more mass participation at the district level in order to build a stronger sense of community.[29] Most of these suggestions have been adopted or were already in place.

The following sections will explore some further examples of the new approaches to political and social control in China, the antidotes to potential challenges to state security. I will focus on four new control/management chains: (1) the localizing of Party power from the workplace to the residential area, which relates to management of the urban subject; (2) the reform of the content of mass persuasion messages to the Chinese public, which relates to the moulding of public opinion; (3) Reform of the means of control/management of the public sphere, which relates to guiding the exchange of ideas and information; and (4) promoting volunteering as a managed device to increase popular participation and a sense of ownership in the Party-state system. Highlighting the fact that these new methods take a lighter approach than that adopted in previous eras it should be noted that Party *apparatchiks* now tend to avoid using the word 'control' (*kongzhi*). The preferred terms to describe the multiple 'chains of silver' are terms such as *guanli*, 'to manage'; *suzao*, 'to mould'; and *yindao/zhidao*, 'to guide'. Moreover, instead of the Party-state's previous policies of micro-controlling any forms of resistance, the government now prefers a strategy of macro-management.[30] Predictably though, the micro-control approach is still followed in crisis situations/ environments, such as in Tibetan areas since 2008; in Xinjiang since 2009; and in March 2011 in Beijing and Shanghai following calls for a 'jasmine revolution'.[31]

Localized governance

Currently 60 per cent of the Chinese population are living in urban areas and 75 per cent of the Chinese urban workforce are employed in the private sector. Residents' associations (*jumin weiyuanhui*) fill in the gap of services (and means to monitor the individual) formerly provided by the *danwei* or the rural collective. Residents' associations administer districts (*shequ*), the smallest unit of the Chinese urban administrative system.[32] The district is the new basic model for urban organization.[33] Each district consists of around 4,000 people. Residents' associations had strong powers in the Mao years, then declined in importance in the 1980s and 1990s. In the 1990s some residents tried to form their own representative groups, which challenged the Party's existing structures.[34] But since the early 2000s, the CCP has clawed back its authority at the local level by giving increased powers, duties, and resources to the residents' associations. China's updated residents' associations have been modelled on certain aspects of local government bodies found in the West, especially in France or Germany.

The functions and activities of the residents' associations have been greatly expanded, but the administrative unit's basic organizational role has not: it is still the bottom rung of the Chinese Party-state. The Party's influence remains strong, albeit more disguised than in the past. According to the Party secretary of one residents' association I interviewed, these changes are designed to bring China's public administration closer in line with 'international practice' (*guoji jiegui*).[35] These days the CCP is anxious to be seen by both the Chinese people and outside observers alike, as democratizing and modernizing China's system of government, to make it more in accordance with 'global norms'.

China is in the process of creating a network of social welfare not connected to the individual *danwei*, and local residents' associations are taking over many of the administrative tasks related to social control formerly assigned to the work unit, the Public Security Bureau, and other administrative agencies.[36] Residents' associations also have a role in many other local welfare issues, in maintaining public security, health and family planning, education and sport activities, protecting the local environment, and promoting government policies to the general populace within their area. All cultural and social activities in a given district must be supervised by the residents' association. It is illegal to organize events without their permission. The residents' associations are supposed to organize cultural activities for the elderly such as fan dancing and arts and crafts.

The residents' associations approve who is entitled to receive social security payments (*di bao*) due to unemployment, illness, or lack of retirement pension.[37] Those who have a computer, keep a dog, possess a motorbike or car – and the residents' associations have the on-the-ground knowledge to check this – are not entitled to receive any social security payments.[38] Designated staff can also assist the unemployed to find work and arrange for them to attend re-skilling classes. They have the authority to order those receiving social security payments in their area to take part in 'voluntary' activities such as collecting monthly facilities fees from residents, helping keep public areas tidy and clean, or forming a 'rent-a-crowd' for mass propaganda performances.[39] The residents' association also supervises the payment of retirement pensions in their area. Previously this was paid directly by the former employer to the employee. The leader of one residents' association explained to me, without any irony, that they had been given this role because they are more familiar with conditions at the local level and are better able to verify that the person receiving the pension 'is still alive'.[40]

The residents' associations are the eyes and ears of the Party-state at the local level. Local 'activists' pass on information to the residents' association about any illegal or suspicious behaviour, such as a woman who is pregnant with her second child, illegal gatherings, and whether there are foreigners living in Chinese residential areas who have not yet registered with the police. In the case of family planning matters, the residents' associations have dedicated staff in charge of passing on information about family planning to local residents. These staff have only an educational role; any breach of family planning regulations is the responsibility of higher authorities. The residents' associations collect information on residents for local government; for example the figures on who in their area doesn't have health insurance, the level of education of residents, their age, and who lives where. This information is also passed on to the police, who provide information to the residents' association such as the names and details of foreigners who are living in their area and legally registered with the police. In July 2007 the residents' associations in Beijing's Dongzhimen district were the first to be given the task of registering all non-Beijing residents who came to live in their area.[41] This experimental policy, which has since been more widely adopted, enabled the floating population in the district to better access local services; but it also made it easier to manage and monitor them. The residents' associations in these areas enter migrants' details on a national database accessible to the police. This change in approach is related to reforms in the household registration policy; and allows the police to focus on criminal matters. It is similar to the approach utilized to keep track of foreigners' movements in China since 2002. Most foreigners are probably unaware that when they register in a Chinese hotel and many other forms of accommodation open to foreigners such as foreign students' dorms and apartments, their details are also being registered on the police national database of foreigners in China.

In some more longstanding residents' associations personnel are mostly, but not all, retired residents of the area. But in newer areas the employees are younger, and they are not necessarily residents there. All are Party members. The residents' associations are led by a Party secretary who is also the district manager. The Party branches in residents' associations take responsibility for all local Party members who do not have a Party branch at their work unit or are retired or unemployed. A key role of the district manager/Party secretaries is pastoral care; David Bray calls this 'bringing the Party back to the people'.[42]

Party membership is increasingly going local, rather than being enterprise-based as in the past. This is because some private employers don't like the Party's interference in their operations, employees feel awkward about their status, and the former central role of the Party in urban enterprises doesn't match the new market economy. Moreover, as a result of the rapid changes in the Chinese workplace in the last fifteen years, many long-standing Party members have lost touch with the Party organization. When SOE's closed down, their Party organization closed with them. The Party's role in the politically sensitive industrial and technical sectors was particularly affected by these changes. This led to a situation of '*shuang zhao*', or 'both sides searching', meaning that Party members were trying to find a Party organi-zation to belong to and the Party organization was trying to re-organize former Party members. The Chinese media are forbidden from mentioning this phenomenon and may not publish statistics on exactly how many Party members have been lost, as Party organization work is meant to be 'all action and no talk' (*zhi zuo bu shuo*).[43]

A new terminology has been coined to reflect the transitional stage of CCP organization work: Party members who work for foreign companies are commonly known as '*yinxing dongyuan*' (hidden Party members) and '*dixia dongyuan*' (underground Party members); unemployed graduates are 'pocket' Party members (*koudai dongyuan*); while poor Party members are '*kunnan dangyuan*' (Party members with 'difficulties'). However the Chinese media are also forbidden to use such terms and must use euphemisms to refer to these groups.[44] As Ji Fengyuan has discussed in her essay earlier in this volume, the eighteen-month long 'Party Progressiveness Movement' (*Xianjinxing jiaoyu huodong*) from 2004 to 2006 was aimed at strengthening Party organization at the local level. Some local Party branches spent large sums on organizing 'Party membership construction' (*jiandangyuan*) activities such as all-expenses-paid tours and concerts to motivate 'lost' Party members to return to the fold. Currently there are proposals under discussion that in future *all* Party membership will be linked to one's residency, not one's work unit. This would bring China in line with political party membership in other modern industrial societies.[45]

Party meetings are meant to be held monthly. Oftentimes the meetings are just social gatherings, such as outings to scenic attractions. Just like members of political parties in many other modern industrialized countries, some Party members hardly ever attend a meeting. For adults, political study in China today mostly involves 'self-study'. This is all part of the overall watering down of political education that has gone on since 1989. It is as if the government was somehow engaging in a step-by-step reverse of the process of the radical transformation of Chinese society of the Mao and immediate post-Mao years. The selective rendering of modern Chinese history plays an important role in this, creating a collective amnesia about the events of the recent past and their impact on life in contemporary China. However, unlike the previous eras, each new stage of this reverse transformation is being introduced with as little disruption to social and political stability as possible.

Persuasion not indoctrination

As shown throughout this book and as party propaganda theorists constantly point out, despite the dramatic changes in Chinese society over the last thirty years, propaganda and thought work continues to be an essential tool of CCP rule. Although in the 1980s some argued that the Chinese government should put its emphasis on economic development alone (thereby implicitly rejecting the role of political activities), after 1989 Deng Xiaoping set the new bottom line: that the CCP should manage China's economic reform process with the help of assiduous 'thought work'.[46] Yet political indoctrination has become considerably less onerous than in the past. In a reaction against the excesses of the Mao years, there is a strong popular distaste in China for political campaigns and mass indoctrination. Reflecting this there has been a refinement in understanding of what constitutes 'thought work'. In addition to political education, thought work now incorporates civics education (*gongmin jiaoyu*) and patriotic education (*aiguozhuyi jiaoyu*), as well as education on concepts related to health, psychology, morals, and the environment.[47] This adjustment in approach builds on the traditional division of CCP propaganda activities into four types: political, economic, cultural, and social propaganda.

Nowadays only youth in the education system, Party members, and the military receive direct political instruction. Even to such groups, the central theme revolves around loyalty toward the Chinese Party-state.[48] Not unlike political parties in other modern industrial societies, from time to time the CCP updates its vision for leading Chinese society. In the last ten years the party has introduced policies which show that it is: attempting to become more representative of the whole of society (the theory of the Three Represents, introduced in 2000); becoming more democratic (political civilization, introduced in 2002); developing a social welfare system and basic standard of living for all (moderate prosperity or *xiaokang shehui*, introduced in 2002, and harmonious society, introduced in 2007); and developing a knowledge economy in China (scientific development, introduced in 2007). As noted, *only* youth, Party members and the military are required to have close familiarity with these policies. As mentioned in the previous chapters, the rest of Chinese society receives guidance in various aspects of what the CCP refers to by the umbrella term 'spiritual civilization'.[49] Rather than revolution and radical social transformation, the goal of China's propaganda work is now – understandably – social unity and cohesion. It is well understood that social stability equals political stability.

As discussed in previous chapters, the stated goal of the 'construction of spiritual civilization' is to attempt to maintain CCP influence over the socialization of Chinese people.[50] Any problems within this environment are dealt with by other bureaux.[51] Party propaganda departments and the spiritual civilization offices are separate, but very closely linked. Spiritual civilization offices engage in mass work activities, their tasks have more abstract goals and their officers have much weaker powers. Following the crackdown on Falungong in 1999 there was a tightening up of control over social groupings in China. In theory, any social group now requires permission from the district spiritual civilization office in order to organize an event. However the prevalence of the house church movement in China, which is technically illegal according to China's laws on religion, indicates that theory does not always meet practice at the local level. Party theorists refer to spiritual civilization as a soft form of social control that is backed up by the legal system.[52]

As discussed in Chapter 2 of this volume, on top of the deliberately non-political messages of 'spiritual civilization', one of the most dominant themes of modern thought work is economic development. China's modern economic propaganda has both political and economic goals. It must provide 'spiritual impetus, intellectual support and positive public opinion on economic development', as well as introducing 'successful methods and experiences for accelerating economic development'.[53] Such an approach is necessary in order to guide public opinion as China negotiates the difficult waters of a shift from a centrally planned economy to a mercantilist one – at the same time as retaining its communist government. Remarkably, these efforts have been extremely successful and there is widespread public support for China's current economic model.

An additional strong theme in the CCP's contemporary thought work promotes patriotism and loyalty to China. Here patriotism means supporting the political status quo, the Party-state system and the leadership of the CCP over Chinese society. This approach has also been extremely successful both within China and as a message to the Chinese diaspora, as shown when hundreds of thousands of Overseas Chinese participated in pro-China demonstrations during the 2008 Beijing torch relay around the world. Patriotic propaganda is usually positive propaganda (*zhengmian xuanchuan*). Party propaganda specialists frame any activity that could engender pride in the might of the Chinese state as patriotic. Hence, in addition to their normal duties, Chinese polar scientists and astronauts are required to spend large amounts of their time giving talks to youth and fronting up to the media, and major events such as the 2008 Beijing Olympics and the 2010 Shanghai Expo are promoted as heavily as any political campaign in the Mao years. In times of crisis, patriotic propaganda will focus on negative aspects, the aim being to unite the population against a common enemy such as US hegemony and imperialism, Taiwan independence, or Tibetan and Uighur separatism. These tropes have also been extremely successful in building loyalty to, or at the very least acceptance of, the current political status quo in China.

Television is now the main organ for Party thought work directed at the masses, which means it is the most heavily censored tool of mass communication in China. Most Chinese people have access to a TV; as part of a national project even nomads have been given TVs (with portable satellite dishes and solar power generators) and migrants have special facilities available to them in many cities. China's primetime TV dramas and documentaries always feature an underlying educational message, intertwined with the usual mix of sexual titillation, violence, and unfulfilled romance which is the stuff of popular TV drama series around the world. CCP propaganda specialists have long understood that political messages are best presented to the masses through entertainment. In the Yan'an era the CCP incorporated the *yang'ge* dances of the local people; nowadays they invite popular culture figures to participate in television propaganda so that more people will be attracted to watch.[54] Newspapers still have an important role in moulding public opinion, especially among China's intellectuals and the older generation. As they cater to a more educated audience, the print media tend to have more leeway in covering sensitive stories.

The Internet is now a key organ of persuasion, particularly for Chinese youth. According to the China Internet Network Information Centre, in 2009 61.5 per cent of the country's 384 million Internet users were under the age of 29. Just like advertising campaigns, the effectiveness of Party propaganda messages is now measured in terms of website hits. In 2007 an internal bulletin of the Central Propaganda Department claimed that there had been 210,000 hits on the CCTV site after the new Olympic slogans such as 'Participate, contribute and be happy' were released, and that there were 1,469 messages left on the bulletin boards.[55]

Traditionally the CCP referred to the media as the 'tongue and throat' of the Party. Nowadays it is called the 'tongue and throat' of the people and the government. This change in terminology is a reference to the watchdog-on-a-leash role of some Chinese journalists. The influence of this role has waxed and waned in the last fifteen years, depending on the political climate. Formerly CCTV's primetime show, *Focuspoint* was renowned for its exposés, but official interference has led to it becoming a shadow of its former ferocious self. These days it only manages a few yaps of critique alternating with programmes praising some aspect of government policy. This is a deliberate strategy, in order to evade official censure. *Focuspoint* journalists and editors are too mindful of the consequences to do otherwise.[56] Instead, most watchdog journalism appears in the print media. But even here, journalists are careful to write about individual issues, not structural problems. Investigative reports are regarded as a useful barometer – and release of tension – for politically sensitive issues which stir up public opinion.[57] According to Party *diktat*: 'The media's watchdog role should be of benefit to the party and government's work it should help to solve issues and it should help to protect social stability ... All stories on sensitive matters must be approved and censored before publication.'[58] Nonetheless, despite all the limits, except on a few key issues, China currently has a freer media environment than at any other time since 1949. This more tolerant attitude to a greater diversity of views in the public sphere has done much to create acceptance of the continuation of CCP rule.

Updating the means to manage the public sphere

In the last fifteen years there has been a radical transformation in the approach to managing the Chinese media and the public sphere. This reflects the new 'macro-management' approach to information control. According to Harold Lasswell, the mass media have an essential role in political and social control in modern industrialized societies.[59] The media are the means for moulding public opinion, an important tool for governments to garner the imprimatur of public support for their rule. The media also comprise the route by which other alternative perspectives may enter the public sphere, hence the crucial role of censorship in any mass persuasion endeavour.[60]

In China the most central organization with a censorship role is the CCP's Central Propaganda Department and its local equivalents. These bodies 'lead' (*lingdao*) the General Administration of Press and Publishing; the State Administration of Radio, Film, and Television; the Ministry of Culture; State Administration of Industry and Commerce. They also 'guide' (*zhidao*) the Public Security Bureau, and the Ministry of State Security, on ongoing censorship concerns. On top of this all other state and Party organizations also have a censorship role if a sensitive issue touching on their activities becomes public knowledge. The Central Propaganda Department is not just a gate-keeper, it is also an upholder of standards, similar to broadcasting standards authorities and press councils in Western democratic societies. So, in addition to politically sensitive items, the Central Propaganda Department also cracks down on fake advertising, paid-for news stories, and restricts coverage of suicide from the point of view of avoiding copycat attempts.[61]

There are also a multitude of smaller groups and individuals with censorship – or what the CCP prefers to call 'guiding' – roles in the public sphere. In 1994 a system of readers' groups was set up to monitor the national- and provincial-level print media. Each local group produces a bulletin as a guide for editors.[62] The advent of the Internet has greatly increased the challenges of managing the Chinese public sphere, but technological controls and a multitude of human censors make it possible for the Chinese government to manage the worst of online content while encouraging the advantages the knowledge economy can bring. Since the late 1990s many of the most popular web discussion groups in China such as Strong Country Forum on the *People's Daily* website or university-based student forums have had dedicated staff to observe web postings as they come in, delete inappropriate ones, and add constructive comments when necessary. From the early 2000s local governments began to set up their own mini-teams of online censors to monitor debates regarding local and national issues. Chinese netizens sarcastically refer to these individuals as the '50-cent Party' for the amount of money they are alleged to receive for each pro-government posting they contribute.[63] Many websites display a logo from the Public Security Bureau reminding users that their online activity is being observed. Both approaches enhance self-censorship as the authorities *want* netizens to be aware they are being watched and moderate their behaviour accordingly.

One of the most important means by which information is controlled in China is through naming (*tifa*) and framing (*kuangjia*) what can and cannot be said in the public arena. The Central Propaganda Department and its local equivalents regularly issue detailed materials that set the correct wording and 'frames' for public discourse in China, and, in some cases such as on how to refer to Taiwan, even internationally. These guidelines are given out orally at regular update meetings which the central and provincial level propaganda departments hold with senior media personnel and other leaders in the propaganda sector. They are also issued in written form via classified publications, faxes, and emails. Not all media guidance is political; a lot of it is in the form of public service messages such as conserving resources and protecting electrical supplies.[64] The CCP desires to control the public sphere and prevent alternative voices from entering, but not necessarily to fill it with political messages.

In a major shift from past practice, since the debacle of the 2002–3 Severe Acute Respiratory Syndrome (SARS) outbreak the CCP's information management strategy in crisis situations now includes releasing selective negative news. China's modern propaganda specialists argue that releasing negative (*fumian*) information during crisis situations creates popular confidence in the government's ability to manage the situation.[65] SARS spread worldwide as a direct result of the CCP propaganda gag on mentioning the new disease (and any other politically sensitive matters) during the Jiang–Hu leadership transition, and there were massive domestic and international consequences. As part of this new strategy, government agencies have been increasingly privileging the Chinese media in covering breaking news stories, allowing them to scoop the foreign press and get China's 'frames' out first.

The importance of this new policy was demonstrated in September 2008 when the Chinese media 'broke' the story of poisoned infant formula immediately after the New Zealand government contacted relevant authorities in China to inform them of what they already knew, but had been suppressing for political reasons.[66] As discussed in Chapters 1 and 2, due to restrictions on reporting food safety stories in the lead up to the 2008 Beijing Olympics, Chinese journalists had been banned from reporting on this shocking story. However, once the information was forced out in the open by a foreign government, the Chinese media were sent into overdrive to manage Chinese and foreign opinion on the subject, scapegoating a handful of individuals and, after a very brief period of factual reporting, keeping information from the 300,000-plus victims away from the public eye. The father of one of the infants with kidney damage, Zhao Lianhai, refused to be silenced and set up a website for the families of victims. In 2010 he was sentenced to prison for 'disturbing social order'. The wording of his 'crime' shows how the Party perceives individuals speaking up against social and political injustice as a direct threat to social and political control.

The *nomenklatura* system (in Chinese *zuzhi gongzuo*) has an essential part to play in maintaining the CCP's influence over the public sphere. *Nomenklatura* are senior management positions within state and society which are Party-appointed. The *nomenklatura* are gatekeepers, they control the flow of information and establish the norms within their own work unit, as well as making personnel decisions about lower level staff. The powers and responsibilities of the *nomenklatura* have actually increased as a result of economic restructuring. Senior managers of China's new media conglomerates are in charge of controlling the content of their subsidiary newspapers, magazines, radios or TV stations and must take responsibility if anything goes wrong. All editors, journalists, and other employees such as part-timers or interns must be strictly checked for their 'political thought quality', 'professional news quality', and 'professional morals quality'. Only the politically reliable can be employed, and all media employees must pass an exam in order to enter the profession.[67] Unlike the Mao era there is no attempt at the 'thought reform' of media personnel who cross the line. Nowadays, if you break the rules you are out and banned from working in the media ever again; some journalists have even been imprisoned.

Economic measures are an important means for managing the public sphere. The central and provincial Party propaganda departments have the power to allocate or take away lucrative contracts or permission to engage in business with suitably obedient state and commercial organizations within the public sphere. This covers everything from advertising agencies to Internet companies and popular festivals. Since 1994 profit-making enterprises within the propaganda system have been measured for their 'social efficiency' (whether or not they follow the Party line) and 'economic efficiency' (whether or not they make a profit or are regarded as superfluous). Economic reasons have frequently been used as a pretext to close down organizations which push the censorship boundaries too far.

'Rule by law' (not rule *of* law) is also a further important new means to control China's public sphere. In the last twenty years a vast new body of laws has been created which affect the Chinese media, backed up by a complicated net of local and national regulations. Laws unrelated to media matters are also frequently used as a means to control journalists who push the boundaries of public debate. From the government's perspective, Chinese law is a tool of governance aimed at strengthening state power. It is not meant as a balance to state power. The Soviet Union and other Eastern Bloc countries also took this approach to law.[68] Stanley Lubman has called the Chinese legal system a 'bird in a cage', which is still very much constrained by the Party-state system.[69]

Constructing a sense of social belonging

While Harold Lasswell was exploring the ways in which mass persuasion was useful in binding together modern industrial societies, in the same decade industrial psychologist George Elton Mayo explored ways to bind the modern workplace. Mayo argued that monetary incentives and good working conditions are less important for the individual worker than the need to belong to a group, hence senior management must be aware of workers' social needs and cater to them, rather than suppressing them.[70] Mayo's theories on industrial psychology have become extremely influential on contemporary approaches to public administration and management in China. Some Chinese scholars are applying Mayo's theories on the worker in industrialized societies to the Party-state's management of individuals within modern day Chinese society.[71] Critics of Mayo accuse him of being anti-democratic;[72] perhaps this is why his ideas appeal in China today. Mayo is not the only influence on this approach; scholars are also turning to research on civics education in the US and Singapore, and other approaches to community building.

Mayo emphasizes the importance of a sense of community and belonging. Feeling that you belong in a society comes from participation, because when you participate in something, you make it your own. 'Participation' was one of the central slogans of China's Beijing Olympics propaganda directed at the Chinese population. As discussed in the first chapter of this book, there were 1.47 million volunteers (*zhiyuanzhe*) in the Beijing Olympics. Only 400,000 of them were based in Beijing. The volunteers were primarily selected from university students, a key target group of the CCP's patriotic education.[73]

Many other Chinese citizens were also given many opportunities to not just be spectators, but actually 'participate' in the 2008 Olympics through classes in 'civilized behaviour' and other activities. In the Mao years activism and volunteering formed an essential role in the construction of New China, helping to build new social values and new infrastructure in a remarkably short space of time. Since 2005, the CCP has been advocating and overseeing a number of large-scale volunteering projects. This is in response to the ever-increasing rise in the numbers of non-governmental organizations (NGOs) in China and the government's awareness that such groups could become agents for political change, as they have been in other authoritarian societies.

Modern participatory activities in China include online forums, public opinion hotlines, and service activities such as working with the disabled or elderly or otherwise disadvantaged groups. The Party is still trying to organize the masses, but using different methods and organizations from previous eras. Party members, especially those who are retired, fit and able, are all expected to be involved in some form of voluntary work. These can range from helping local disabled people, to participating in 'rent-a-crowd' activities when foreign dignitaries visit. Youth are particularly encouraged to be involved in volun-tary work such as taking time out from university studies to teach in China's remote rural areas or acting as translators and guides during China-based international sporting events such as the 2010 Asian Games in Guangdong. Government-sponsored volunteering efforts have to compete with a host of legally registered and non-registered NGOs currently operating in China, many of them with an international support base. Volunteer groups (non-governmental and government-directed) are considered to be mass organiza-tions (*qunzhong quanti*), which means they are considered to be part of the Party propaganda system. The CCP is working on building up a managed civil society in China,[74] one which has a collective sense of ownership for maintaining the current social and political order.

Conclusion

> There are currently over 20,000 Chinese students studying in the US and other Western countries, almost all of them the children of the Chinese elite. It is hard to believe that when they return home to run the country they will be content for China to be the only country in Asia unaffected by the larger democratizing trend.[75]

In 1989, in his highly influential article 'The End of History', US scholar Francis Fukuyama famously predicted that China's overseas students would soon return to democratize China. Fukuyama also stated that 'China can no longer act as a beacon to illiberal forces around the world'.[76] Fukuyama was wrong on both counts. Twenty-two years after Fukuyama's predictions, the CCP still maintains a firm hand on Chinese politics and as the worldwide pro-China demonstrations of China's overseas students in April and May 2008 vividly illustrated, the regime has regained a high level approval rating from the majority of its citizens, both within China, as well as without. The lack of popular response to public calls for a 'jasmine revolution' in March 2011 further underline that the popular consensus supports, or at the very least accepts, the political status quo in China. China in 2011 is a very different society to the one which Fukuyama so confidently predicted was doomed. The collapse thesis has dominated scholarship and journalism outside China throughout the 1990s and into the 2000s, but within China perceptions of the regime's survival tend to be much more optimistic and confident.[77]

Beginning in 1978, but rapidly accelerating since the turning point of 1989, China has undergone major economic and political change. Remarkably, while many of the economic and political policies of the Mao era have been jettisoned, the core political status quo has been retained. Coercive means for controlling the population have not been discarded, but as in most modern industrialized societies, these are now relegated to a more secondary role and only affect a minority of the population.

The current CCP leadership clearly understands that in order to stay in power it needs to focus on policies which satisfy the human craving for stability. In an already risk-averse society, which knows all to well the trauma of revolution and other violent forms of social upheaval, these strategies are proving to be an effective means to maintain social and political control. The violent images of the 1989 crackdown persist in the Western world as the symbol of the CCP's rule over China. However, the reality is that such public and large scale displays of force by the regime are rare indeed, and a sign of the failure of gentler interventions. The preferred tactic in the current era is putting in place policies which avoid the eruption of conflict, and the Hu-era stress on 'harmony' is a reflection of this.

China's new order tends to be less violent; hence following Foucault's 'physics of power', it engenders less resistance. Chinese society is more fragmented than in the past, but the new methods of social and political control draw closely on methods utilized in other modern industrialized societies which are similarly fragmented and individualistic and yet politically stable. Though there is mainstream acceptance of the current political regime, there is also inevitably some resistance, both attacking the system as a whole, as well as particular aspects. In the words of Michel Foucault, 'there are no relations of power without resistance'.[78] Indeed power actually feeds on resistance as the justification for its existence. However as Foucault accurately predicts, in modern industrialized societies this resistance is marginal and marginalized. Despite the international reputations of leading Chinese dissidents such as Liu Xiaobo, Wang Dan, Wei Jingsheng, and Ai Weiwei, they do not have a wide following in China and the public reaction to their activities is indifference. When Liu Xiaobo won the Nobel Peace Prize in November 2010 a Wuhan taxi driver incredulously told me, 'A Chinese criminal has won a Nobel Peace Prize!' Similarly, the public reaction (except perhaps amongst some in the tiny Tibetan and Uighur communities) to the government's violent crackdown on ethnic violence in Tibetan areas in 2008 and in Xinjiang in 2009 was one of strong support. Rather than feeling intimated by the heavy police presence in Tibetan areas and Xinjiang, many residents – both Han and non-Han – told me it actually made them feel safer, and they were universally critical of the local authorities for not acting sooner to control the ethnic violence.[79] As the words of Czeslaw Miloscz accurately predict, the average Chinese citizen – whether Han or non-Han – craves stability, harmony, and happiness. In this they are no different to individuals in other modern industrialized societies around the world.

Notes

1 Czeslaw Milosz, *The Captive Mind*, translated by Jane Zielonko (London: Penguin, 2001), p. 6.
2 David Shambaugh has summarized Western thinking on China's political future in *China's Communist Party: Atrophy and Adaptation* (Washington, DC: Woodrow Wilson Press, 2008), pp. 23–40.
3 Bertram H. Raven and John P. French, Jr, 'Legitimate Power, Coercive Power, and Observability in Social Influence', *Sociometry*, vol. 21, no. 2 (June 1958), pp. 83–97.
4 Anne-Marie Brady, *Marketing Dictatorship: Propaganda and Thought Work in Contemporary China* (Lanham, MD: Rowman and Littlefield, 2008).
5 I have borrowed this term from Han S. Park's analysis of propaganda and thought work in North Korea, see Han S. Park, *North Korea: The Politics of Unconventional Wisdom* (Boulder, CO and London: Lynne Rienner Publishers, 2002), p. 178.
6 Mao Zedong, 'Report on an Investigation of the Peasant Movement in Hunan' (March 1927), *Selected Works of Mao Tse-tung, Volume I* (Peking: Foreign Languages Press, 1965), p. 28, cited in *Quotations from Chairman Mao Tse-tung* (Peking: Foreign Languages Press, 1966), pp. 11–12.
7 Lowell Dittmer, *China's Continuous Revolution: The Post-Revolution Epoch, 1949–81* (Berkeley: University of California Press, 1987).
8 See David Bray, *Social Space and Governance in Urban China: the Danwei System from Origins to Reform* (Stanford, CA: Stanford University Press, 2005); Lu Xiaobo and Elizabeth Perry, eds, *Danwei: The Changing Chinese Workplace in Historical Comparitive Perspectives* (Armonk, NY: M. E. Sharpe, 1997); Victor Shaw, *Social Control in China: A Study of Chinese Work Units* (Westport, CT: Greenwood Press, 1996); Eddie U, *Disorganising China: Counter-Bureaucracy and the Decline of Socialism* (Stanford, CA: Stanford University Press, 2007).
9 Bray, *Social Space and Governance in Urban China*, p. 144.
10 Max Weber, *Economy and Society: An Outline of Interpretative Sociology*, edited by Guenther Roth and Claus Wittch (Berkeley: University of California Press, 1978), pp. 987–88, cited in U, *Disorganising China*, p. 11.
11 Chinese scholars have written scores of papers on this theme in recent years; the following are just a selection: Liu Zhenglan and Shi Zhifeng, 'Dui Weibo lixing guanliaozhi de zai shenshi' (Reassessing Weber's Theory of Rational Bureaucracy), *Wuhan ligong daxue xuebao* (Shehuikexue), vol. 19, no. 2 (April 2006), pp. 172–76; Liu Zhiping, 'Guanliaozhi lixing yu Zhongguo xingzheng xiandaihua' (The Rational Bureaucracy and China's Administrative Reform), Fujian guanbo dianshi daxue xuebao, no. 6 (2007), pp. 4–10; Zhang Dingzhun, Huang Guoping, 'Xifang lixing guanliaozhi yu wo guo gonggong xingzheng de fazhan quxiang'

(Rational Bureaucratic System in the West and the Development of Public Administration in China), *Shenzhen Daxue xuebao* (Renwen shehuikexue ban), vol. 22, no. 2 (2005), pp. 47–51.

12   See Anne-Marie Brady, *Marketing Dictatorship*. For more on the relationship between mass persuasion and political control in Western democratic societies see Kevin Robins, Frank Webster, and Michael Pickering, 'Propaganda, Information and Social Control', in *Propaganda, Persuasion and Polemic*, ed. Jeremy Hawthorn (London: Edward Arnold, 1987), p. 7.

13   Bray, *Social Space and Governance in Urban China*, p. 120.

14   Lora Sabin, 'New Bosses in the Workers State: The Growth in the Non-State Sector Employment in China', *China Quarterly*, vol. 140 (1994), pp. 944–70.

15   'China Vows Equal Treatment for Private Sector Talents', *China Daily*, 9 June 2010, www.chinadaily.com.cn/china/2010-06/09/content_9953634.htm

16   'Shi-er-wu qi mo chengzhenhua lu jiang chao 50% chengxiang renkou geju jubian caijing' (China's Urbanization to Reach 50 per cent in the Latter Half of the 15th Five Year Plan) *East Money*, July 3, 2010, http://finance.eastmoney.com/news/1350,2010070381699116.html

17   'Migrant Workers in China Will Hit 350 mln by 2050', *People's Daily*, 28 June 2010, http://english.peopledaily.com.cn/90001/90776/90882/7042480.html

18   Li Qiang, 'Zhongguo yuji dao 2010 nian chengxiang renkou jiangge zhan yiban' (China's 2010 Urban Population predicted to reach 50%), 12 December 2006, *CCW Research*, www.ccwresearch.com.cn/store/article_content.asp?articleId=15774& Columnid = 139&139& view = #

19   See www.npfpc.gov.cn/en/about/detail.aspx?articleid=090427111022687682.

20   'Beijing "fengcun" guanli zhen xiang' (The True Face of Sealed Villages in Beijing), *Caixin*, 30 April 2010, http://policy.caing.com/2010-04-30/100140248.html

21   Quanguo xuanchuan ganbu peixun cankao ziliao, ed., *Xuanchuan ganbu peixun cankao ziliao* (Propaganda Cadre Training Reference Materials) (hereafter XCGBPX), 4 vols (no publisher or place of publication identified, 1999), vol. 1, p. 133.

22   Fei-ling Wang, 'Reformed Migration Control and New Targeted People: China's Hukou System in the 2000s', *China Quarterly*, vol. 177 (2004), pp. 115–132.

23   Ding Yuanzhu, 'Dang qian wo guo shehui guanli mianlin de zhuyao wenti ji zhengce xuanze' (Contemporary Policy Choices for the Main Challenges Facing China's Social Management) in *Shiliu Da yilai dang he guojia fazhan daju zhi guan zhongyao de ruogan wenti, Xia ce* (An Overview of Party and State Development and Important Issues Since the 16th Party Congress, volume 2), Zhongguo guanli kexue yanjiuyuan, September 2007 (neibu yantao yong, internal reference), p. 593.

24   I first heard this phrase in an interview with a Party propaganda specialist, December 2007. Bray also notes this phrase in his research, Bray, *Social Space and Governance in Urban China*, p. 157, citing Zhu Huaxin, 'From a "Person of the Work Unit" to a "Social Person": Pyschological Evolution Under the Impact of Reform', *Renmin Ribao*, 14 December 1993, p. 11.

25   See Michel Foucault, *Discipline and Punish: The Birth of the Prison* (New York: Vintage Books, 1979).

26   Harold Lasswell, *Propaganda Technique in the World War* (London: Kegan Paul, Trench, Trubner, 1927), p. 222.

27   See Brady, *Marketing Dictatorship*.

28   *Shanxi fazhan daobao* (Shanxi Development Guide), 14 September, cited in *Shisan nian lai yingxiang Zhongyang gaoceng jingji juece de lundian huiji* (Collected Debates Influencing the Central Authorities' High Level Economic Decisions in the Last Thirteen Years), ed. Shisan nian lai yingxiang Zhongyang gaoceng jingji juece de lundian huiji bianji zu (Beijing: n.p., 2003), p. 23.

29 Ding, 'Dang qian wo guo shehui guanli mianlin de zhuyao wenti ji zhengce xuanze', p. 594.

30 Xuexi chubanshe, ed., *Quan guo xuanchuan sixiang gongzuo huiyi wenjian hui bian* (Collected Articles from the National Conference on Propaganda and Thought Work) (Beijing: Xuexi chubanshe, 1994), pp. 358–61.

31 In March 2008 a series of peaceful protests developed into violent ethnic conflict in Tibetan areas in China, while in early July 2009 a similar situation occurred in Urumqi, capital of Xinjiang Province. When I visited a Tibetan prefecture in Yunnan Province and the Tibetan Autonomous Region in September 2010 and Xinjiang Autonomous Region in October 2010, both locations had heavy concentrations of armed police in riot gear and People's Armed Police, also in riot gear, patrolled the streets. The political atmosphere was extremely tense. It was a completely different atmosphere from the rest of China, where the police presence is extremely muted.

32 This section draws on my own fieldwork and the writings of David Bray, *Social Space and Governance in Urban China*; David Bray, 'Building "Community": New Strategies of Governance in Urban China', *Economy and Society*, vol. 35, no. 4 (2006), pp. 530–549; Thomas Heberer, 'Institutional Change and Legitimacy Via Urban Elections? People's Awareness of Elections and Participation in Urban Neighbourhoods', in *Regime Legitimacy in Contemporary China: Institutional Change and Stability*, edited by Thomas Heberer and Gunter Schubert (London: Routledge, 2008), pp.79–106; Zhang Jing, 'Neighbourhood Level Governance: The Growing Social Foundation of a Public Sphere', in Jude Howell, ed., *Governance in China* (Lanham, MD: Rowman and Littlefield, 2004), pp. 121–42.

33 Bray, *Social Space and Governance in Urban China*, p. 182.

34 See Zhang Jing, 'Neighbourhood Level Governance: The Growing Social Foundation of a Public Sphere', in Jude Howell, ed., *Governance in China*.

35 Interview with Party secretary of a Beijing resident's association, September 2007.

36 Some individuals may work in still-powerful work units such as the armed forces, railways, and banks. However, even in these units the range of social services provided to employees has declined markedly and employees are also no longer so dependent on their work unit for resolving multiple matters, as in the past.

37 Only those people who had a long term employment contract with a *danwei* receive a pension in China. Many people who only had intermittent and short term contract work do not receive pensions; women are most likely to be in this situation. Peasants are also not entitled to pensions. Workers whose *danwei* went bankrupt do not receive pensions.

38 Interview with unemployed worker, Beijing, September 2007.

39 Interview with unemployed worker, Wuhan, November 2007.

40 Interview with residents' association director, Beijing, September 2007.

41 'Dongzhimen wailai renkou guanli huan "Dong jia"' (Controls on Dongzhimen's Non-Resident Population Returns to 'Dong Families'), *Beijing Wanbao* (Beijing Evening News), 29 August 2007, p. 4.

42 Bray, *Social Space and Governance in Urban China*, p. 190.

43 'Zai xianjingxing jiaoyu huodong xuanchuan zhong ying zhuyi bawo de jige wenti', Neibu tongxin (hereafter NBTX), 17/2005, p. 5.

44 'Zai xianjingxing jiaoyu huodong xuanchuan zhong ying zhuyi bawo de jige wenti', NBTX, 17/2005, p. 5.

45 Interview with Party policy analyst, December 2007.

46 Deng, X. P. (1989) 'Address to Officers at the Rank of General and Above in Command of the Troops Enforcing Martial Law in Beijing', *Deng Xiaoping wenxuan* (Deng Xiaoping, selected works), vol. 3, accessible at http://english.peopledaily.com.cn/dengxp/

47   Interview with thought work policy adviser, December 2007.

48   Ding, Guangen, 'Guanyu xuanchuan sixiang gongzuo de jiben silu' (The essentials of propaganda and thought work), in Zhonggong Zhongyang xuanchuanbu zhengce fagui yanjiushi, ed., *Shisi dai yilai xuanchuan sixiang gongzuo de lilun yu shixian* (Theory and Practice in Propaganda and Thought Work since the 14th Party Congress) (Beijing: Xuexi chubanshe, 1997), pp. 62–97.

49   The term 'socialist spiritual civilization' was first used in 1979 by Marshal Ye Jianying, a Party conservative. It was used as a criticism of the Deng government's perceived emphasis on 'material construction', i.e. economic development. In response, in 1981 Deng proposed the 'Five Stresses and Four Beautifies'. These are: stress culture, manners, hygiene, order, and morality; and beautify soul, language, behaviour, and environment. These nine categories still consist of the agenda for promoting 'socialist spiritual civilization' in China, Cheng Hsiao-shih, *Party-Military Relations in the PRC and Taiwan* (Boulder, CO: Westview, 1990), p. 117; see also Ding Xueliang, *The Decline of Communism in China: Legitimacy Crisis, 1977–89* (Cambridge, MA: Cambridge University Press, 1994), p. 123; Stuart R. Schramm, 'Ideology and Policy in China since the Third Plenum, 1978–84', Contemporary China Institute Working Paper no. 6, School of Oriental and African Studies, SOAS, University of London, 1984, pp. 30–33.

50   Chen Junhong, ed., *Jiaqiang he gaijin sixiang zhengzhi gongzuo xuexi duben* (A Reader on Strengthening and Reforming Political Thought Work) (hereafter JQGJSXZZGZ) (Beijing: Zhonggong zhongyang dangxiao chubanshe, 1999), p. 149.

51   Resident's association propaganda cadre, September 2007.

52   JQGJSXZZGZ, p. 152.

53   Neibu tongxin (hereafter NBTX), 2005/4, p. 1.

54   NBTX, 2007/15, p. 7.

55   NBTX, 2007/15, p. 8.

56   Interview with former Focuspoint staffer, March 2009.

57   NBTX, 2007/15, p. 18.

58   NBTX, 2007/14, p. 18.

59   Harold Lasswell, 'The Vocation of Propagandists', in *On Political Sociology* (Chicago: University of Chicago Press, 1977 [1934]), pp. 234–35.

60   Lasswell, H. D., 'The Theory of Political Propaganda', *American Political Science Review*, vol. 21 (1927), pp. 627–31.

61   NBTX, 2005/13, p. 21.

62   NBTX, 2004/13, p. 5.

63   http://chinadigitaltimes.net/2010/08/an-inside-look-at-a-50-cent-party-meeting/

64   See for example NBTX, 2004/13, p. 7.

65   Dong Guanpeng, ed., *Zhengwu gongkai lilun yu shiwu* (English title, Theory and Practices of Transparent Government) (Beijing: Xinhua chubanshe, 2007), p. 380.

66   See 'China Contamination of Milk Supply', 10 September 2008, CHN/NZ/1/4, New Zealand Ministry of Foreign Affairs and Trade cable.

67   NBTX, 2007/14, p. 17.

68   Martin Krygier, 'Marxism and the Rule of Law: Reflections after the Collapse of Communism', *Law and Social Inquiry* (Chicago), vol. 15 (1990), pp. 602–31.

69   See Stanley B. Lubman, *Bird in a Cage: Legal Reform in China after Mao* (Stanford, CA: Stanford University Press, 1999); Randall Peerenboom, *China's Long March to Rule of Law* (Cambridge: Cambridge University Press, 2002).

70   Elton Mayo, *The Human Problems of an Industrialized Civilization* (New York: Macmillan, 1934).

71   Zhang Shiwen, Xu Yangtao, Wang Xinshan, eds, *Xin shiqi sixiang zhengzhi gongzuo yanjiu lunwen ji* (Collected Articles on Political Thought Work Research of the New Era) (Wuhan: Wuhan Daxue chubanshe, 2001), p. 449.

72 Daniel Bell, 'Adjusting Men to Machines: Social Scientists Explore the World of the Factory', *Commentary*, vol. 3 (1947), 79–88; James Hoopes, *False Prophets: The Gurus who Created Modern Management and Why Their Ideas are Bad for Business Today* (Cambridge, MA: Perseus Publishing, 2003), pp. 129–59.

73 http://en.beijing2008.cn/20/95/article212019520.shtml

74 Gao Yanqing, 'Gongmin shehui yu sixiang zhenzhi gongzuo fazhan de xin qushi' (New Developments in Civil Society and Political Thought Work), *Dang zheng ganbu luntan* (Political Cadre Forum) (September 2007), pp. 28–30.

75 Francis Fukuyama, 'The End of History', *The National Interest*, issue 16 (Summer 1989), pp. 3–18.

76 Ibid.

77 See senior leader Li Dongsheng's comments on how the risk of China's youth turning against the party has been eradicated here. http://blog.newsweek.com/blogs/beijing/archive/2008/08/04/even-state-media-must-break-records.aspx

78 Michel Foucault, *Power/Knowledge: Selected Interviews and Other Writings 1972–77*, ed. Colin Gordon (Brighton: Harvester Press, 1980), p. 142.

79 Interviews in Yunnan, Tibet, Xinjiang, September and October 2010.

Index